# The Canon
and the Archive

# The Canon and the Archive

## Configuring Literature in Modern Spain

Wadda C. Ríos-Font

Lewisburg
Bucknell University Press

© 2004 by Rosemont Publishing & Printing Corp.

All rights reserved. Authorization to photocopy items for internal or personal use, or the internal or personal use of specific clients, is granted by the copyright owner, provided that a base fee of $10.00, plus eight cents per page, per copy is paid directly to the Copyright Clearance Center, 222 Rosewood Drive, Danvers, Massachusetts 01923. [0-8387-5554-2/03 $10.00 + 8¢ pp, pc.]

Associated University Presses
2010 Eastpark Boulevard
Cranbury, NJ 08512

The paper used in this publication meets the requirements of the American National Standard for Permanence of Paper for Printed Library Materials Z39.48-1984.

Library of Congress Cataloging-in-Publication Data

Ríos-Font, Wadda C., 1964–
    The canon and the archive : configuring literature in modern Spain / Wadda C. Ríos-Font.
      p.    cm.
    Includes bibliographical references and index.
    ISBN 0-8387-5554-2 (alk. paper)
    1. Spanish fiction—20th century—History and criticism.  2. Spanish fiction—19th century—History and criticism.  3. Canon (Literature)  4. Literature and history—Spain.  5. Popular literature—Spain—History and criticism.  I. Title.

PQ6072.R55   2004
863'.609—dc22

                                                2003060691

PRINTED IN THE UNITED STATES OF AMERICA

# Contents

| | |
|---|---|
| Acknowledgments | 7 |
| Introduction | 11 |

### Part I: The Nineteenth Century

| | | |
|---|---|---|
| 1. | Refashioning the Canon: The Nineteenth-Century Serial Novel | 35 |
| 2. | Benito Pérez Galdós and the Canon of Spanish Literature | 75 |

### Part II: The Twentieth Century

| | | |
|---|---|---|
| 3. | Literature and Propaganda: Agustín de Foxá's and Ramón J. Sender's Novels of the Civil War | 121 |
| 4. | Eroticism and Canonicity at the Spanish *Fines de Siglo* | 164 |
| 5. | Manuel Vázquez Montalbán and the Spanish Literary Institution | 187 |
| Afterword: Rummaging Through the Archive | | 216 |

| | |
|---|---|
| Notes | 233 |
| Bibliography | 252 |
| Index | 269 |

# Acknowledgments

Work on this book was made possible by grants from the Ministerio de Asuntos Exteriores de España, the Program for Cultural Cooperation between Spain's Ministry of Culture and United States Universities, and Brown University's Salomon Faculty Grant program. For this institutional support I am extremely grateful.

I also want to express my appreciation for the personal and professional support of wonderful colleagues, students, and friends. Most especially to Christopher Maurer and John Kronik, admired mentors and dear friends whose example I have tried to follow.

To Geoffrey Ribbans I am thankful for his readings and guidance, and to Dru Dougherty for his constant help and counsel. I owe Randal Johnson for his invaluable early advice about the theoretical grounding for the book, and my friend Itamar Even-Zohar for a healthy dose of iconoclasm and insight. Anne Cruz's razor-sharp critique was priceless in reworking the manuscript.

I am indebted to three research assistants, Camille Cruz, William Worden, and Jennifer Rains, for innumerable library expeditions, photocopying, and proofreading. My seminar students at Brown, and especially Leigh Mercer, my first-born, were the best audience before which to work through ideas.

Antonio Monegal and Harry Vélez held my hand and filled my glass through eight years of writing and writer's block.

Y a mi madre, Ada Font, y mi abuela, Esther López de Font, a quienes dedico este libro, en agradecimiento por el amor y la fuerza.

# The Canon
and the Archive

# Introduction

THIS IS A BOOK ABOUT FRONTIER TEXTS. IT IS NOT ABOUT "POPULAR" literature, although it includes forms, like the nineteenth-century serial novel and the erotic novel, widely considered so. It is not about "noncanonical" literature, since any production by Benito Pérez Galdós, even his lesser-known journalism and underestimated theater, could hardly qualify as such. It does not posit a tradition that includes these, as well as the propagandistic novel of the Spanish Civil War, and the more recent detective novel of Manuel Vázquez Montalbán. Though all the writings analyzed in the following pages could be grouped by vague classifications such as "popular" or "noncanonical," the great differences between them allow no incontestable categorical grouping. What they have most in common is that, within modern Spanish literary history and criticism, at one time or another they have been deemed just "outside" literature, either because they were considered part of a different type of nonartistic corpus of imaginative writing, or because they weren't judged of enough "quality," or because they were defined as a different type of discourse.

The texts addressed in this book have been sites of friction between the "literary" and the variously "nonliterary"; academic debates about the nature of these terms have actually taken place or become especially relevant around them. It is precisely this liminal position that brings them together as readings with the potential to stir up both established literary history and ingrained critical methodologies. The specific interpretations and the type of reading practiced here bring up questions about how we understand literature (in general) or modern Spanish literature (in particular) as objects of study, in the context of a discipline that is probably much more elusive than physics or mathematics, and yet must have, and does have, a tangible content. What falls within its boundaries is at the same time a matter of extensive agreement, and a collection of constantly renewed (or potentially renewable) acts of choice. In other words, the theoretical impossibility of finding a once-and-for-all definition of literature has had limited bearing over the form and content of literary studies, national or comparative.

In recovering and analyzing the texts included here, I have attempted to bring together questions of theoretical, critical, and historical nature. What mark does or should contemporary theorizing about the nature of literature leave on its ongoing study? What are our unstated assumptions about what comes within this category and what doesn't, and how connected are they to theoretical acceptance of the "relativity" or "contingency" of the notion of literature? How does "formalist" or philosophical thinking about this topic merge with the cultural, especially in the culture of the academy? To what extent does thinking of literature as a cultural phenomenon, a field of production, a network of contingencies, or a mutable institution in fact affect traditional dealings with it as a sacred collection of texts representative of a national patrimony? While I do not purport to reach decisive answers to these questions, I propose readings that force us to keep them in mind, in order to attempt a self-reflexive critical practice that acknowledges the simultaneously stable and dynamic shape of the field of modern Spanish literature.

The issue of value is always implicit in the criticism and teaching of literature. Specifically in institutions of higher learning, selecting something for inclusion in a limited curriculum already implies evaluative choice, however varied the criteria for such selection may be in today's academia. Whether guided by traditional notions of canonicity, of quality, of cultural significance, or representativity and social progressiveness, scholars enter a terrain theoretically divided between "Western and multicultural, canonical and noncanonical, hegemonic and nonhegemonic" (Guillory, *Cultural Capital,* 45) and establish their own guild-canons, local canons, or even "private" canons (Charnon-Deutsch, "When the Canon," 475). To the extent that these become shared, they assume relative stability and endurance, even if their continuity is to some extent generational, destined to be modified when new theoretical paradigms, and the new crop of scholars who represent them, come of age.

Despite such diachronic change, any synchronic slicing into what literature and culture scholars teach and write about will show a measured consensus over the works and authors included, from an almost invariable core of historical and modern "classics," to a moderately fluctuating register of others widely considered meritorious and sometimes forming alternative canons, to a more diversified and narrow "fringe" covered here and there because of local or private interest. The greater proportion of stability to instability, of agreement to disagreement, can be seen, in the case of Spanish literature, in the extremely interesting statistical study of Ph.D. program reading lists carried out by Joan Brown and Crista Johnson in 1998. The researchers set out to answer the question "does consensus . . . exist for most eras and genres, and, if so, what is our shared literary canon at this time?" ("Required Reading," 5), and, though they surprisingly reach the conclusion that there isn't one (in an analysis that is less engaging than their data), they nevertheless provide a list of core authors who appear in 95 percent or more of the lists. This core coincides largely with the names one might spin off almost automatically if asked about a Spanish canonical tradition: "Cervantes, Galdós, Calderón, Rojas, Lope, Tirso, Cela, Ruiz, García Lorca, and Unamuno" (5).

It seems that apocalyptic fears that the "opening up" of the canon would do away with Cervantes certainly overestimated the danger to Spanish classical tradition. Those names whose inclusion might seem to some even slightly more "disputable" (as in the case of all women writers except for Emilia Pardo Bazán—the only one with a representation higher than 77 percent) are very irregularly included in Brown and Johnson's "canon"—but this is partly a function of their methodology, and there would certainly be more consensus if the study included, for example, *course* curricula at the graduate and undergraduate levels (where an alternative canon of women authors, relatively agreed upon, would surely make a very strong appearance, because of the popularity of courses on their writing). Even when contesting a nuclear, classical literary tradition, the tendency in our profession is still to put together such an exemplary grouping of texts, though perhaps updated to include recent work, or to be more representative of minorities.

The limited dissension about a canon of Spanish literature parallels the limited dissension regarding the operations of criticism that we perform on the texts selected for reading and interpretation. As John Beverley points out, even cultural studies unconsciously perpetuates the modernist ideology it supposedly displaces "by transferring the formalist program of dehabitualization of perception from the sphere of high culture to the forms of mass culture, now seen as more aesthetically dynamic and effective" (*Subalternity and Representation*, 111). In a similar way, the critical methods favored in the academy over a wide spectrum of disciplinary and political approaches maintain the legacy of New Critical studies. Academic interpretation of texts derives in the main from the traditional literary close reading, in which the trained eye guides the eye-in-training in the discovery of textual deep structures not immediately apparent to any nonspecialist reader. The general beliefs and debates held by a particular discipline at any particular period also determine the questions asked of texts, so that even when individuals hold contrary opinions, their disagreements are often reflections of divergent views on the same topics and approaches.

In this context, it is interesting to look at Barnet and Bedau's *Critical Thinking, Reading, and Writing: A Brief Guide to Argument*, a handbook widely used by university students learning to write critical papers. In a chapter on literary criticism, the authors divide writing about literature into three categories, stated in implicit hierarchy: "interpreting, judging (evaluating), and theorizing" (339). In interpretation, a writer offers evidence for setting forth the meaning (or "a" meaning) of a text. Judging entails the assessment of quality, although that quality may be appraised according to varying assumptions, such as:

1. A good work of art, although fictional, says something about real life.
2. A good work of art is complex yet unified.
3. A good work of art sets forth a wholesome view of life.
4. A good work of art is original.
5. A good work of art deals with an important subject. (341)

Barnet and Bedau quickly gloss over theorizing, perhaps considered beyond the capabilities of their desired audience, and define it tautologically as "concerned with . . . theoretical questions" (244). Presumably a writer engaged in literary theorizing, rather than analyzing particular texts, is laying out and probing the foundations for the work of judging and interpreting.

The authors obviously did not intend this short chapter as a definitive guide to literary criticism. But especially if one considers it an oversimplified delineation for beginning writers, the extent to which its premises apply to advanced and professional critics is remarkable—though not surprising, since most of us probably began our early ventures into criticism under the guidance of some text of that sort. The manual's first underlying assumption is that "literature" is an object of study, understood as such and deserving special attention insofar as it can be judged exemplary in its formal complexity and originality, and/or its thematic engagement with valued cultural issues. The implicit point of view from which this is to be assessed is that of the proficient and qualified (academic) reader, since these categories have little to do with the readings nosnspecialist audiences might perform (despite the fact that the interests of those other audiences or "subjects" are often identified with the valued cultural issues). The second implication of the manual's definitions is that criticism (interpretation and judgment) and theory are separate exercises, of different nature; and particularly, that criticism may "apply" theory or function without it (or without direct reference to it), but in any case is not concerned with the diacritical thought that pertains to it. Underlying the exercise of literary criticism is the presumption that one already knows what literature is, and can recognize the fundamental character and corpus of one's discipline.

In consequence, a good part of academia, especially those who have remained committed to the study of *literature* in the context of the boom of cultural studies, exists in a state of scholarly schizophrenia—a fragmented praxis in which the choice of an "applied" field (Spanish literature of the nineteenth and twentieth centuries, in my case) almost functions as a damper on the kind of theoretical thought that questions precisely essentialism, canonicity, and traditionally understood notions of "competence." Particular literary corpuses thus assume relative historical stability in contrast to the apparent state of constant renewal marked by theory. This may be partly because some reject or have not even considered the currents of thought that question the necessity for specific (national or comparative) canons, chronicled according to geographical areas and chronological periods, that structure most programs of study—the much-proclaimed antitheoretical bias of resistant groups, believed within Hispanic studies to be particularly entrenched in the peninsular field.[1] But perhaps the protective shields are not as impenetrable as is commonly thought; the fact is that these specific theoretical issues, even when carefully pondered and substantially accepted, trigger all the danger signals for critics and teachers.

At the most evident level, relativist thought about literature disputes the quintessential existence of the very fields that we are supposed to be experts in, as well as the need for that expertise in today's academia (and in today's society). At another level, it seems to place the logical and the experiential into conflict. One may find, in consonance with Stanley Fish, that "literature" is "a conventional category . . . a function of a communal decision as to what will count as literature" (*Text*, 10). One may believe that the notion of literature, as well as the shape of literary canons, is culturally determined and therefore potentially and actually mutable; one may even see it for the instrument of hegemony that it conspicuously is. Yet one may also "know" the difference between Cervantes and Cuca Canals, and state it in terms of substance, quality, and canonicity. And evidence such as that Brown and Johnson present shows that among those who "profess" the field of Spanish literature, judgment of that sort is almost universally present. Even when interest in feminism, popular culture, postmodern creation, or Catalan literature might prompt a writer like Canals into inclusion in a specific course, for example, it is hard to envision her occupying the canon-curriculum's center; and not simply because that "center" is most often a result of passing "the test of time."

The fact is even the most relativistic professionals of Spanish literature, myself included, may be uncomfortable doing away with a basic notion of "canon," a core of authors and texts accorded special cultural value *in comparison with others*. Does this mean that the relativistic critic is hypocritical when he or she affirms that the category of literature is conventional and not essential, that evaluation is a function of specific values, that canons are hegemonic structures that objectify subjective understanding, or that any such cultural construction—assuming it should even exist—should allow for the inclusion of diversity in judgment? Not necessarily. The disparity may arise from both institutional constraints on change in any particular field, and personal quandaries about how to collate the "theoretical" and the "applied" in literature. The translation of the theoretical into the critical is by no means obvious; it is not immediately clear how the conceptual acceptance that a particular practice is not intrinsically necessary, or that a given canon is historically and culturally determined, should be transposed into the critical field. In other words, the kinds of changes in reading and writing that should in principle follow the retreat from a sacralizing, essentialist view of literature are open to experimentation and debate.

The theoretical thinking that grounds this book deserves some attention at this point. I have already mentioned as one of its influences that of Stanley Fish, whose early epistemological theorizing insisted on the relativity of literature, and on the constituent character of perception over the perceived phenomenon: "linguistic and textual facts, rather than being the objects of interpretation, are its products" (*Text*, 9). Fish's work was concerned with how it is, or isn't, possible to know that a discourse is literary (and thus how readers produce the interpretations that texts seem to evoke *because* they are literary), and one of his answers was that such knowledge depends on the consensus of an interpretive community. His groundwork therefore arrived at the threshold of cultural and political analysis: if what counts as "literature" within a given society is the decision of a community, then that community's beliefs and characteristics, as well as its power relations—the very same ones that allow it to institute and uphold such a category—come to be at issue.

It is at this point of juncture between the philosophical and the cultural that Barbara Herrnstein Smith's groundbreaking *Contingencies of Value* takes up. According to Smith, "literary value is radically relative and therefore [at least hypothetically] 'constantly variable'" (11). She analyzes the factors on which that value depends, from the "personal economy" (30) of an individual receiver to the interdependency between it and the cultural determinants that generate personal values, expectations about the literary, and either convergence or divergence of taste within given communities. To the extent that there is consensus among a certain group of people, the contingencies—Smith uses the word to refer both to the relativity of value and to the conditions that determine it under given circumstances—that govern value for them will be perceived as noncontingencies, and the illusion of objective or intrinsic value will be created within that community. Nonetheless, complete agreement is rare, and is always "implicitly threatened or directly challenged by the divergent tastes and preferences of some subjects within the community . . . as well as by most subjects who are outside it, or, more significantly, on its periphery" (40). For Smith, canonicity and value always reflect the tension between the contingencies of those in positions of power and those of others who might jeopardize their ascendancy, and who are consequently discounted or pathologized. Thus, Smith locates aesthetic value in *values*—personal and communal—that allow subjects to perceive certain texts as performing the (privileged) functions that they, from their specific positions, consider literary.

The emphasis on community, especially as present in Smith's work, opens the door to critiques of the canon that dispute any supposedly objective accounts of the aesthetic and turn to the contingencies and values of the individuals and groups engaged in the production and evaluation of texts. Such views govern the reading practices of what John Guillory terms the "politics of representation" (*Cultural Capital*, 5). The ideal negotiation between contingencies advocated by scholars of feminist, queer, ethnic, and some sectors of cultural studies—

which see the matter of the canon as one of representation and exclusion, analogous to those occurring in society at large (6)—would lead (has led) both to a more inclusive, more socially representative core canon, and to the construction of alternative canons for the subcommunities or peripheral communities. But the perspective of "identity politics" (11) on the canon debate posits a whole new range of problems. For one, these standpoints often fail to problematize notions like gender, race, or sexual orientation in themselves, to explore the ways in which they are constructs, or performances, that may not completely define individuals (and consequently communities of individuals) or encompass their various attributes. The necessary political pragmatism of such identity politics, which aims for the recognition of concrete rights, often addresses these concepts as essential categories in themselves. Additionally, these approaches provide little space for engagement (except adversarially) with works that, though noncanonical, might be at odds with the currently acceptable categories of vindication. There is no ground from which to recover forgotten texts not understood as marginalized for reasons of minority exclusion, and in this way the new liberal critical approaches can become as prescriptive as more traditional ones. Likewise, the displacement from essence to shared contingency does not sufficiently explain disagreement and struggle within a group of individuals that might reasonably be considered a community, or, conversely, "agreement between parties whose total economies manifestly diverge" (286).

Most importantly, approaches that hinge on the recouping of the marginalized often leave untouched the binomial structure of canonical thought, a fact Smith already suggests in her account: "Insofar as . . . marginalized groups . . . constitute social communities in themselves, they also tend to have prevailing structures of tastes and may be expected to control them in much the same ways as do more obviously 'establishment' groups" (*Contingencies*, 41). The dis-authorization of essentialist thought does not necessarily exclude its replacement by analogous, and equally unexamined, structures of discrimination. Moreover, changes in the names and titles included in the canon (or the curriculum or the critical corpus), as well as in the criteria for selection, generally replicate and reinstitute the oppositional thought that grounds canon formation. Even when such changes are widely embraced, as in the expanding attention to women or Latino writers in American academia, they do not symbolize the deposition of the canon, but rather the creation of a newer version.

In his book *Cultural Capital: The Problem of Literary Canon Formation*, already alluded to above, John Guillory affirms that both the defenders and attackers of the canon are united by an obsession with the form of the canonical list. Lists are essential to the contemporary social imagination, from the domain of mass culture to that of "high" culture. From David Letterman's Top Ten to collections such as the *Cien mejores poemas de la literatura española* to the canon itself, the notion of the list provides a sense of organic plan, of order, of unity, of achievable mastery. We derive from lists a sense of direction, and especially a sense of community:

> A nostalgia for community pervades the debate about the canon on both the right and the left sides . . . on the one side as the unity of Western Culture, and on the other as the unity of its individual countercultures, represented by canons of "noncanonical" works. Both unities contend with the actual dominance of mass culture by projecting an imaginary totality out of mass culture's image of cultural diversity—the form of the list [itself]. (36–37)

By predicating the necessity for women, homosexuals, or minority writers to be represented in the canon, critics and professors perform an admirable cultural duty that nevertheless repeats the same static structure in which certain authors and works (even if they are not the "usual" ones) occupy the privileged position of an inheritable treasure transmitted and administered by the university.

There are, of course, approaches based on vindications of gender, race, sexual orientation, or subaltern status that distance themselves from canonical thought through the rejection of literature itself as an inherently hierarchical tradition, and its replacement by "culture." One of the assumptions behind a large sector of cultural studies is that literature is one of the several interrelated institutions and discourses which, together, produce hegemony, defined as "a situation in which a provisional alliance of certain social groups can exert 'total social authority' over other subordinate groups, not simply by coercion or by the direct imposition of ruling ideas, but by 'winning and shaping consent so that the power of the dominant classes appears both legitimate and natural'" (Hebdige, "From Culture to Hegemony," 366). In this context, the study of literature is absorbed into a larger ideological critique of culture, whose primary objective becomes the deciphering of the ways in which dominant ideologies codify themselves, and the furnishing of alternatives that give voice and standing to the marginalized. The goal of a representative canon is no longer central, because canons, being hegemonic constructs, are an inherent part of cultural alienation. Insofar as literature remains an object of study, it remains so on par with any other sort of cultural "text," onto which, as Beverley noted, the same sort of analysis is projected. In the most radical forms of this critique, "literature" is a negatively charged term, that incarnates in and of itself forms of political domination and is therefore the legitimate object of a socially responsible repression.

The readings in this book are not a rejection of identity politics or cultural studies, many of whose values I share. They are, nevertheless, concerned specifically with literature as an autonomous and extremely powerful social system, worthy of study in its own right. Neither the fact that literature has long served as an asset that empowers certain classes, nor the fact that it is a constructed rather than essential category, detract from its fundamental role as one of the axes around which cultures define and consolidate themselves. "Literature" (as a special, and privileged, kind of text) and "value" (as a quality of literature) are not objectifiable terms, and their definition depends on interpretive consensus—even, granted, on interpretive consensus among people with authority. But the terms nevertheless have an important social existence as instruments of symbolic cohesion within collectives that include many individuals beyond those in power. In the case of Spain, for example, *Don Quijote* serves as a culture-building and culture-maintaining tool for people who may not identify with the values that produced this "classic" as a cornerstone of the literary canon of a(n imagined) strong, unified nation. Many persons who may not even have read it would agree not only that it is an important text, indeed a classic of literature, but even that it conveys something about a Spanish "spirit"—that the characters of Don Quijote and Sancho could be regarded as specific national types (whether or not that is demonstrably true). In other words, even those who might ostensibly be outside of the field of power, indeed the "victims" of the power relations that support themselves through the hegemonic command of canons, participate in the framework of canon making. And this is not only because the most complete power is that which seeps throughout the culture so as not to have to be "imposed" from above; it is also because literature and high culture represent something in which all classes of individuals have different types of investment.

The need for and existence of canons cannot, then, be unproblematically related to a clearly binomial structure of domination. In view of this fact, the readings in this book are implicitly grounded on a Foucauldian view of power relations: though power is exerted through the shaping of individuals' consciousness, it is not a structure of domination unilaterally wielded by one group over another. Rather, it is a network of complex relations in which dominance and resistance are never static. In Foucault's words:

> Power comes from below; that is, there is no binary and all-encompassing opposition between rulers and ruled at the root of power relations, and serving as a general matrix—no such duality extending from the top down. . . . One must suppose rather that the manifold relationships of force that take shape and come into play in the machinery of production, in families, limited groups, and institutions, are the basis for a wide-ranging whole. These then form a general line of force that traverses the local oppositions and links them together; to be sure, they also bring about redistributions, realignments, homogenizations, serial arrangements, and convergences of the force relations. Major dominations are the hegemonic effects that are sustained by all these confrontations. (*History*, 94)

The social field of literature constitutes one of the most active networks of power relations in culture, and perhaps one of the reasons why the notion of canon is so difficult to dispense with is the intricacy of those relations. The existence of a national literary patrimony may be at once against and in the interest of specific parties, and, furthermore, individuals who debate it may simultaneously belong to (or consider themselves advocates for) different groups that may actually conflict among themselves. In circumstances like these, there is no direct line from the profession of nonessentialist thought to the presumably logical consequence of repudiating the concepts of the literary (as a discourse empirically distinguishable from others according to criteria ruled and possessed by a few) and the canonical (as a privileged class of texts that represents hegemonic or otherwise esteemed values).

The literary and the canonical thus remain extremely enduring cultural institutions, surprisingly stable considering the degree of controversy that surrounds them. Literature subsists as a strong index of cultural uniqueness and endowment; some sense of "canon" survives, always already established and yet somehow in need of, on the one hand, protection and transmission, and on the other hand, questioning and challenge. And because these operations are never performed once and for all, but need to be constantly reenacted, even the highly technological Western societies—commanded by what Guillory calls the "professional-managerial class" (*Cultural Capital*, 45)—preserve one of the least manifestly "productive" and most paradoxical social functions: that of the intellectual, largely rooted, in the American context from which I write, in the academy (though in Spain, with its engrained tradition of public investment in culture, there remain other obvious quarters).

Representations of the intellectual are many and varied, and it is not pertinent here to give a comprehensive outline of them. I will allude only to two views that in my opinion reveal strong reasons for the critical hesitation between relativistic questioning and stalwart preservation of the canon I have commented on: those of Edward Said and Pierre Bourdieu. In a sense, "professionals" of literature, as intellectuals, are impelled toward the transcendent role envisioned by Said:

> The intellectual is an individual with a specific public role in society that cannot be reduced simply to being a faceless professional, a competent member of a class just going about her/his business. The central fact for me is . . . that the intellectual is an individual endowed with a faculty for representing, embodying, articulating a message, a view, an attitude, philosophy or opinion to, as well as for, a public. And this role . . . cannot be played without a sense of being someone whose place it is publicly to raise embarrassing questions, to confront orthodoxy and dogma (rather than to produce them), to be someone . . . whose *raison d'être* is to represent all those people and issues that are routinely forgotten or swept under the rug. The intellectual does so on the basis of universal principles: that all human beings are entitled to expect decent standards of behavior concerning freedom and justice from worldly powers or nations, and that deliberate or inadvertent violations of these standards need to be testified and fought against courageously. (*Representations*, 11–12)

The powerful ideal of being a cultural advocate motivates the intellectual who studies literature to assume that study as political at heart. Nevertheless, the powers fought are contradictory. Is one to confront the "orthodoxy and dogma" that have produced literature and the canon as hegemonic tools, or those that threaten humanistic knowledge—so linked to the post-Enlightenment values of freedom and democracy—in the accelerated transit toward a technology- and market-based world? Perhaps the answer is a double "yes," in which case it propels the intellectual in two different directions, precisely because the field of power is not univocal but multiple. If, on the one hand, canonical thought is inherently exclusive, on the other hand canons are one of the chief written records of cultural collectives as human ventures, and the individuals who form those collectives perceive them as repositories of positive communal values. The cultural tool that serves to keep many out of the power spheres to which representation in it and command of it give access also gives tangible shape to the "universal principles" Said refers to. Given this quandary, it is no wonder that "opening up" the canon in order to bring it closer to a liberal political ideal has proved to be much more practicable than leaving it behind.

Pierre Bourdieu, whose view of intellectuals is much more pragmatic than Said's, insists on their "paradoxical" and "*bidimensional*" character, due to the fact that their existence "calls into question the classical alternative of pure culture and political engagement" ("Fourth Lecture," 656). Beginning with Emile Zola's *J'accuse*, intellectuals have derived cultural authority from their standing in the ostensibly autonomous and disinterested fields of artistic or scientific knowledge, and invested that authority in the political arena. It is this crossover that makes an intellectual, and in this sense it can be inferred that his or her social position is different from that of a political activist, even if both obey analogous mandates and may coincide in the same person. According to Bourdieu, the very essence of intellectuals' position in society is precisely that they are

> a dominated fraction of the dominant class. They are dominant, in so far as they hold the power and privileges conferred by the possession of cultural capital . . . ; but writers and artists are dominated in their relations with those who hold political and economic power. . . . This contradictory position of dominant-dominated, of dominated among the dominant or, to make use of the homology with the political field, of the left wing of the right wing, explains the ambiguity of the positions they adopt, an ambiguity which is linked to this precariously balanced position. (*Other Words*, 145)

Bourdieu's statements point to a conclusion that anchors the chapters in this book. Returning once more to the dilemma of essentialism versus radical relativism, and to the failure of applied literary studies to reconcile relativistic theoretical positions with actual critical practice, it should be noted that such a move is almost unfeasible for the literary scholar as an intellectual. If an essentialist position regarding literature and the canonical may be associated with the avowal of distinction and knowledge characteristic of the dominant, and a relativistic position is most readily assumed by the dominated who challenge hegemony, the intellectual's contradictory social position would logically translate into ambivalence regarding these literary matters.

Additionally, literature and the canon are not simply the patrimony of dominant classes. They are, quite particularly, the asset of intellectuals, and not only insofar as they themselves belong to the dominant, but also as the jurisdiction of knowledge that endows them with the cultural authority they might use politically against the dominant. In other words, part of the paradox of the literary intellectual's position arises from his or her gain of self-identity through the keeping and management of the literary tradition, an operation that is at the same time against the interests, and in the interest, of the marginalized. In order to be who they are, and perform what they perceive as their social function, literary intellectuals require their role as priests and priestesses of the canon—a capacity even critics who would "depose" it are fully conscious of, and fully assume (they know themselves to be in a position to modify canonical thought). In possession of this role, nevertheless, most intellectuals will understandably lean toward self-preservation through the preservation of the canon in some form, even if they understand its part in actual structures of domination.

Such an assertion of interest in a supposedly disinterested field does not amount to bad faith; in fact, for Bourdieu, an indispensable "conscious and organized mobilization of intellectuals" ("Fourth Lecture," 662) for the public good has to go through a defense of their own welfare: "The first objective of intellectuals should be to work collectively in defense of their specific interests and of the means necessary for protecting their own autonomy.... One defends the universal by defending the defenders of the universal" (660–61). This is "the homage that vice pays to virtue" (669). If, for a follower of Said's idealistic view of the intellectual, the complexity of power relations and the contradictory nature of the powers perceived as inimical may lead to the ambiguous preservation of canonical thought, from Bourdieu's pragmatic standpoint that preservation acquires added symbolic significance.

All of this is not to say that intellectuals are hypocritical—on the contrary, the "professional" of literature exists within a "universe of belief" (Bourdieu, *Field*, 164) that more often than not obscures the stage machinery behind the action, and I believe one would be hard-pressed to find a critic or professor who has not felt seduced by the "magic" power of a literary work. The task of interpreting and judging literature is not an empty exercise done for the sake of cultural authority. In the Spanish and American societies in relation to which I work, literature remains, as I said before, a crucial cultural force—as a patrimonial collection of texts (a canon), as an educational discipline, and as a field of social relations. Individuals in academic posts are among those on whom is bestowed the very special function of participating prominently in its administration. And this effort can be undertaken, in good faith, in a variety of ways.

For myself, at this juncture, and in this book—a very personal project—the endeavor implies the embrace of the contradictions of our field and of our position within it and within society at large. It involves personal acceptance of the role of literary scholar and professor as a place of tension, and reflection on the explicit and implicit negotiations behind it. Every scholar of literature exists personally and professionally in a world of complex power relations, of which he or she forms a multifaceted part. And it is precisely from the acknowledgment of this complex situation that one can begin a study of literature that attempts to go beyond the repetition of the dual structure of canonical thought while at the same time acknowledging the historical existence of canons and making fruitful use of one's knowledge of them. This book embarks on the possibilities of such a study, centered on the effort to bring the theoretical and the critical together. I believe that any answers to the great questions of what literature is, how it coincides with the canon, what the latter signifies in a culture, and how it should be treated are bound to be provisional and local, that they are resolved differently at different places and times, and from different angles.

Therefore, although the work that I do in the following chapters is theoretically inspired, it is also eminently "applied." Additionally, it is eminently self-reflexive, for the issue of literature and the canon is, as John Guillory has pointed out, an academic one. Especially in the United States, but also, to some extent, in Spain, most of the pertinent debates are held in the school and within its curriculum, and it is there that what the culture has (contradictorily, varyingly) judged its heritage can be passed on to new generations. Consequently, this book pays particular attention to the history of how the academy has determined the canonical fortunes of the works studied, and what networks of intricate relations have in turn dictated its choices. It is clear from everything I have already written that I am not only interested in textual analysis—despite that fact that I do give great importance to close reading—but also in these works' trajectories through literary history, and in the transactions between various agents that have determined it.

My approach owes much to two complementary systemic, relational views of literature: that of Pierre Bourdieu, to whom I have already alluded, and that of the Israeli theorist Itamar Even-Zohar. Although they will be referred to and quoted often in the body of the book, some of their basic ideas bear review here. Both theorists turn away from a text-centered approach to literature, and toward an institutional, *relational* account. For Bourdieu, literature is not a set of texts delimited according to given criteria, but a *field of production* whose apparent autonomy masks its active interconnection and homology with other fields of cultural production (such as those of the other arts) and with social fields in general—including the fields of power (economic and political), to which it is subordinate. As Randal Johnson explains,

> the formulation of the notion of field . . . [represents] an attempt to apply what Bourdieu . . . calls a relational mode of thought to cultural production. This requires a break with the ordinary or substantialist perception of the social world in order to see each element in terms of its relationships with all other elements in a system from which it derives its meaning and function. ("Editor's Introduction," 6)

Concepts such as value, canonicity, literariness, or even specific postulates about a work's meaning or impact acquire their significance in the context of the functioning of the field and the struggles among agents within it (an agent may be an author, but also a reader, a critic, a publisher, etc).

Bourdieu's account of the interactions within the field of cultural production sees literature, and generally artistic fields, as "social microcosms, separate and autonomous spaces, in which works are generated" (*Rules*, 181). The structure of the field is not immanent, but historically developed. Specifically, throughout the nineteenth century (and at different paces), the literary and artistic fields divide into two spaces, the space of large-scale production, and the field of restricted production ("high," "aesthetic," or "serious" art). In the latter subfield, the stakes of competition between agents are largely symbolic, involving prestige, consecration and artistic celebrity. This . . . is production for producers. Economic profit is normally disavowed (at least by the artists themselves), and the hierarchy of authority is based on different forms of symbolic profit, e.g. a profit of disinterestedness, or the profit one has on seeing oneself (or being seen) as one who is not searching for profit. It is in this sense that the cultural field is a universe of belief. The symbolic power of this sub-field's products is sustained by a vast social apparatus encompassing museums, galleries, libraries, the educational system, literary and art histories, centres for the performing arts, and so forth. (Johnson, "Editor's Introduction," 15)

In the kind of analysis proposed by Bourdieu, the comprehension of a text or an author entails a comprehension of the workings of the literary field—that is, of the positions and possibilities available at a certain point in time and place to any particular agent, and the social value attached to them, as well as of the culturally determined structures of perception that enable the agent to identify those possibilities and to act accordingly (what Bourdieu calls the *habitus*). In short, studying literature involves reconstructing, historically when necessary, the multiple variables forming part of the conditions of production and consumption of any given work—a process that I have tried to follow as far as possible, especially in the sections of the book dealing with nineteenth- and early twentieth-century literature.

Another relational approach I have found useful is the polysystem theory developed by Itamar Even-Zohar. The theory posits the notion that semiotic phenomena—including "culture, language, literature, society" (*Polysystem*, 9) are aggregates of systems in interaction, where the word *system* is taken to mean "*the network of relations that can be hypothesized for a certain set of assumed observables*" (27). Within culture, the literary system is formulated as a "complex of activities" (28) rather than a collection of texts. This complex of activities includes

as "internal" rather than "external," all factors that are involved with the set of activities for which the label "literary" can be used more conveniently than any other. The "text" is no longer the only, and not necessarily for all purposes the most important, facet, or even product, of this system. Moreover, this framework requires no *a priori* hierarchies of importance between the surmised factors. It suffices to recognize that the *interdependencies* between these factors which allow them to function in the first place. Thus, a CONSUMER may "consume" a PRODUCT produced by a PRODUCER, but in order for the "product" (such as "text") to be generated, a common REPERTOIRE must exist, whose usability is determined by some INSTITUTION. A MARKET must exist where such a good can be transmitted. None of the factors enumerated can be described to function in isolation, and the kind of relations that may be detected run across all possible axes of the scheme. (33–34)

Like Bourdieu's, Even-Zohar's theory affords the possibility of approaching literature as a social network of dynamic complexity. It also affords the possibility of transcending the limitations of canonical thought, since it specifically rejects "value judgments as criteria for an *a priori* selection of the objects of study" (13). Stated otherwise,

> If one accepts the polysystem hypothesis, then one must also accept that the historical study of literary polysystems cannot confine itself to the so-called "masterpieces," even if some would consider them the only *raison d'être* of literary studies in the first place. . . . As scholars committed to the discovery of the mechanisms of literature, there seems to be no way for us to avoid recognizing that any prevalent value judgments of any period are themselves an integral part of these mechanisms. . . . [However,] excluding the selection of objects to be studied according to taste does not mean that either particular "values" or evaluation in general are excluded by any section of the [human] sciences . . . as active *factors* to be accounted for. Without a study of such evaluative norms, there is no way of understanding the behavior of any human system. (13)

A particularly appealing feature of this approach, thus, is the possibility for the researcher to acknowledge his or her personal values without necessarily making them the central legitimation of the research, even if the latter concentrates on political and social values and the canonical structures they have engendered and continue to engender. Taking for granted that all humans, including literary researchers, are political beings, and that everything one does is marked by one's beliefs, it must also be possible to distinguish between actions that are directly civic, and actions that have their origin in a systematic quest for knowledge about the substance of cultures and their institutions. If the nature of the intellectual is that she or he uses the social strength gained in the field of letters in the political arena, there is something to be said for maintaining the space for crossover. I therefore approach the subject of this book not as a political activist, but as a humanist worker concerned with objective understanding (literally the understanding of certain objects) as well as with the possible ways of practicing my profession according to my political beliefs.

The chapters in this book are an attempt to practice a relational criticism that incorporates the lessons of the theories that inspired it. I have referred to the works chosen for study as both "noncanonical"—outside the range of literary works commonly valued and read in academic environments—and "frontier"—in some peripheral relationship to what is ordinarily included in such a canon or curriculum. Although each chapter focuses on a particular text or form, and although interpretation is a key resource used to understand them, my "readings" emphasize eventualities of production and reception as an intrinsic part of each works' very being, trajectory, and status. While I may or may not sympathize with the structures of evaluation and the values that have functioned to make these works noncanonical—I attend to works that are ideologically and stylistically very different—I consider their relationship to "literature" and the "canon" especially revealing. In other words, the study of these works affords factual and historical knowledge (valuable in and of itself) that sheds light on the processes through which the literary, Spanish literature in particular, has come to be understood in the ways that it is, in the cultural contexts around which I work.

It can therefore be said that I juxtapose and compare the literary and the nonliterary, the canonical and the noncanonical, but not by recognizing them as distinct categories of literary objects. The categories are, in my view, historical, relational, and fluid, and it is as such that I probe them. The notion of canon in particular is one that I attempt to acknowledge without seeking to destroy or perpetuate it. Canons and canonical works are a fact of national (and even international, as in "Western" or "Eastern") histories. Their existence and their consequences, negative and positive, cannot be ignored, much less retroactively amended through curricular revisions. The past cannot be rewritten or erased; it cannot be undone, nor can it be melodramatically characterized as a binomial relationship between power and its absence. It can only be recontextualized in the present, engaged with in a new way; and for this, it needs to be recognized.

Similarly, literary canons are extremely important cultural testimonies that cannot be erased or destroyed, that incarnate many-sided power relations, and even today serve crucial functions for certain collectives—functions in which academics and intellectuals in general take substantial part. They are, however, there, to be engaged with again and anew, and perhaps it is their relation to the totality of "literature" or "imaginative writing" within a culture that needs to be rethought. In the context of this book, I attempt to do so through the notion of "archive," a term that John Guillory puts forth, almost in passing:

> The historical condition of literature is that of a complex continuum of major works, minor works, works read primarily in research contexts, works as yet simply shelved in the archive. Anyone who studies historical literatures knows that the archive contains an indefinite number of works of manifest cultural interest and accomplishment. While these works might be regarded as "noncanonical" in some pedagogic contexts—for example, the context of the "great works" survey—their noncanonical status is not necessarily equivalent in anyone's judgment to a zero-degree of interest or value. (*Cultural Capital,* 30)

An "archival" rather than "canonical" view can recognize the cultural importance of the texts either traditionally included in the canon, or written according to the criteria by which texts have been included in the canon, without submitting to those criteria or relying on conventional categorization. It approaches literature as an unendingly increasing repository of texts in an unending series of possible readings, understandings, and characterizations. Like Jorge Luis Borges's library of Babel, it is an infinite supply, "*ilimitada y periódica*" [unlimited and recurrent] (*Obras completas,* 471) of works that do not simply contain meanings, but acquire them according to changing readings *and* relationships. The fact that some texts have been selected, displayed, canonized, should not obscure the corresponding fact that they are only a fraction of the possible readings, and that they have been made what they are through their contact with successive and different eyes.

The five chapters in this book thus look to the archive to find specific tomes that will elucidate the shaping of the institution of literature at a particular time and place: Spain in the nineteenth and twentieth centuries. The works on which I write may seem disparate in kind and in chronological context, and they may not always be the works that appear to make the most "sense" as illustrations of the problems that concern me. They are not only chosen according to personal interest and circumstance, but also in an attempt to stay away from artificial unity, alternative tradition, or excessive academic neatness. Nevertheless, they all belong to a period that loosely coincides with the lifetime of the disciplines of Spanish literature and literary history. José-Carlos Mainer, in his indispensable article "La invención de la literatura española" [The Invention of Spanish Literature], points to the period of consolidation of such a concept beginning in the 1830s. It is in 1836 that the National Library is established—signalling the perceived need for a national patrimony—and the university discipline of Spanish literature, with its corresponding professorships, is created by Royal Decree. This critical mood leads also to the production of "the first Spanish university handbook of *national literature,* published in 1844" (34), as well as to other efforts toward the constitution of a national literature, for example, the publication in 1846 of the first volume of the *Biblioteca de Autores Españoles* [Library of Spanish Authors] (36). José María Pozuelo, following Leonardo Romero Tobar, points to the significance of the 1845 reform of curricular programs, "which . . . definitively established the institutional independence of literary history studies, and gave rise to the massive publication of instrumental texts, anthologies, and support handbooks" (*Teoría,* 127). It is thus after the 1830s and 40s that a canon of Spanish literature is, as Rosa María Aradra also points out, retroactively constituted. And it is in this period that criteria of distinction begin to be exercised, laying the ground for the later consolidation of the divided literary field. All the chapters of this book are concerned with how these processes of discrimination have played out from that initial point in time through the very recent past.

The five chapters of the book reflect on borderline texts of the past two centuries in their contexts; and they are all "borderline" or "frontier" in different ways. The first chapter considers the canonical history of nineteenth-century Spanish serial fiction, a kind of writing that simultaneously institutes the novel as a modern genre with a continuous history, and the market that will lead it to the split between high and low, restricted and large-scale production. My second chapter analyzes Benito Pérez Galdós's novel, theater, and journalism as the complementary works (though with very different fortunes) of the author who most symbolizes the transition in Spain from the earlier (unified) to the modern (divided) state of the literary field. Agustín de Foxá's and Ramón J. Sender's novels of the Civil War, to which the third chapter is dedicated, are read as works whose fall through the cracks of literary history brings to the fore many of the premises and presuppositions inherent to the universe of belief. Similarly, in the fourth chapter attention is paid to turn-of-the-century (nineteenth and twentieth) erotic novels as texts that incarnate the tension between "aesthetic" eroticism and pornography, as a metonymy for the anxiety of literary differentiation. Finally, I examine the position of a contemporary author, Manuel Vázquez Montalbán, and his "borderline" place between the canon and mass culture as exemplary of the problems of contemporary canon formation, when critical judgment occurs simultaneously with original reception.

What unites these works and authors is, in the end, their problematic nature. They are not volumes lost in the dusty, never-visited hexagons of the Library of Babel; they have been borrowed and read, but never quite classified. They are sources of confusion, discomfort, or embarrassment, and accordingly bring out the effort to categorize and control. Because of this, they challenge critics. They make us confront the historicity of our universals, and realize that rather than priests and priestesses, we are librarians, keepers of a treasure that includes the known and revered, yet goes beyond. That the treasure is not only in our hands, or in the hands of those trained by us, but open to all who can bring their own experiences to it. And that the treasure is not the list, or the catalogue, but the library itself. It cannot be "mastered," only used, again and again, in search of the ever-replenishing combinations of the twenty-five orthographic symbols.

# I
The Nineteenth Century

# 1
# Refashioning the Canon: The Nineteenth-Century Serial Novel

THE IDEA OF BENITO PÉREZ GALDÓS AS THE CREATOR OF THE MODERN Spanish novel, who reclaims for Spain the genre Cervantes had given the world, persists in literary studies, perhaps as a self-perpetuating misreading of his own remark in "Observaciones sobre la novela contemporánea en España" [Observations on the Contemporary Novel in Spain] (1870) that "no tenemos novela" [we have no novel] (162).[1] Attention is selectively paid to the earlier historical novel (Gil y Carrasco, Larra, Espronceda, López Soler) and to Gertrudis Gómez de Avellaneda's *Sab* (1841) in the context of Romantic expression, or to Cecilia Böhl de Faber's *La gaviota* (serialized in *El Heraldo* in 1849) as the *costumbrista* prehistory of the realist novel. Less studied, and even less read, is the abundant production of novels, principally in serialized form—as *folletines* in newspapers, or as *novelas por entregas*, sold in fascicles by subscription—that flourishes between the 1840s and the 1860s.[2]

One of the first scholars to concentrate substantially on this period of the history of the novel is José F. Montesinos in his 1955 *Introducción a una historia de la novela en España en el siglo XIX*. Nevertheless, this study virtually ignores Spanish writers—even one as well-known in the 1840s as Wenceslao Ayguals de Izco—and emphasizes instead the mass of translations that proliferated in the period between 1800 and 1850. Montesinos's focus does not follow from unawareness of autocthonous novelistic production, but from a value judgment about its consequence, since it is evident from his argument that he finds Spanish novels neither quantitatively nor qualitatively comparable to those imported from abroad. Thus, his general condemnation of Spanish novelists of the moment—"se obstinaban en escribir novelas los menos dotados" [only the least gifted insisted on writing novels] (xiv)—saves only Böhl de Faber from the crowd of translators and imitators: "Sólo Fernán Caballero, entre las gentes de aquella generación, supo lo que quería y podía hacer" [Only Fernán Caballero, among the people of that generation, knew wht she wanted to and could do] (xvi). Again, we have to wait for Galdós to rescue Spanish artistic prose from lethargy: "Galdós, para llegar a esas alturas, había tenido que rehacer por sí mismo la experiencia de su nación y de su siglo, penetrarse de las mejores esencias artísticas del mundo, fundirlo todo en el crisol de la gran tradición cervantina, y excederla según el uso de los tiempos" [In order to reach those heights, Galdós had had to rebuild on his own the experience of his nation and his century, become imbued of the best artistic essences in the world, smelt it all in the melting pot of the great Cervantine tradition, and surpass it according to the fashions of time] (xvii).

Serial novels were more systematically studied during the 1970s, when Iris Zavala's *Ideología y política en la novela española del siglo XIX* was followed by several books and articles on either the *folletín,* the *novelas por entregas,* or both, including those by Ferreras, Díez-Borque, Goldman, Botrel, Amorós, Romero Tobar, Rubio Cremades, Carrillo, Benítez, Ouimette, and others. These instructive contributions invaluably advanced the knowledge of what were then almost completely eradicated authors and texts; information is now readily available on names and biographies of writers, titles and dates of works, favored plots, narrative structure, ideological contents, mode of production and distribution, and readership.[3] Without attempting to lump these analyses together or reduce them to a single point of view, there emerges from the reading of several of them (especially those that least limit themselves to a strictly sociological, descriptive approach) a sense that a certain embarrassment about their subject prevents them from reaching different conclusions based on the data they handle.

Most of these scholars address the serial novel as an extraliterary phenomenon which they variously label as "paraliteratura o paranovela" (Ferreras), "subliteratura" (Amorós, Díez-Borque), "infralittérature" (Carrillo), or "novela popular" (Romero Tobar, Ouimette). Especially the more analytical works—those that come closer to performing the reading operations one would perform with any literary text (although all shy away from full-force "literary" or "aesthetic" treatment)—often appear apologetic, justifying to their audience their attention to the serial novel. Thus, on the first page of his book, Benítez, for example, feels the need to specify about Ayguals's popularity that "I don't know if this justifies a book, but it does justify at least the study of the author" (*Ideología,* 1). Later on, he also appeals to the reader's sentimental, archaeological sense of pleasure: "I trust the reader will find, as I have, a certain nostalgic pleasure in the reading of these serials. If, on the one side, they age irreparably, on the other they have the endurance of feeling, even if that feeling verges on the maudlin and on bad taste" (6).

Peter Goldman, in his two-part article "Toward a Sociology of the Modern Spanish Novel: The Early Years" implies that the history of the serial novel *is* the history of the Spanish novel; he also argues convincingly that this novel is not "popular," if by that one means read mainly by a working- or lower-class public, or even chiefly concerned with this class. Nevertheless, his particular focus on "sociology" rather than "literary analysis" seems to qualify his forceful implications. He suggests as one of the relevant questions that might come up in the context of the serial novel: "Is a *bad* novel necessarily popular culture?" (part 2, 184, my emphasis)—apparently taking for granted that these are bad novels, without going into the implications of the word "bad." He also suggests, as a reason for its study, "the need to illuminate the boundaries between high and low culture." In this way, he restates the good/bad, high/low differentiation that has kept in the realm of the noncanonical an entire literary form whose original reception allowed for novel-by-novel evaluation. Even for Goldman, the facts of print culture that noticeably shape the serial novel are negative, so that the "certain degree of originality" (part 2, 190) one might grant a writer like Wenceslao Ayguals de Izco is countered by his characterization as an "unprincipled opportunist."

After the surge in serial novel studies during the 1970s, it seems that their insights fall onto dry ground, and attention to the genre again lulls until, more recently, a few scholars rediscover it. On the one hand, a renewed interest in the sociology of literature has produced critical works such as that of Brigitte Magnien's research group in Paris, *Hacia una literatura del pueblo: del folletín a la novela (el ejemplo de Timoteo Orbe)* (1995). This collection of essays is primarily concerned with the late nineteenth-century use of serialized fictions by workers' presses and authors associated with them (i.e., Timoteo Orbe), providing a summary of the genesis and development of the *feuilleton* in the Spanish press as a background to its primary subject. On the other hand, a small group of scholars has revisited the serial novel, though tangentially, from the point of view of feminist theory, most notably Catherine Jagoe in her groundbreaking article about the relationship between Galdós's novelistic project and the earlier production which he "feminizes" and discredits, as in her 1994 *Ambiguous Angels*. One should also refer to, among others, Lou Charnon-Deutsch's research on desire and domesticity in nineteenth-century women's novels; to Cristina Enríquez de Salamanca's remarkable work on the contribution of domestic discourse to the formation of women's political subjectivity in nineteenth-century Spain; and to the suggestive MLA session on nineteenth-century women's novels and the canon (with the participation of Jagoe, Charnon-Deutsch, Enríquez de Salamanca, John Sinnigen, Alda Blanco, and Stephanie Sieburth) published as a "Diálogo crítico" by the *Revista de estudios hispánicos* in 1993. Although, as a group, these critics are not focusing on the form of production, but rather on the issue of gender in the mid-nineteenth-century novel, obviously the corpus they handle largely coincides with that of the serial novel.

The approach to nineteenth-century serial novels written by women is of great use to feminist criticim of Spanish literature. It is an essential step toward the understanding of the development of the figure of the woman author, and of how this figure fostered a conception of woman as intellectual property owner (see Enríquez de Salamanca, "The Question"), which in turn led to the creation of a space for women in the public sphere (culminating with the relatively early movement for women's suffrage in a country in which feminism had not developed as it had in England or the United States). This approach is also key to the comprehension of how the modern concept of "woman" itself was constructed—literally formed for the first time—throughout the nineteenth century, and how texts by women and texts written by men about women coincided or diverged in this construction. This acknowledged, one must also say that as an approach to the serial novel, or to novelistic production preceding the Revolution of 1868 in general, feminist theory, as it has been applied, is insufficient. The singling out of women's novels from the larger corpus of which they were a part does not take into account that many of the traits attributed to these novels were also traits of novels written by men, and not necessarily for female audiences. The consequent, voluntarily or involuntarily implied, equation between serial or popular novel and women's novels does not, then, follow from available data, and sometimes obscures the study of the genre.

Lou Charnon-Deutsch defines the noncanonical "private canon" she addresses as one of women's novels: "In the latter half of the nineteenth century a small group of mostly upper-middle class women began to consume and write large quantities of novels popularly dubbed 'women's literature' . . . [and] scarcely represented in the canon . . . of nineteenth-century novelists" ("When the Canon," 475). Those novels would exhibit a "*poetics* of women's literature" (476), and the rationale for studying them is that "nineteenth-century women writers . . . discovered in the novel an ideal vehicle for imagining a way for women to become the best they could be, and in turn we find in them an ideal source for exploring the connections between gender ideology, gender oppression and canonical and cultural prestige." Thus, "quality aside, we cannot afford *not* to study them" (474) because "we owe it to our students . . . to assess marginal literary traditions *differently* than the men we had as our teachers." By "we," Charnon-Deutsch means "a somewhat ghettoized group of Hispanists, still mostly women, to or for whom the canon too often fails to speak" (472). For this interpretive community, noncanonical texts are of interest for one of two reasons: because of a private need for "catharsis, closure, sexual release, acute sensitivity" that might transfom us into "closet consumers of romance, spy or science fiction novels," or because we consider the texts transcendent in the sense of "counter-cultural and subversive" (472).

Leaving aside the matter of whether women scholars in general or women Hispanists in particular were "ghettoized" (thus powerless) in 1993 academia (especially American), the basic principles that Charnon-Deutsch uses in the "Diálogo crítico" to explain her approach to nineteenth-century women's novels isolate these from male-authored novels with which they shared many thematic, structural, and physical traits, and would seem to suggest that only women novelists, as opposed to men novelists, were erased from the canon after 1870. It also suggests that the main reason for the academic recuperation of these novels is a particular countercultural or subversive point of view: that of women at odds with patriarchal culture. Although there were many women novelists—and those who published in *folletín* form did not always publish in women's magazines, but also in the major newspapers and journals—most of the authors of serial novels were men. María del Pilar Sinués de Marco or Angela Grassi shared in popularity with Ayguals de Izco, Fernández y González, Antonio Flores, or Enrique Pérez Escrich. Male or female, these novelists tended to publish in the same formats, and their works shared common views on desire, domesticity, class relations. They have *all* disappeared from the Spanish canon, and it is imperative to consider the factors that contributed to their *collective* dismissal.

In this context, Catherine Jagoe's argument that in order to contest the hegemony of the serial novelists (male and female), realists, led by Galdós, first had to stage their identification with feminine values, and that by doing this they were instituting a divide between a "literary" and a "nonliterary" or "popular" novel that did not exist before, is both perceptive and pertinent. Before 1870, serial novels were not a countercultural or subversive product, or rather, they were not so primarily in terms of gender but of literary and class status. On the one hand, the very fact of writing novels in the early and mid-nineteenth century is an assault on existing ideas of the aesthetic, and on the order of literary genres. On the other hand, the issue of gender, while significant, was subsumed within the issue of class ideology. As I will argue further on, these novels were a central part of the bourgeois capitalist revolution directed against the aristocratic social standard prevalent at the onset of the century. Consequently, serial novels became "establishment" (ripe for Galdós's vilification) when the middle class had achieved, or was close to achieving, establishment status.

While Alda Blanco too observes that "the exclusion of a prolific generation of *women authors* writing between 1850 and 1870 can be seen as a result of a series of critical moves which began to take place in Spanish literary historiography with the appearance of the Realist novel" ("But Are They," 464, my emphasis), she opens up an interesting avenue by making it clear that "not only have the women writers been erased from the canon, but in fact the whole period between 1850 and 1870 has disappeared from the text of the history of the novel" (466). Like Jagoe, Blanco recognizes that "what Galdós undertakes is the construction of a realist theory of the novel in opposition to, or in contradistinction to, contemporary forms of novel writing" (468). Nevertheless, she goes on to re-gender those forms of novel writing in terms that should be qualified. Blanco argues that they are critically devalued because of their "predominantly female *readership*" (468, my emphasis), appropriating the argument made by Terry Lovell in *Consuming Fiction* that "a condition of literary canonization, then, may have been not so much that the author must be male, as that the work must be addressed to men and read by them, and not addressed exclusively to women" (83, qtd. in Blanco, "But Are They," 468–69).

The view of serial novels as addressed in large part to a feminine audience has been widely held. In her study *La mujer en la novela por entregas del siglo XIX*, Ángeles Carmona affirms that "these are works fundamentally addressed to women" (118). Montesinos points out that "the names of those collections indicate how editors sought the favor of women" (*Introducción*, 128), and that "woman, and especially the young woman, contributes powerfully to the triumph of an art that fashions itself young" (129). Botrel posits that "it can be assumed that city women, much more literate than their fellow province women and traditionally idle, constituted a privileged audience for this type of novel" ("La novela por entregas," 133–34). Juan Ignacio Ferreras assumes the same readership: "If we go by the topic of many serial novels, of female protagonist and 'feminine' issues, it would seem that the serial novel must have been read by a great number of women" (*La novela por entragas,* 25).

Taking for granted that many *folletines* were specifically marketed for women—Angela Grassi's texts, for example, were serialized in *El correo de la moda,* which she directed, and Faustina Sáez de Melgar wrote in *La violeta*—statistics about Spanish literacy should serve to qualify the assumption of *majoritary* female readership (and note that Montesinos, Botrel, and Ferreras do not refer to a *predominance* of women readers). In 1860 the census counts roughly 3,130,000 literate persons in Spain; of those, 716,000 are women (less than 23 percent) (Botrel, *Libros,* 310).[4] A successful market genre such as the serial novel, with printings and reprintings of around two hundred thousand copies each (see note 1 of this chapter) could not have been geared *mainly* to those who constituted a minoritary section of that market. It is logical to assume that men, who formed the greater part of writers, were also, based on such literacy figures, the greater part of readers, even if women were a *significant* part of that readership (especially in urban areas). One should furthermore be careful not to make the jump implicit in the above quote by Ferreras, who presumes a female readership based on the appearance of female protagonists and "feminine problems." The presence of sentimentality and domesticity do not necessarily signal the search for a female audience, and elements such as what came to be named *lo cursi* [the affected, maudlin] are central to nineteenth-century aesthetics in general. The popularity of the serial novel (of the early novel) was most likely due to its appeal for a large audience, across gender lines, and this despite the significant noise nineteenth-century intellectuals made about the dangers such texts posed for their female readership.

I made earlier the rather strong statement that the feminist approach to pre-1870 Spanish novels can obscure their study. This is not to denigrate this perspective—useful, as I pointed out, to study certain novels, and from the point of view of a narrative of literary history that takes into account the important contributions of women to the genre's development. My point is rather that the general isolation of women's writing or women's reading encourages a certain kind of attention to the genre, clearly described by John Sinnigen. In his participation in the "Diálogo crítico" he refers to his own position (contested by Jagoe) as related to Nancy Hartsock's concept of an "epistemology of the dominated" ("Symbolic Struggles," 443):

> According to this view, cultural production by the dominated is to be valued as an achievement in the face of unfavorable material conditions and a hostile ideological environment. This epistemology necessarily decenters the question of quality, since quality as difference (different conditions of production as well as different types of texts produced) competes with quality as aesthetically "better," and social achievement competes with aesthetic achievement, as reasons for being studied.

Addressing mid-nineteenth-century novelistic production as women's production, or identifying it chiefly with the mark of the feminine leads one to look for a certain kind of "subversiveness" in it, namely the subversiveness of an oppressed gender fighting for its voice. This projects onto the early and mid-nineteenth century a current notion of what it means to be a woman, and of how the novel can serve a specific suppressed form of subjectivity, minimizing at the same time the way in which men's and women's novels shared an epistemology.

Additionally, Sinnigen's stand on the notion of quality—the conviction that these novels should not be judged on the same aesthetic standards as canonical novels, but rather according to a different but equally significant *symbolic* standard of value, dependent on their power relations to social and political institutions (445)—might, paradoxically, discourage the researcher from assuming a historical, contingent view of specifically *literary* value. In other words, the qualities we presently value in novels (either the realist aesthetic, or the various types of self-reflexive complexity of "good" modern and postmodern novels) were not the qualities valued in mid-nineteenth-century novels by their original readers. It is not that serial novels were produced or read according to a different standard of value than other novels of the time (although, as we will see, the introduction of the novel in Spain did demand a change of the evaluative strategies used for other genres), but that standards of value changed with time, feminizing and "disinheriting," to borrow Jagoe's terms, the earlier aesthetics of novels written by both men and women.

The approach described by the above-mentioned critics conceals the fact that between the 1840s and the 1860s the serial novel was not an extracanonical form subordinate or oppositional to other, already prestigious and "canonized" novels but, simply, the novel. Men and women writers shared in the development of the form and participated equally, depending on the specific work, in the revolutionary or reactionary ideology (i.e., Böhl de Faber) it carried. Men and women novelists participated in the same literary market, and very often published in a format that would itself be equated with the noncanonical. Men and women readers impatiently awaited the next installment, to follow the adventures of characters about whom they worried as if they were real. It is as the early history of the novel—not a prehistory, not an inferior "paranovel," not a countercultural liberatory discourse—that the serial novel can be most fruitfully addressed at this point. This outlook, suggested in 1974 by Goldman, has yet to lead to a comprehensive study of the form, both thoroughly researched and theoretically informed. While such a project definitely exceeds the bounds of an essay like this one, what follows is an attempt to point in the direction of this type of revision of the narrative of nineteenth-century literary history.

Why has serial novel production, chronologically contemporaneous with the Romantic historical novel and hegemonic until the advent of Galdós's prose, not fully made it into such a narrative of literary history? One answer, if somewhat redundant, is that from the late nineteenth century on, critics with considerable cultural prestige have characterized it negatively. A model to understand what happened to the Spanish novel after 1870, and consequently what happened to the novel before that point, is provided by Pierre Bourdieu's consideration of the literary field. According to Bourdieu, literature is a field of struggles, structured primarily by the opposition between a subfield of large-scale production and a subfield of restricted production (strictly "aesthetic" creation by and for a limited number of initiates). Secondarily, already within the field of restricted production, literature is structured by the opposition between consecrated writers and the newcomers who seek to displace their cultural orthodoxy. This configuration is not, however, a constant. Different genres advance at different paces toward the split between the two subfields of production. What Galdós and the important realist writers who soon followed him achieved, supported by the cultural institutions of the moment, was precisely the division of the territory of the novel into the space of aesthetic, restricted production, and the space of large-scale, "popular" or "mass" production (as I will argue in the following chapter, Galdós led the same movement also in the case of theater).

Catherine Jagoe has alluded to the arguments Galdós mounted against previous novelistic creation in the essays "Observaciones sobre la novela contemporánea en España" [Observations on the Contemporary Novel in Spain] (1870) and "Un tribunal literario" [A Literary Tribunal] (1872), and in the novel *La desheredada* [The Disinherited Lady] (1881). To these texts one should add, at the very least, the short story "La novela en el tranvía" [The Novel in the Tram] (1871) and the necrological articles on Manuel Fernández y González published in 1888 (singled out by Victor Ouimette). Several types of objections appear in these texts. First, Galdós attacks the serial novel's sentimentality (Jagoe, following Naomi Schor as well as nineteenth-century nomenclature, calls it "idealism") and its failure to truly reflect the life of the Spanish middle class. Second, he characterizes it as a "novela de impresiones y movimiento" [of impressions and movement] ("Observaciones," 164), dizzying readers with its lack of verisimilitude. Third, he accuses these novels of favoring entertainment rather than fashioning themselves as "obras serias y concienzudas, de puro interés literario" [serious and conscientious novels, of pure literary interest] (163). Fourth, he derides the novels as mass productions, both in the sense that masses of novels were produced by one author at a breakneck pace, and in the sense that they were addressed to the necessarily undistinguished mass of readers. Fifth, he associates them with an unquestioning, uncultured, feminine reader who confuses their contents with reality. And sixth, he brands the novels, the writers, the readers, and the entire publishing process as consumerism (somewhat ironically, since one of the vices most often attacked in the earlier novels had been consumerism itself, the desire for luxury and leisure).

All aspects of this criticism are reflected in Galdós's articles on the death of Manuel Fernández y González, where he writes:

> Meditando un poco sus obras, habría llegado adonde pocos llegan. Pero la tarea febril de su composición a destajo no permitió que todas sus facultades brillasen por igual. Era un temperamento enemigo del reposo y de la concepción lenta y madura. Necesitaba producirse constantemente, y la abundancia de su fantasía, estimulándole a la creación incesante, perjudicaba a la misma creación como obra literaria. Lo escrito por Fernández y González debe juzgarse y apreciarse en conjunto, más que en la unidad de cada obra; es una monstruosa fecundidad, un derroche de in-

genio, y un amontonamiento de cualidades que se oscurecen las unas a las otras por falta de ponderación. ("Fernández y González," 106–7)

[Had he carefully thought out his works, he would have arrived at where few did. But the feverish task of his piecework composition did not allow all his faculties to shine equally. His was a temperament opposed to rest and slow, mature conception. He needed to produce himself constantly, and the wealth of his fantasy, stimulating him to incessant creation, was detrimental to that very creation as literary work. The writing of Fernández y González should be judged and appreciated as a whole, rather than in the unity of each work; it is a monstruous fecundity, a waste of wit, and a piling up of qualities that obscure each other for lack of restraint.]

The above judgment is complemented with the observation that "sus novelas le produjeron cantidades fabulosas" [his novels earned him fabulous sums] (110), followed by the vividly related tale of how Fernández y González squandered his earnings, dying in misery.

Thus, the writer's method of feverish composition, at the expense of thought, meditation, and slow maturing of the works, prevents these from achieving literary quality. This criticism, though directed specifically at Fernández y González, really affects all serial production; in it, a different standard of quality from the one that had formed the context of the serial novel is put forth. Ferreras, Botrel, and several other scholars have documented how the idea for a work often came from an editor, who would then assign a writer to produce it; how, often, a writer might be replaced midnovel by another; how Fernández y González himself was famous for dictating to his secretaries (one of whom was Vicente Blasco Ibáñez) several novels at once. Works produced in this way would, for Galdós and his followers, necessarily remain impersonal and unindividuated, and could therefore only be considered "as a whole, rather than in the unity of each work." For Galdós, novels should be the unitary work of "unique creators irreducible to any condition or conditioning" (Bourdieu, *Field,* 29). Individual works are not to be considered as part of the whole of the other works of the author or the time, but as *singular* works of art, designed according to an aesthetic plan (this will manifest itself concretely in the realists's relative abandonment of the formerly frequent device of the continuation, whereby a new novel, with a different title, would use characters and situations from a previous one).

Galdós's choice of words in the above quote reinforces Jagoe's contention about his impulse toward the feminization of the existing novel (an impulse which would have been unnecessary had the genre already been widely considered as feminine). He refers to Fernández y González's prolificacy through a curious, ungrammatical use of the reflexive (*producirse,* to *produce* oneself) allusive to the function of reproduction, and as fertility gone awry—"monstrous fecundity" or "fecundidad más prodigiosa" [most prodigious fecundity] ("Fernández y González," 105)—reminding one of the madwoman and monster figures often used in Western traditions to characterize women authors of the period. But the idea of a monstruous or excessive production also represents a reflection on the novel's participation in the literary field as *market.* "Un número increíble de lectores en todas las clases sociales" [an incredible number of readers of all social classes] (105) produces astonishing amounts of money, but the exchange is characterized as squander. Fernández y González's efforts are a "waste of wit," the input incommensurate with the value of the output, because that output is to be measured in a new way. Galdós's notion of quality is at odds with the concept of literature as *primarily* a salaried profession—though, as evident in "Un tribunal literario," he obviously thinks writers should be properly remunerated—and thus the "waste" has strong monetary connotations. The earnings are disproportionate with regard to the product, and consequently irresponsibly dissipated by an author who doesn't seem able to control his wealth.

In other words, literature assumes the form of the commodity, an objectified form of men's (and women's) labor characterized by an arbitrary exchange value that replaces, or obscures, the true social relationships behind it.[5] For Galdós the waste, and the relations of exchange from which it springs, qualify the existing novel as mass culture that fails to enact the necessary demarcation between the discourse of art and the discourse of commerce (as was indeed the case with the serial novel). In opposition, he proposes a new model of novel—also about the middle class, but in a different, more critical and distanced way—that will contest the ascendancy of bourgeois capitalism, even while participating, quite actively, in the culture industry. The novel as literature, from this moment on, will be ostensibly separated from the economic world; in Bourdieu's terms, it will become "the economic world reversed" (*Field,* 29).

Galdós's characterization of the serial novel as *popular,* in the sense of mass-produced, mass-consumed, nonartistic literature, separate from a different corpus of aesthetic creation which he represents, succeeds. It is the view Menéndez y Pelayo, authorized by his own cultural prestige and his power to consecrate, reiterates in his much cited 1897 speech on Galdós's induction to the Royal Academy of Language: "Entre monstruosidades y ñoñeces dormitaba la novela por los años de 1870" [among monstrosities and inanities slept the novel around 1870] (qtd. in Jagoe, "Disinheriting," 225; and Blanco, "But Are They," 466). It is the view adopted by most of the 1970s critics of the serial novel, who start their investigations from it, and adopt the perspective of trying to assess the symbiotic relationship between the "popular" and the "literary." And the same view is, I would argue, inherent in the approaches to the serial novel as noncanonical "feminine" literature (inasmuch as they emphasize its *difference* from the canonical novel, and inasmuch as the popular is often implicitly gendered). While this kind of "popularity" is at least partly attributable to post-1870 serial production (although quite respectable authors, including Galdós and Clarín, would often publish in serial format), earlier novels were not in the relational position to "serious" literature ascribed to popular or noncanonical texts. Galdós's triumph in creating the modern novel is therefore a triumph in creating the field of restricted production, but also in the struggle of neophytes to replace the aesthetic norms of already consecrated writers, and achieving, in this case, their relegation to the domain of the subliterary.

Another key reason why the serial novel has not been widely studied as the early development of the genre in Spain is its categorization as mimicry of a foreign form. Galdós laments in 1870 that the prevailing novelistic model signifies "la sustitución de la *novela nacional* de pura observación por esa otra convencional y sin carácter, género que cultiva cualquiera, *peste nacida en Francia* y que se ha difundido con la pasmosa rapidez de todos los males contagiosos" [the substitution of the *national novel* of pure observation for that other one, conventional and without character, genre that anyone can practice, *pest born in France,* and which has spread with the amazing speed of all contagious maladies] ("Observaciones," 164, my emphases). In addition to marking the difference between the novel he will attempt and the novel as it exists—observation vs. convention—the postulate rests on the assumption that whatever novel there is in Spain, it does not amount to *the* Spanish novel, but remains a foreign imitation; thus, "we have no novel." As Jesús Torrecilla amply documents, the opinion was shared by many of his contemporaries. During the period 1860–1908, systematic attempts were made to spur the creation of a national novel:

> In order to counter the importation of French *feuilletons,* and at the same time stimulate the creativity of national writers, literary contests are organized, with an adequate protectionism. The initiative of those contests is taken by the Royal Academy (two), [and the journals] *La Ilustración Española y Americana* (1874), *El Mosquito* (1879), *El Imparcial* (1883); the will, on the part of newspaper directors, to promote "the national novel" . . . and "encourage, on the other hand, writers not yet well known, but considerably talented" . . . manifests itself repeatedly. International agreements between Spain and France, and Spain and Italy, are also signed, in order to control the "commerce" of novels from beyond the Pyrenees and fix very high copyrights for Spain. (Lecuyer and Villapadierna "Génesis y desarrollo," 29–30)

Iñigo Sánchez Llama mentions a similar novel-writing contest sponsored by the Royal Academy in 1866 (Angela Grassi won second place), and details the requirements: the original novels presented should not be historical, but should feature contemporary customs and give primary importance to linguistic purity and morality.

Galdós's position about the lack of a native novel before 1870 is echoed, as we have seen, by Menéndez Pelayo. Sixty years later, Montesinos still affirms that there was no Spanish novel in the first half of the century (since he writes about the period 1800–1850). His study consequently concentrates on what was translated in those years: Fielding, Chateaubriand, and Scott before the 1840s, followed by Balzac, George Sand, Soulié, Nodier, Sue, Dumas, and Hugo after that. Of particular interest in this context is Montesinos's observation that

> one gets the impression that the concept of novel, which only very recently has begun to include lengthy works of fiction, is still not clearly fixed. Or rather, it can be affirmed that editors and audience fix it at that time, not without resistance from old-fashioned folks, who did not always understand that a ten-volume work could be called a novel. (*Introducción*, 139)

Into the 1850s, the name *novela* alternated with others like *romance* or *cuento* (story) to designate the same kind of lengthy fictions, and verse novels coexisted with prose novels. This hesitation suggests, rather than the absence of the form, the importance of the period as a formative point in its Spanish history. It is evident from Montesinos's remarks that in Spain there is, by the 1830s and for some time after that, a concern over what exactly will constitute the novel as a genre.

From early on, there is also a simultaneous anxiety over the creation of a *national* novel. Lamentations over the excess of foreign, and especially French, translations are common. Romero Tobar quotes an 1834 statement by Alcalá Galiano (the first native historian of Spanish literature) that "en conjunto, los españoles, son muy dados a la lectura de novelas y están provistos con abundancia por los franceses" [as a whole, Spaniards are very given to the reading of novels, and are well-provided by the French] (*La novela popular,* 36). The "anonymous" author of the following article in an 1839 *Semanario pintoresco español* (actually Mesonero Romanos) ascribes devilish deeds not to the serial novel in general, but to French novels in particular:

> Siguiendo la misma influencia periodística, hasta las obras de más unidad y trabazón, han dado en publicarse por entregas.... Todo se achica y estruja lo suficiente para poder entrar por bajo de las puertas ó caber en la cartera del repartidor; y los más abultados mamotretos ... filtran, insensiblemente, su quinta esencia en los más indiferentes lectores, que sin saber cómo, se encuentran al cabo del año con que han leído diez grandes volúmenes y tragado inadvertidamente todo el veneno ó narcótico que contienen. A favor de esta subdivisión infinitisimal [sic] van inundando los tocadores, las chimeneas y hasta las alcobas, las novelas de Balzac, Soulie, G. Sand y otros ingenios transpirenáicos, ... contribuyendo poquito á poquito a la perpetración de nuevos crímenes y al aumento de nuevas y curiosas páginas á las *Memorias del Diablo.* ("Crónica literaria," 191)

> [Following the same journalistic influence, even the most unified, cohesive works have begun to be serialized.... Everything is shrunk and crumpled up to fit in the newspaper boy's bag, and the thickest tomes ... imperceptibly filter their essence into readers who, without knowing how, find at the end of a year that they have read ten huge volumes and inadvertently swallowed all the poison or narcotic they contain. Aided by this infinitesimal subdivision, boudoirs, chimneys, and even bedchambers are gradually flooded by the novels of Balzac, Soulie, G. Sand and other trans-Pyrenean wits, ... contributing little by little to the perpetration of new crimes and the addition of new and curious pages to the *Devil's Memoirs.*]

In an 1840 piece, he advises the reader to peruse French newspapers and count: "a cuántos desgraciados han conducido esas máximas al Sena, cuántas seducciones, adulterios, violencias, separaciones han causado" [how many wretches those maxims have driven to the Seine; how many seductions, adulteries, violent acts, separations, they have caused] (qtd. in Romero Tobar, *La novela popular,* 36).

Romero Tobar shows that the the rejection of foreign novels was accompanied by an insistence on the need for indigenous production, and that the need to produce original texts, even if they followed the French model, "drove some very notable cultivators of popular literature to present themselves as pioneers in the creation of the *national novel*" (36–37). He mentions Juan Martínez Villergas, Gregorio Romero Larrañaga, Fernán Caballero (based on the tertulia in *La gaviota* where the type of novel best suited to Spanish sensibility is discussed), and, especially, Ayguals de Izco.[6] Rubén Benítez details how Ayguals, who essentially originates the *novela por entregas* with his 1845–46 *María o la hija de un jornalero* [Mary, or the Labourer's Daughter], "is conscious of his innovativeness. He warns that *María* is a protypical product of Spanish literature, explicable only from the model of the Cervantine novel. In the prologue to *María* he attempts to differentiate himself from the French *feuilleton*" (*Ideología*, 47).[7] As he also makes clear, Ayguals nationalizes the foreign model, focusing on Spanish political and social history rather than on foreign history, and thus turning it into material worthy of writing about.

The same preoccupation with producing a particularly Spanish novel, connectable with Cervantine tradition, appears in Antonio Flores's prologue to the volume edition of his *Fe, esperanza y caridad* [Faith, Hope, and Charity] (originally serialized in 1857), one of the most successful serial novels ever. Just as in their historical novels Larra or Gil y Carrasco looked to *Don Quijote*, Antonio Flores also evokes the model as he self-consciously wonders how to proceed with the writing.[8] His lengthy comments on the difficulty of writing a prologue, patterned after Cervantes's, constitute a reflection on the nature of that nonfictional discourse in relation to the fiction that follows it, as well as on the intricate balance between formulas and original writing:

> Yo he visto muchos prólogos; casi tantos como libros; pero ¿qué relación guardan la mayor parte de ellos con el texto de las obras que los acompañan? ¿No están todos calcados sobre un mismo patrón . . . ? ¿Pues cuanto mas valdria que hubiese un prólogo que sirviese para muchos libros, que no el que haya muchos libros que se sirvan del mismo prólogo? ¿No sería mejor que un mismo ingenio inventase una fórmula, que no el ponerlos á todos y para cada una de sus obras, en el compromiso de discurrir algo nuevo . . . ? (vi)

> [I have seen many prologues; almost as many as books; but, in what relationship do most of them stand to the works that accompany them? Are

they not all copied from the same pattern? So, would it not be better to have one prologue to fit many books, than many books using the same prologue? Would it not be better to have one sage invent a formula, than to place them all, and for every one of their new works, in the position of having to come up with something new?]

Such a brief quote shows a marked intertextual exchange with a text (*Don Quijote*) that functions as blueprint, model, and measure for writers of the nineteenth century who are concerned with the status of fiction, as well with as the generic parameters of the novel. It also shows an attempt on the part of these authors to give respectability to their practice of a new, scarcely prestigious genre, by emphasizing its connection with what had already become a Spanish classic.

We see, then, how the early and mid-nineteenth-century serial novelists precede Galdós in deploring the nonexistence of the Spanish novel, and how they actively attempt to produce it. Ayguals, in his double character as editor and writer, worries about acclimating Spanish audiences to the then current concept of the novel through the publication of translations (the public's favorite was Eugene Sue's *El judío errante* [The Wandering Jew] in 1844). As Elisa Martí López has shown in *Borrowed Words,* Ayguals and other serial novelists are aware of the novel's roots in Spanish tradition, and look to Cervantes as an archetype (although the mention of his name seems to be more frequent than the actual attempt to emulate his fiction). They dream of making a significant contribution to the development of the genre, which might be acknowledged by succeeding generations. They consciously distance themselves from French production, even when, as in the case of Ayguals, they seek the support, in the form of letters of evaluation, of famous French novelists who will lend them prestige.[9] They describe in detail the contemporary life and customs of Spaniards of all classes—portraying a decadent aristocracy, a rising bourgeoisie, the environment of the urban workers, and the criminal underworld—so that it is somewhat inaccurate to say of later realism that "for the first time in Western literary history, [it] portrayed mundane, non-aristocratic, and even ugly characters at the centre of serious narratives" (Jagoe, "Disinheriting," 232). In short, although they did not succeed in being perceived by posterity as having created, once and for all, the authentic Spanish novel—it was too soon for this, perhaps—they did take the first steps to bring it into being, and they *were* Spanish writers writing what was then considered the novel in Spain. As it turns out, there was indeed a Spanish novel.

The entire controversy over whether the Spanish novel existed, and the struggle on the part of particular writers to be the ones to institute it, must be understood in the context of Spanish nationalism—a very strong force behind cultural movement throughout the entire nineteenth century, beginning with the aftermath of the Napoleonic invasion. As cultural theorist Itamar Even-Zohar points out, within a culture literature can function as a set of goods representing something, or as a set of tools to achieve something. Literature as goods—as a valuable canonical endowment—has been crucial to the concept of nation since antiquity. Even-Zohar traces the existence of this type of endowment, part of "the *indispensabilia* of power" ("Literature as Goods," par. 6.4, n. 3), back to the civilizations of Sumeria, Akkad, Babylon, Egypt, and Assyria. Nevertheless, the transformation of abstract cultural products into valuable symbolic goods "has not been a linear process, nor a unique event that might have occurred once and for all in some yore. On the contrary, it has been a permanent struggle" (par. 6.2).

In this struggle, and quite importantly in the context of our attention to the serial novel (which always shared the market with innumerable translations), production need not be extensive in order to become valuable as patrimony:

> Value, being above all symbolic, does not necessarily require ample production. Sometimes, the capacity to produce can be sufficient in order for "the obligatory list of indispensable goods" [of the culture] to be checked off in the relevant category. In very extreme cases, the persons that are potentially capable of producing texts are more important than the products. I cannot avoid thinking, for example, of Cacofonix, this bard of the Armorican village of Asterix, who is never allowed to sing his poems, although his role as "the village bard" is indispensable. (6.3)

The function of literature is, as pointed above, *symbolic*. As such, it is also central to the power of a state: "'possessing a literature' is thus equivalent to 'possessing riches appropriate for a powerful ruler'" (6.4).

This function is nevertheless only initially limited to the state as a political institution. It eventually becomes relevant for much larger human collectives that need to strengthen their group ties through a sense of cultural unity and common nationality:

> In the history of literature as goods, these goods change proprietors. From a state in which in order to be valuable they must belong to a ruler, they become goods belonging "to everybody." As such, instead of "en-

nobling and consolidating" the political power of a ruler, they then ennoble and consolidate the sense of identity and the welfare of large collectives. . . . Since the Eighteenth century, the foundation of some national languages and literatures has then been equivalent to the acquirement of goods for self-identification and self-construction, which in other times had been characteristic of leading groups only. (6.5)[10]

The effort of Spanish intellectuals to "create"—repeatedly—the national novel, as well as to link it to linguistic purity, is inseparable from the communal effort to come to terms with the cultural hegemony of France in Europe; with the centrifugal forces already present, most strongly, in Catalonia and the Basque Country; with the instability of the monarchy and the confusion over lines of succession; with the century-long decline of imperial power; and especially with the radical social transformation produced by the rise of the bourgeoisie.[11]

Thus, the intellectuals of the early nineteenth-century observe the absence in Spain of something that France and England produce in abundance, and explicitly declare that it is necessary to have it too, if Spain is to be considered on par with other European nations. The imitative effort to develop a genre that exists elsewhere (*because* it exists elsewhere) is, by itself, enough to have produced the exclusion of the pre-1870 novel from Spanish literary history. As David Perkins has shown, literary history developed throughout the nineteenth century as a narrative that "traced the phases or sometimes the birth and/or death of a suprapersonal entity" (*Is Literary History Possible?* 2), and suprapersonal entities were "'ideal unities' or 'logical subjects,'" such as nations, religions, and classes" (3). For a discipline that sought to explain literature as an aesthetic evolution conditioned by, or even naturally springing from, a unified national conscience, (overt) imitation and exchange—such as Martí López has traced in *Borrowed Words*—were anathema. Galdós's formulation of a particularly Spanish novel, "donde respire y se agite todo el cuerpo social" [in which the whole social body breathes and moves] ("Observaciones," 166), was more likely to find its way into the history of literature.

Although in the 1840s and 50s the claim to national distinction already exists—manifest in the stress on Cervantes—it works chiefly as an assertion of Spain's nuclear position in the creation of the European novel, a claim to have given it to the now powerful England and France. As there is more production of native works, however, the problem of competition with the French market emerges. While at that point the Spanish novel as an endowment of cultural goods definitely exists (the preponderance of its production over foreign translations not being a requisite for its reality as a national institution), it is not succeeding in *displacing* the foreign novel—partly because it is scarcely differentiated from it, and partly because the publishing infrastructure cannot match that of the other countries (especially France).[12] By the time Galdós arrives on the literary scene, it is already becoming possible to improve the material production of the book (one reason why serial publication will diminish), recovering that production industry for Spain.[13] It becomes necessary to create a fully distinct Spanish novel as well. The process begun at this point will be successful in both literary and cultural terms. In the last years of the century the existence of an *artistic* national novel will begin to be acknowledged by all. But this achievement will be reached at the expense of forgetting the genre's local history.[14]

What, then, was the serial novel like? Despite the great variety in contents, scholars have insisted on one formal feature: that of conventionality, repetitiveness, lack of originality. This criticism too was already present in Galdós, as I pointed out in my earlier discussion of his obituary for Fernández y González: the existing novel was that of *convention;* his, that of *observation*. Botrel, Ferreras, and Romero Tobar, among others, describe the serial novel's formulaic nature as both structural and thematic. At the structural level, the precarious literacy of its readers, together with the publisher's financial interest, dictate a certain typographical design, with large, clear fonts, and lots of blank space on the page. The novel's marketing in serial format necessitates the use of techniques like the suspense with which each installment ends (a technique not entirely absent from nonserialized novels divided into chapters), and even leads to thematic continuity beyond the boundaries of a single novel.[15] There is also an insistent use of some devices, such as the ubiquitous presence of a very conspicuous author/narrator, who not only tells, but extensively comments and explains, in didactic dialogue with the reader (see Romero Tobar, *La novela popular,* 153).

At the level of contents, one notes the repetition of certain themes, among which critics have noted those of illegitimate children and, in general, family relations (within which I would note the importance of incest, or the risk of incest, since it is not uncommon that a character will feel love or sexual tension with regard to someone who turns out to be a brother or sister); *costumbrista* description of customs; crime and the *lumpen;* etc. (for an inventory of themes, see Ferreras, *La novela por entregas,* 254–55). Apart from the usually noted sentimental, familial, or patriotic story lines, and as I will explain below, I consider money and social mobility the dominant themes of the majority of serial novels. The story types are also repeated often, so that Ferreras and other scholars can make inventories of the kinds of *novelas por entregas* published. Instead of attempting to define further a typology of serial novels, I will come back to some important lines in my analysis.

Scholars of the serial novel are, of course, right in their observation of its formulaic nature. But rather than taking for granted the equation between the formulaic and the "popular" or subliterary, one can analyze why this quality, so prevalent in the nineteenth-century Spanish novel (as it also was in the theater), did not automatically signal the presence of an inferior work. It is possible to reconstruct moments in the history of a genre in which literary value is placed precisely on conventionality, and the first half of the nineteenth century in Spain is very plausibly one such moment (in fact, both theater and poetry are also highly conventional at the time). Without a continuous tradition stemming from *Don Quijote*, the novel was still a young genre, and individual texts were not just exponents but also preceptive constituents of the form. Any one text—historical or *costumbrista* novels (often published serially) as much as the majority of serial novels—would structure itself not through departure from a pre-established set of conventions, but through an "original" use of the very sets of conventions they all sought to establish. Critics of the moment defined this originality in widely varying and often vague terms, and praised authors whose personal touch or elegant prose distinguished them from others, or who successfully adapted an avowedly foreign model to national circumstances. Furthermore, originality was not necessarily opposed to imitation of such models. As Torrecilla has noted, originality can be conceived in two distinct ways: "the 'originality of the latest' and the 'originality of the authentic'" (*La imitación colectiva*, 34). Those novelists who first see themselves as innovators against the antiquated Spanish tradition understand their adaptation of a French form as a venture into modernity. The rejection of this sort of originality in favor of its second sense (national authenticity) is always "a second movement, subsequent to the attraction felt towards the trends in vogue, and conditioned by it" (42).

In pre-1870 Spain there existed also the problem of intelligibility with regard to readers who not only were to a large degree unfamiliar with the novel as a genre, but also with the practice of reading in itself. As both Goldman and Jean-François Botrel have shown, at that time literate persons in Spain were few in relation both to its own population and to the literacy rate of other European countries. Nevertheless, the extremely rapid rate of increase in the number of literate persons indicates the appearance of a growing group of individuals who could enjoy a cultural product that was also available as never before. The structure of the serial novel responded to the needs of this emerging public. Its conventionality worked indeed as a narrative grammar containing, in Thomas G. Pavel's words, "information on narrators, on the contents of narratives, on events and their organization" ("Literary Conventions," 56). It not only facilitated the generic definition of the novel, but also the audience's progressive maturation through the development of reading strategies based on recognition of a precedent.

As Pavel puts it in his essay on literary conventions, "archaic formulaic works, which usually presuppose a heavy battery of known prescriptions, do not direct the attention of their readers toward the same kind of effect as a modern text: reading strategies based on precedent differ from those searching for novelty" (54). In his account, an individual who encounters a literary form for the first time reacts to it through "strategies of discovery" (58)—every element of the text will be new. The subject who applies "strategies of recognition" (who looks for elements he/she knows will appear), though unsophisticated in comparison with present-day, academic, innovation-seeking practices, is already at a second stage of reading and interpretation, and deriving a very specific pleasure from it:

> The transition from novel solutions to solutions based on precedent helps to emphasize an important component of aesthetic pleasure, which the romantic and modernist traditions . . . unfortunately neglect. Like all games in which skill improves with training, literary games enhance the pleasure of taking fewer and fewer risks, of feeling oneself more and more in control. . . . The practicing reader senses the growing of his power and dexterity; he enjoys his progress and loves to continue the practice. (58)

Highly formulaic forms such as the serial novel—and twentieth-century forms like the *novela rosa* or the detective novel—allow their readers to develop and show a high degree of competence. In the early nineteenth century, the insistence on the formula was also instrumental in educating readers about what the term *novela* would thereafter designate.

John Cawelti has concisely defined a formula as the "combination or synthesis of a number of specific cultural conventions with a more universal story form or archetype" (*Adventure*, 6) that translates into "particular sorts of story patterns and effects." Such a definition provides very clear terms with which to approach the analysis of the serial novel's formula: what are its specific conventions and figures? what are its story patterns? what kinds of cultural preoccupations do they evidence? Care should be taken in this approach, however, since the concept of "serial novel" defines first and foremost a novel published in installments, and not all serial novels conformed to one pattern. Many followed the conventions of historical novels or *costumbrismo*, and many which did not mainly obey these conventions partly incorporated them. Nevertheless, there is an archetype that appears at the same time as (and is partly determined by) the printing and marketing technology of serialization, and which together with this technology can be seen as a foundation of the nineteenth-century Spanish novel. In general terms this archetype is characterized, as several critics have noted, by the attention to sentimentality. It posits a specifically domestic idea of morality, establishing the separation between the public and private spheres (and definitely feminizing the latter). Most centrally, I believe, it is concerned with urban class relations, and particularly with stimulating, recording, and confirming the ascendancy of the bourgeoisie; it can therefore be called, years before Galdós, the Spanish bourgeois novel.

It will be helpful at this point to recall the plots of some sample novels. It is unfornately necessary to summarize these works at length, since they are largely unknown and also quite convoluted. Ayguals's *María o la hija de un jornalero* tells the story of María, daughter of the brave urban policeman Anselmo (a former soldier in the War of Independence) and his good wife Luisa, who is blinded after years of hard work as a seamstress. The innocent María and her family undergo a long series of mishaps and disgraces—some the result of poverty and illness, some provoked by the ungodly lust that Fray Patricio, "usurer and Carlist, gluttonous and lascivious cleric" (Benítez, *Ideología*, 48) feels for her. As a result of her *temple* (character) and *templanza* (moderation, restraint, frugality), and supported by some virtuous benefactors, María eventually overcomes adversity and marries her beloved Don Luis de Mendoza, noble Marquis of Bellaflor, effectively producing, through the union of aristocracy and *pueblo*, a new class. In *Pobres y ricos, o la Bruja de Madrid* [The Poor and the Rich, or The Witch of Madrid] (1849–50), by the same author, Eduardo, the secretly illegitimate son of the formerly dissolute Duque de la Azucena, falls in love with Enriqueta, the daughter of an honest and honorable painter. Their love is impeded by the duke's insistence on Eduardo's marriage to an aristocratic but inconstant and immoral young woman, and also by the inexplicable opposition of a horribly disfigured, yet virtuous, beggar (the *bruja*) who had previously been a friend to both lovers. She objects to their union on the grounds that aristocrats (not all the rich) are naturally perverse, and only disgrace can come from an inter-class marriage. In the end, she turns out to be the poor woman the duke had seduced and abandoned, and Eduardo as well as Enriqueta and their long-lost children. Because their kinship prevents their marriage, Eduardo commits suicide and Enriqueta joins a convent.

In Manuel Fernández y González's *Los desheredados* [The Disinherited] (1857)—note the explicit connection with the title, and content, of Galdós's later *La desheredada*—Gaspar Media-Noche is a hunchback with a beautiful soul. An orphan adopted by a poor family, he becomes doubly orphaned when his step-parents die, and is subsequently raised by a good priest (an uncommon figure in Fernández y González's novels) who teaches him that "la caridad es . . . la virtud de las virtudes, la base del cristianismo, *pero* toda virtud, al exagerarse, puede convertirse en vicio. . . . No debe entenderse por caridad la que á todo tiende la mano, hasta al crímen" [charity is the virtue of virtues, the foundation of Christianity; *but* any virtue, overdone, can become a vice. . . . One should not understand as charitable reaching out to anything, even crime] (10, my emphasis). Upon the priest's death, Gaspar inherits enough money to live comfortably, but predictably his generosity becomes excessive. He marries the beautiful Isabel, and when she leaves him for a series of lovers, he sends her a monthly allowance. When she ends up in jail for theft, he spends his entire fortune to bail her out, and brings her back to his household. When she dies in childbirth, he adopts her newborn daughter. Eventually, he falls in love with a second woman, María, even as a third young woman, Clara, falls in love with him. The mysterious duke of Castro (Cesáreo) then appears, to reveal that Gaspar is the son of the late first-born duke, and María his sister. Gaspar assumes his true social position and marries Clara, although he still harbors feelings for María. At the same time, he loses Isabel's baby, whom Cesáreo has had kidnapped so that she will never inherit the title (two people are killed in the process). At the end of the novel, Cesáreo is punished for his crime, Gaspar repents his love for María, Clara attends to his Christian death, and all returns to a state of order—except that the baby girl never reappears.[16]

These summaries should suffice to give a concrete idea of some patterns in the archetype. At the most basic level, it is obvious that these are all love stories, and, more particularly, love stories protagonized by virtuous characters, whose moral rectitude is their most salient feature. Insofar as love, ethics, and justice are primary concerns in these novels, one can refer to them, in the terminology of Catherine Jagoe (often used in the nineteenth century), as *idealist*—engaged in the representation of "'noble feelings and superior souls'" ("Disinheriting," 231). I would, however, dispute Jagoe's assertion that

> the *novela moral y recreativa* [moral and recreational novel] in vogue from 1850–1870 was ontologically idealist in that it privileged the spiritual over the material: descriptions of the physical world and the body are important in these texts only as they are suffused by and express changing states of mind or mental characteristics exterior and prior to them.

On the contrary, the material is in no way subordinate to the spiritual, and these novels are about the distribution of wealth and social position as much as they are about "noble feelings and superior souls." The rewards of virtue are both moral and tangible, and good characters work hard and enjoy (or hope to enjoy) the comforts that money can provide.

New Testament Catholic doctrine says that it will be harder for a rich man to enter the gates of Heaven than for a camel to pass through the eye of a needle. In its attitude toward riches, the serial novel can truly be considered a foreign product, since it is a lot closer to non-Catholic conceptions of wealth as a reward of virtue than to this social and religious outlook. As we will see below, the masculine figure the novels most praise is that of the self-made man, for Gaspar Media-Noche's title is only icing on the cake, and in *Los desheredados* as elsewhere, earned money is the best money. This feature relates the serial novel to nineteenth-century American literature, and to authors such as Horatio Alger.[17] In general, "good" characters desire money, and their wish is not at odds with their moral nature. A character comments about Gaspar, "es muy buen hombre.... Siempre está diciendo: ¡Si yo fuera rico! ... ¡Si yo fuera rico! ... Y no tiene por qué quejarse, porque mire usted ... lo que es treinta reales diarios se los saca ... pero, ¿qué quiere usted? siempre está con esa canción" [He's such a good man.... He's always saying: If only I were rich! ... If only I were rich! ... And he has no reason to complain, because he makes at least thirty *reales* a day ... but, what do you want?

He's always singing the same song] (1:228). And there is no better pairing than that of gold and virtue, as the Enriqueta of *La bruja de Madrid* so eloquently expresses:

> Desearía que mis padres pertenecieran a la alta aristocracia. . . . Habitaría un magnífico palacio, me vería rodeada de criados sumisos, y si algún joven marqués o duque se enamorase de mí, me hallaría digna de él, y no tendría que sufrir las humillaciones a que está sujeta la pobre hija de un pintor. . . . ¿Por qué no he de hallar un esposo rico y noble que enaltezca mi posición social? . . . No es una ambición criminal, porque yo no deseo hacer mal a nadie. Quisiera ser noble porque se me figura que no puede haber nobleza sin virtud. . . . Quisiera ser rica para socorrer a los pobres . . . de consiguiente nada tiene de punible mi ambición. (153)

> [I wish my parents belonged to the high aristocracy. . . . I would live in a magnificent palace, I would be surrounded by obedient servants, and if some young marquis or duke fell in love with me, he would find me worthy of him, and I wouldn't have to suffer the humiliations befalling the poor daughter of a painter. . . . Why shouldn't I find a rich and noble husband who might elevate my social position? . . . It is not a criminal ambition, because I wish to harm no one. I would like to be noble, because it seems to me there can be no nobility without virtue. . . . I would like to be rich in order to sustain the poor . . . consequently, there is nothing reprehensible in my aspiration.]

In this novel's value system, as in that of the bourgeois novel archetype as a whole, the ideal society is not one without class divisions, but one in which rich and poor coexist peacefully. The rich should be generous and the poor hard-working, and all of them united by a single moral standard.

The repeated claims among the serial novel's initial readers about its immorality, about the danger it posed for the foundations of society, have less to do with actual immoral acts portrayed in the novels—these are always performed by "bad" characters who receive their deserved punishment at the end—than with their attack on existing social and class structures. In this context, the attitude of Ayguals de Izco is paradigmatic of the bourgeois serial novel. As Rubén Benítez shows, Ayguals is an anti-aristocratic, anticlerical, federalist, democratic republican who defends education for the poor (*el pueblo*), correctional reform, and suffrage for all men not convicted of any legal offense. This does not mean that he was in any way socialist (as Zavala suggested), insofar as that term would designate a primary concern with the working class.[18] Ayguals's portrayal of workers and of the lower class in general is the condescending, if benevolent, portrayal of the subaltern. He was, above all, a champion of the industrial bourgeoisie, a "pre-capitalist, pro-free-trade, anti-protectionist" (Benítez, *Ideología*, 95) defender of the right to the accumulation of private property by those individuals who have worked their way up the social ladder:

> El desnivel de fortunas, consecuencia inevitable de mil vicisitudes y causas infinitas, no da derecho a los ricos para avasallar a los pobres e insultar su indigencia con provocativas miradas de desprecio.
> Tan insensata y absurda es la conducta de esos magnates . . . como anárquico, disolvente y criminal es el aserto de los flamantes abogados de los pobres que aseguran que la propiedad es un robo hecho al pueblo y que este pueblo tiene derecho a exigir la restitución de lo que se le ha arrebatado y apoderarse de las fortunas de cuantos poseen para repartirlas entre la comunidad.
> ¡La propiedad un robo! Imposible parece que haya en el presente siglo hombres tan osados que tengan la avilantez de confundir la rapiña del bandido con la honrada adquisición. (*La bruja*, 66–67)

> [The disparity of fortunes, inevitable consequence of a thousand difficulties and infinite causes, does not give the rich the right to subjugate the poor and insult their indigence with provocative looks of disdain. As senseless and absurd is the conduct of these magnates . . . as anarchic, dissolute, and criminal is the assertion of the flamboyant advocates of the poor, who affirm property is a theft perpetrated on the lower classes, and they have the right to demand restitution and seize the riches of those who have them, to distribute them among the community. Property a theft! It seems impossible that in the present century there are such daring men who have the vileness to confuse the pillage of the bandit with the honorable acquisition.]

This ideology might seem reactionary today, when aristocracy does not mean "ruling class" and social alternatives to bourgeois capitalism in the Western world have all but failed. In the 1840s, however, it was perceived as profoundly radical, because it posited an order of society entirely different from the one that saw the beginning of the century. The most common archetype in the serial novel, the bourgeois narrative, in fact contributes to the creation of an anti-aristocratic feeling, and of the sense that social mobility is possible; it is, then, from its very inception in Spain, an integral part of the bourgeois revolution.

More than ten years after the publication of *María*, Fernández y González echoes and intensifies the same politics. In *Los desheredados* he praises the Constitution of 1812 as the "primer hálito de libertad que los españoles lanzaban después de trescientos años de despotismo" [first breath of freedom that Spaniards exhaled after three hundred years of despotism] (1:7). His view of the reign of Fernando VII is that of an anti-Spanish tyranny (1:142). Where Ayguals reminds aristocrats that they are like all other men, Fernández y González preaches their decadence: "La aristocracia . . . es un enfermo débil que agoniza por consunción" [The aristocracy . . . is a feeble patient who agonizes from consumption] (1:331). If Ayguals writes that "LOS FRAILES NO SON . . . COMPATIBLES CON LA CIVILIZACION Y LIBERTAD DE LOS PUEBLOS" [Friars are not . . . compatible with the civilization and freedom of countries] (*María*, 1:56), Fernández y González accuses them of greed, gluttony, and treason: "[During the Napoleonic invasion,] los frailes andaban gordos, orondos y satisfechos: disponian de todo, eran un componente indispensable de todo" [friars were fat, smug, and satisfied: everything was at their disposal, they were a necessary component of everything] (*Los desheredados*, 1:128). Both writers, and serial novelists in general, are concerned with a new order of things, dominated by a secular middle class.

In this new order, power, wealth, and influence shall no longer be acquired by birth, but by effort, and thus the serial novelists propound a new social organization.[19] In this, the Spanish serial novel serves a purpose similar to that of the early English novel. Nancy Armstrong has shown how the latter has a paramount role in positing, and thus contributes to the creation of, a society not organized around generation and genealogy, but around merit. This society is overtly gendered, since it will depend at its core on the existence of a new ideal of woman, desirable because of her virtue rather than her lineage, and on her surveillance over the realm of the household. Moreover, the idea of woman as essentially different from man because of her psychology—that of morality and domesticity—appears for the first time at this point in history: "My argument traces the development of a specific female ideal in eighteenth and nineteenth century conduct books and educational treatises for women, as well as in domestic fiction. . . . One cannot distinguish the production of the new female ideal either from the rise of the novel or from the rise of the new middle classes" (Armstrong, *Desire*, 8).

In Spain, serial novels were obviously instrumental in creating the modern conception of woman that we now often take as timeless, and it is extremely illuminating to study the way in which they did so. The sanctity of the bourgeois household, and the responsibility of the woman in its maintenance, are readily observable in their archetypal plot. In *Los desheredados,* Isabel's adultery is equivalent to a breach in the social contract:

> La moral lo ha definido todo, y es necesario no rebelarse contra la moral; porque la moral es obra de los siglos, la esperiencia de la humanidad: el que falta á un contrato, debe ser obligado á cumplirle, ó ser castigado, si es imposible el cumplimiento: el que roba debe ser considerado como un ladron: la mujer adúltera no puede ser perdonada mas que por Jesús, y despues del arrepentimiento. (1:288)

> [Morality has defined everything, and one must not rebel against morality; because morality is the work of centuries, the experience of humanity: whoever defaults on a contract must be made to honor it, or be punished: whoever steals must be considered a thief: the adulterous woman cannot be forgiven except by Jesus, and (only) following repentance.]

No such fuss is, however, made about a male character, Don Restituto, who frequently visits a lover (a former servant) in the apartment he has given her, or about prostitutes, who are overtly acknowledged and integrated into the novel's social world.

In addition, the way in which the serial novel constructs women's sexual desire reflects its preoccupation with the channeling of that desire through the institution of matrimony. Also in *Los desheredados,* on recounting Gaspar and Isabel's wedding night, the narrator underlines the importance of a wife's devotion being both physical and spiritual: "Isabel había cumplido con su deber [sex]; pero cumplir con su deber una esposa, no es satisfacer el amor del marido; no es refundir su alma a la suya" [Isabel had performed her duty (sex); but for a wife to perform her duty does not amount to satisfying the husband's love; it does not necessarily amount to fusing her soul to his] (1:34). In *María,* the protagonist experiences what certainly sounds like an orgasm while dreaming, not about physical contact with Luis, but about the consecration of their vows: "Al oir el mismo *sí* de los labios de su amante, sobrecogióla un estremecimiento delicioso, á cuyo violento impulso despertó fatigada, desfallecida y bañada en copioso sudor" [Upon hearing the same *yes* from the lips of her beloved, she was moved by a delicious shudder, under whose violent impulse she awoke fatigued, exhausted, and bathed in copious sweat] (1:211). In these novels, women's desire is not denied, but curbed, so that it will identify as its object the plenitude of the bourgeois household.[20]

As shown above and, more extensively, by feminist scholars of the serial novel, this form was instrumental in the creation of modern female subjectivity. One must not, however, lose sight of the way in which, in these works, the topic of "woman" was framed through the masculinization of public society, and both were part of the larger puzzle of the emergence of the bourgeois imagination. In this context, attention must be paid to the stress serial novels place on the defining traits of the bourgeoisie: the possibility of social advancement through the acquisition of money, and the consolidation of social position through the appropriate distribution and transfer of that money. In *María, o la hija de un jornalero*, the protagonist's misadventures come from her family's poverty, aggravated by the excesses of the church and of the aristocracy. She overcomes adversity through her innocence and her disposition to hard work, and in the end receives the reward of marrying the (morally and socially) noble, as well as rich, Luis. The young marquis clearly states that since "riquezas me sobran . . . virtud y honradez es lo que yo busco" [I have plenty of riches . . . what I seek is virtue and decency] (1:96). In *La bruja de Madrid*, the "witch" (Inés) presumably opposes the union of Eduardo and Enriqueta as an unequal marriage. But what really prevents the lovers' constitution of an ideal household (love, virtue, and wealth) is the Duque de la Azucena's abusive licentiousness, and his failure to legitimize his relationship with Inés. His transgression dooms his offspring to unhappiness, and even to immorality (incestuous passions, suicide).

Of the novels I have chosen to focus on, *Los desheredados* (the title means both "dispossessed" and "disinherited") most overtly shows the concern with the possession and the sanctioned transfer of capital. Gaspar, defined at the beginning by his "desheredamiento completo" [complete dispossession] (1:14)—a baby lost after his aristocratic father's disastrous death—must become the essence of the good bourgeois. He first inherits the life-long savings of Father Anastasio (with his advice about cautious charity), but wastes this wealth because of his passion for the wrong woman (Isabel): first, on her undeserved alimony, then by replacing the goods she had presumably stolen and getting her out of prison (at a total cost of nine thousand *duros*). Gaspar gets a second chance when a second father figure dies, leaving him another ten thousand *duros*, and this time he seems to make good use of the money. He opens an office and settles down, even urging others to follow his entrepeneurial example: "¿Por qué no deja usted el pordioseo? . . . Puede usted vender quincalla. . . . Yo adelantaré a usted algún dinero, y usted me lo irá pagando. Quien sabe si logrará usted hacer un capitalito" [Why don't you stop begging? . . . You can sell rummage. . . . I will advance you some money, and you'll pay me gradually. Who knows; you might be able to assemble a small capital] (1:229). After Gaspar's aristocratic background is discovered, Cesáreo at first opposes his marriage to the nonaristocratic Clara (as well as his own sister's marriage to a humble military hero). Eventually, however, Cesáreo sees the error of his ways, and the two couples marry (so that the novel advocates interclass marriage). The only wrong *not* rectified at the end of the novel is the kidnapping of Isabel's baby. The perfect deathbed scene—Gaspar reconciled with his faith and with his wife—does not include his "daughter," and he does not lament this fact at that point (as he had earlier). His trajectory as a "found" infant contrasts with that of the little Clara, because he could legitimately inherit the dukedom and its capital, but she, the offspring of *adultery*, cannot.

*Los desheredados*'s bourgeois outlook translates into a predilection for certain images. There is, for example—as in *María* and *La bruja*—a fascination with documents. We literally read the entire contents of letters, contracts, bank drafts, receipts, and legal papers in general. Soon after Isabel's escape from home, her lover leaves her in a Madrid brothel; Gaspar's protector Don Justo commands the chief of police to clean up her record, because her registration with the city defines who she is:

> Lo que yo quiero es que deshagas ese padron, que tendrá puesta una nota infame. . . . Lo que yo quiero es que cuando yo te envie su padron, en que aparecerá como mujer casada, en que yo pondré una nota que diga que viene á vivir á Madrid con licencia de su marido, la pongas el padron que la corresponde, como á toda mujer decente. (1:61)

> [I want you to cancel that registry, which must contain an opprobrious note . . . What I want you to do, when I send you her record, in which she will appear as a married woman, and on which I will write a note saying that she comes to live in Madrid with her husband's permission, is to register her appropriately, like any decent woman.]

Similarly, later on, when she leaves jail, the clerk literally "registra la salida de Isabel Perea, de veinte años de edad, natural de Hortaleza, mujer de don Gaspar Media-Noche, propietario . . . por sobreseimiento en la causa de robo que se le instruia, por no haber lugar á ella, y en virtud del auto del señor juez de primera instancia del distrito del Prado" [records the release of Isabel Perea, age twenty, native of Hortaleza, wife of Don Gaspar Media-Noche, landowner . . . upon dismissal of the charge of theft drawn against her, overruled by order of the judge of first resort of the Prado district] (1:162). Characters' natures as well as their acts are certified in document after document, proving the serial novel's primary concern with social legitimacy. In contrast to the ineffable language of romanticism, this sentimental novel insists on what can be said, and what can be written, as fundamental sources.

The form's crucial interest in emotions and ethical behavior is inseparable from its interest in money, its securing and its bequest. In *Los desheredados,* love is literally given a price, and characters gauge each other's feelings according to the size of their expenditures. When Gaspar bails Isabel out of jail, the warden comments that "tres pesetas no hubiera dado yo por ella" [I wouldn't have given three *pesetas* for her] (1:163). She is morally turned around (though too late) and begins to love Gaspar because of the import of his sacrifice: "Los nueve mil duros gastados por Gaspar la habían impresionado profundamente. . . . No era posible comprender aquel sacrificio . . . sin un inmenso amor" [She had been profoundly impressed by the nine thousand *duros* he had spent. . . . Such a sacrifice could not be understood . . . without an immense love] (1:211). Even Gaspar's *protégé* Pepito Túrdiga appraises his mentor's love through the value of goods received: "Tengo clavados en el corazón los treinta duros que se han gastado en ropa" [The thirty *duros* he spent on my clothes are stuck in my heart] (1:211).

In *María, o la hija de un jornalero,* the young girl first tries to alleviate her family's suffering through a transaction; in order to get some food for her little brothers and sisters, she decides to sell her beloved canary. Her sacrifice does not work because her father commands her to undo the sale, which he understands metonymically as the sale of her honor. Thus, she opts to show her familial love by working as a maid and helping with her hopefully ample earnings: "Tengo unos deseos de aprender mucho y de ganar mucho, porque, la verdad, no hay placer comparable al de proporcionar el bienestar de nuestros padres" [I really want to learn a lot and make a lot of money, because, in truth, there is no pleasure comparable to that of providing for our parents' well-being] (1:153). Although this second plan does not work either, María's resourceful spirit keeps showing throughout the novel, and her final marriage to Luis is described in terms of a paradoxical deal: "El marqués, cuya *hereditaria* nobleza tenia su orígen en la mas remota antigüedad, cifraba SU ORGULLO ... en *adquirir* vínculos de parentesco y de amor con la familia de un pobre albañil, solo porque *atesoraba* virtudes mas apreciables que la necia vanidad de algunos aristócratas" [The marquis, whose hereditary nobility originated in the most remote antiquity, placed his pride ... in *acquiring* ties of kinship and love with the family of a poor bricklayer, only because he *treasured* more substantial virtues than the foolish vanity of some aristocrats] (2:414, my emphases). María and her family have turned virtue into capital that can be coveted by the aristocracy, who will seek to acquire it through marriage.

In summary, the serial novel's idealism, as well as its participation in the nineteenth-century construction of womanhood, form part of its engagement with the project of class upheaval. This preoccupation is evident through its archetypal insistence on a type of formula: the story of how hard work, resourcefulness, virtue, and modesty lead to happiness, defined as the loving environment of the bourgeois home. Because the repetition of this story line again and again is the most salient generic feature of the serial novel (less common plots—for example, historical adventure or rural—are often predicated on the same values), it is useful for the understanding of its importance: both through its form of production and in contents, the serial novel amounts to the early bourgeois novel in Spain. Its eradication has to do with the transcendence of bourgeois concerns and their aesthetics, chiefly dependent on the endlessly reenacted vicissitudes of an archetypal plot for their concrete literary realization.

In this context, yet another possible reason why twentieth-century criticism has been unable to appreciate the serial novel (as well as melodrama, prevalent in nineteenth-century theater) is precisely such emphasis on plot. As Peter Brooks explains,

> modern criticism ... has tended to take its valuation from the study of the lyric. ... The texture of narrative has been considered most interesting insofar as it approached the density of poetry. Plot has been disdained as the element of narrative that least sets off and defines high art—indeed, plot is that which especially characterizes popular mass-consumption literature. (*Reading*, 4)

The serial novel seems to offer little ground for analytical practices. It is virtually impossible for readers to fill in its "gaps" (it appears to have few) in order to find out, or construct, a hidden meaning. Its openness suggests simplicity, and simple texts do not interest us.

This view should be tempered by the observation of an important feature of the serial novel that has nevertheless been upstaged by the obviousness of its formulaic nature. Novels with such clear social and moral theses might be deemed "monological," in the sense that Susan Suleiman gives to the term (and to which I will return in detail in chapter 3 of this book): as works dominated by a single voice seeking to express a particular proposition and demonstrate its validity. On the contrary, serial novels are the essence of dialogism—as the following well-known quote explains, the very essence of the modern novel. In this passage, Mikhail Bakhtin defines the genre's particular stylistics:

> The novel can be defined as a diversity of social speech types (sometimes even diversity of languages) and a diversity of individual voices, artistically organized. The internal stratification of any single national language into social dialects, characteristic group behavior, professional jargons, generic languages, languages of generations and age groups, tendentious languages, languages of the authorities, of various circles and of passing fashions, languages that serve the specific sociopolitical purposes of the day, even of the hour . . . is the indispensable prerequisite for the novel as a genre. . . . Authorial speech, the speeches of narrators, inserted genres, the speech of characters are merely those fundamental compositional unities with whose help heteroglossia . . . can enter the novel; each of them permits a multiplicity of social voices and a wide variety of their links and interrelationships. . . . These distinctive links and interrelationships between utterances and languages, this movement of the theme through different languages and speech types, its dispersion into the rivulets and droplets of social heteroglossia, its dialogization—this is the basic distinguishing feature of the stylistics of the novel. (Bakhtin, *Dialogic Imagination,* 262–63)

Heteroglossia, as described above, is what separates the novel from older genres, and makes preexistent stylistics and poetics insufficient to grasp it. Consequently, the novel's appearance in the modern literary field revealed (or created) a lack in traditional concepts of art. Either it had to be dismissed as nonartistic—and many of the arguments against the serial novel or against individual novelists documented by scholars signal a contemporary dismissal of the genre as a whole—or existing measures of aesthetic value had to be revised.

The serial novel's integration of manifold voices makes it much less "simple" than it appears at first glance. I have already alluded to the presence of "extraneous" documents—letters, contracts, etc.—in serial novels, but there are many other ways in which they incorporate a plurality of discourses. First, as critics have often noted, is the *discurso pintoresco* (discourse of the picturesque) (and, on a related note, travel writing). The serial novels alluded to dwell on descriptions of places and environments—the *Fontana de Oro* cafe, which appears both in *María* and *Los desheredados,* the *Puerta del Sol,* the Prado Museum, and even foreign locales, like Rome, visited by the characters. Second, the serial novel often includes poems and songs. In *La bruja de Madrid,* for instance, the beautiful Juanilla charms the aristocrats she is swindling by singing and playing the guitar (264). Third is the insertion of intercalated stories, like the saga of Gaspar's parents in *Los desheredados.* Fourth comes the imitation of the jargon of different classes and milieus, with special predilection for that of the marginal underworld; an example, from *María,* are the words of *Juana la Esgalichaa* and others from a stock of lowlife characters who reappear in several of Ayguals's novels (1:134). As Benítez and other scholars have noted, Ayguals also likes to reproduce regional languages, and especially Catalan (he was the Valencian-born son of a wealthy Catalan family). Fifth, serial novels often break the flow of the narrative to introduce disquisitions on political history; the narrator of *Los desheredados,* for example, warns his readers that he is about to indulge in "un poco de filosofía de la historia" [a bit of philosophy of history] (1:126), before dedicating almost twenty pages to a depiction of life before and after the War of Independence, and to reflections on the nature of social revolutions. Sixth comes the language of advertising. Botrel has made clear how the first installment of a serial novel was often distributed for free to prospective readers as an incentive for them to subscribe, so that the novel's plot was in itself publicity. In *María* we find a related use of the main text of the novel to sell future works. In the last chapter, in the same narrative and typographical format of the rest of the novel and before the signature of the author and the date, which signal "the end," we read: "Algo debíamos dejar para la segunda época de la historia de MARIA, que con el título de LA MARQUESA DE BELLAFLOR O EL NIÑO DE LA INCLUSA, publicaremos sin dilacion con igual esmero, el mismo lujo é idénticas dimensiones" [We should leave something for the second season of the story of María, which we will publish without delay and with the same care, with the same luxurious presentation and measurements, under the title of *The Marquise of Bellaflor, or the Child from the Orphanage*] (2:450). Rubén Benítez has pointed to another intrusion of advertising into Ayguals's discourse. In his last novel, *La justicia divina o el hijo del deshonor* [Divine Justice, or the Child of Dishonor] (1859), "Ayguals goes on for several pages describing the benefits of Dr. Tendik's Dutch Balm for gout patients, and even its mode of application" (*Ideología*, 69). While for Benítez this refers to Ayguals's personal experience as a gout sufferer, I think the balm might have appeared in the novel as publicity, much in the same way that certain airline or cigarette logos appear in films nowadays.

A very curious seventh type of incorporation of social discourses is the graphic inclusion of posters, signs, or documents in which the visual arrangement of words is as important as their meaning. Thus in *María* Ayguals does not just describe the tavern of *Tio Gazpacho*, but shows us exactly what the placard at the entrance looks like (1:132; see figure).

In this way, the author achieves the vivid participation of the reader in the novelistic world. By *seeing* the sign at the pub's door, we seem to cross it and literally enter this new space, sharing it with *Tio Gazpacho, Juana la Esgalichaa*, or *Curro el Desalmao*. The effect is not unlike that usually ascribed to later realist fiction, in which a strong narrator guides readers through painstakingly described, lifelike, and even recognizable environments. Related to this resource is of course the customary inclusion of captions underneath the requisite engravings, introducing an extranarrative voice in charge of summarizing the action.

The serial novel also approached political or parliamentary discourse in arguing for specific social measures. Especially the novels of Ayguals cry out for the abolition of the death penalty, for the institution and use of savings banks, for a change in the schedule of

Sign at the entrance of the pub door in *María, o la hija de un journalero* (1845–46), by Ayguals de Izco.

trash collection in Madrid (the malodorous task was usually performed just as people were coming out of theaters). Often, the novelist's entreaties are heeded by those in power, and provoke actual social change, incorporated in turn into the novelistic structure. In *María,* for example, the author/narrator asks early on: "¿Por qué no se han de crear en Madrid y en todos los puntos populosos sociedades benéficas en favor de los beneméritos jornaleros, parecidas á la que con el título de *Caja de socorros agrícolas de la provincia de Castilla la Vieja,* se ha establecido en la ciudad de Valladolid?" [Why shouldn't there be established in Madrid and in all other populous locations charities favoring the venerable workers, such as the Fund for Agricultural Aid of the Province of Old Castile that has been constituted in Valladolid?] (1:27–28). Several hundred pages (and several months) later, he confirms the success of his plea:

> Impelidos por el deseo de despertar en España ese humanitario espíritu de fraternidad que moraliza las naciones, nos lamentábamos en las primeras páginas de nuestra historia de la casi absoluta falta de empresas filantrópicas.... Con satisfacción imponderable vimos aparecer la CAJA DE SOCORROS AGRICOLAS DE CASTILLA LA VIEJA, á la que sucedieron en poco tiempo la SOCIEDAD AMIGA DE LA JUVENTUD, la ISABELA y otras de cuyas benéficas miras hemos hablado con la suficiente estension en el curso de nuestra obra." (2:433)

> [Impelled by the desire to awaken in Spain the humanitarian spirit of fraternity which ennobles nations, we deplored in the first pages of our story the almost absolute lack of philanthropic ventures.... With imponderable satisfaction, we watched the Fund for Agricultural Aid of the Province of Old Castile appear, quickly followed by the Friends of Youth Society, the Elizabethan, and others whose charitable ends we have referred to in enough detail throughout our work.]

He proceeds to dedicate nine pages to the literal reproduction of these societies' prospectuses. (Trash collection times, by the way, were also changed.)

The kind of attention that novelistic discourse commanded, and the effects it had over the material world, point to its borderline status. The serial novel blurs the boundary between fictional and factual writing, so that literary discourse is not entirely separate from political, legal, or journalistic discourse. Especially in the case of the *folletín,* journalistic and literary texts were published side by side on the same pages. In the case of the *novela por entregas,* the novel appropriates the format and the distribution system of the newspaper. The fact of the novel's proximity to journalistic writing separates it from the merely imaginary and creates the "danger" seen by the many who—like Mesonero—quixotically viewed the novel as a potentially destructive influence on readers' minds and customs. The danger would have been increased by the cues journalistic discourse seems to have taken from fiction. A present-day researcher reading through Spanish newspapers of the time will inevitably be struck by the "literariness" of their nonfictional sections. Far from the impersonal accounts we have come to associate with journalism, their news and political commentary overflow with rhetoric and even borrow from literature the terms with which they describe events (words like "drama," "argumento," etc.). In the end, the frailty of the boundary between different discursive spaces destabilizes distinctions between "art" and "life," thereby making imaginable the actual practice of the social models the novels present.

At the moment of the novel's appearance, its subversiveness is precisely that of a cultural construct which respects no borders, literary or social. The serial novel's assault on existing social structures is twofold. On the one hand, it overtly ("monologically") attacks early nineteenth-century class distinctions. Its dominant voice loudly preaches the decadence of the aristocracy and the inevitability of a new order: merit over birth. On the other hand, the serial novel's very existence and structure (dialogism) reinforce its blurring of class divisions, helping to fracture further the world whose end it proclaims. Until this time, notions of decorum—that is, of propriety according to preceptive parameters in writing, and according to surrounding circumstances in life—had been dominant, both aesthetically and socially. The novel's textual breach of such norms through the insertion of "nonartistic" languages into the space of literature—and, conversely, of artistic discourse into "ordinary language" (a problematic distinction to which I will return in chapter 3)—is used to encourage other transgressions, such as marrying out of one's station, or displaying the outward signs of power previously restricted to the aristocracy.

Furthermore, the serial novel's, and in general, the novel's, irruption into the world of letters radically changes the configuration of the existing canon. It does not only challenge the ascendancy of the aristocracy, but that of its collection of sacred texts. It is not insignificant that the figure of the *mecenas* (patron) is now replaced by that of the capitalist, and that the genre's birth is simultaneous with that of the modern literary market—as Montesinos remarks, "a poem may be a gift for a few friends; a novel makes no sense if it is not destined to a vast audience" (xii).[21] The serial novel literally forces the members of different classes into one collective (its readership)—any one novel would be purchased and read by the well-to-do in more luxurious bindings, by the lower middle classes and perhaps the literate working class in cheaper versions, and even, as Joaquín Marco shows, reach the lower and illiterate classes through group and public readings. Serial novels thereby force upon the existing literary world the concept that art might be for the many (even for those who cannot pay for an entire volume at one time), and that the sanction of the many might become authoritative. In this way, it changes the existing canon not only by entering and enlarging it, but by changing the nature and the ownership of the cultural capital labeled "literature."

What Galdós so successfully leads after 1870 is, then, a further redefinition of this cultural capital; one that even reverses some of the ways in which the serial novel had affected the world of art and literature. His work, in both novels and critical pieces, was decisive first and foremost in refashioning the idea of the writer. The image of a good novelist will no longer include a sentimental, matronly lady, or a fast-living, fast-writing romantic hurrying to finish his next *entrega,* or a capitalist author-editor (these figures are explicitly caricaturized in "Un tribunal literario"). It will be an intelligent, learned man (or manly woman) devoted to his craft, not worried about money, slowly shaping a unique work of art. The favored audience of the novel will also be knowledgeable, skilled in irony, large but not majoritary, and once again restrictive. In the early century, the community of readers was "naturally" divided between the few who could read and the many who could not; the serial novel, both because of the historical moment in which it appears and because of its structure, erases that division. After 1870, when the numbers of the literate are much larger, a new division appears—largely ushered in by Galdós and other realist writers—between those who own the specialized artistic gaze and those who do not. Later novelistic production both institutes and caters to this mitosis.

Galdós and the generation that follows him thus succeed in bringing about the identification of novels produced in serial format, and characterized by overt sentimentality and conventionality, as popular, mass, nonartistic works. This achievement is not good or bad; it is part of the Spanish history of the genre. It is, however, so complete that it generates the decadence of the serial novel (as a form of production and a formula), occasionally even turning the form against itself: for example, Angela Grassi's 1876 *El copo de nieve* (in *El correo de la moda*), though written in the same class and sentimentality registers as earlier serial novels, is highly critical of such works, and claims only Böhl de Faber as its model. Additionally, the creation of the space of the "popular" for fiction, and the relegation of the serial novel to that space, have as a consequence the form's class redefinition. Once *essentially* bound to the bourgeoisie, serial novels can now appear in socialist and other working-class journals. Although serial novels with a bourgeois outlook continue to exist into the twentieth century (a notable example are those of Blasco Ibáñez), they can now also function as instruments of social protest for the working class, as Magnien and her research group have shown in their study of Timoteo Orbe.

Most importantly, Galdós's accomplishments conceal the way in which the realist novel he initiates shares and develops many features of the serial novel—certain topoi, such as, specifically, *La fontana de oro*, and, more generally, the concentration on Madrid's contemporary urban environment; the strength of the narrative voice; the problematization of the relation of fictional discourse to reality; the focus on the middle class (although post-1870 novels tend not to encourage social mobility, and are more ironically engaged with their social subject); the symbolism of money; the theme of adultery, etc. Works that establish connections between his production and earlier serial production, such as Ynduráin's, Andreu's, and Sieburth's more recent *High and Low,* have only begun to scratch the surface of a field of inquiry that will grow as comprehension of the phenomenon of the serial novel grows, and its separation from what is now widely considered "popular" or "noncanonical" is better understood. The increased reading and study of these texts should not only be part of an interest in the noncanonical per se, or of an effort to construct an alternative, more politically engaged, canon—even if these are attractive enterprises from certain current, and very valid, critical perspectives. Rather, it is of utmost importance for a more thorough understanding of the evolution of the novel in Spain.

# 2
# Benito Pérez Galdós and the Canon of Spanish Literature

IN THE PREVIOUS CHAPTER, I MADE MENTION OF BENITO PÉREZ GALDÓS as the first and most successful reformulator of the concept of quality in the novel. He begins to implement the aesthetic ideals that determine the categorization of pre-1870 Spanish novels as popular or subliterary by fostering the association of their most salient features with the realm of the unartistic. From the rejection of their most common mode of publication and distribution (the installment) to that of their prominent formulaicness and sentimentality, Galdós's disapproval of the serial novel archetype influences contemporary thought, leading to the almost absolute dismissal of the form. It is due to this dismissal that the nineteenth-century realist novel "is repeatedly referred to in manuals of literature as the beginning of the modern novel in Spain" (Gold, "Back to the Future," 180), regardless of variations in its own subsequent canonical fortune. After Galdós's critical and novelistic intervention (followed or accompanied, obviously, by that of other writers of authority), a new standard for the national *literary* novel takes shape, and the field of the novel splits into this aesthetic current and the large-scale production of unartistic, mass, "popular" narratives.

This movement away from a preexisting paradigm does not imply that there is a complete disconnection between Galdós's novels and earlier production—several critics, including Andreu, Yndurain, Jagoe, and Sieburth, have shown many points of contact. Because they have already done so quite suggestively, and because this book focuses on noncanonical or borderline texts, I will not elaborate on such intertextuality and continuity. I do, however, want to dwell on two facets of Galdós that are to a certain extent marginal: the playwright and the journalist. In the two parts of this chapter, I will focus on these comparatively little-known areas of his writing to show how they complement the project of reform he undertakes with respect to the novel. Despite the relative lack of critical attention paid to these facets of Galdós's work, they are essential parts of what amounts to a comprehensive critique of Spanish culture. Though appropriately originating in the field of the novel—the genre arose, after all, as a rupture with earlier literary decorum—this critique reaches out to other interrelated cultural systems, reinforcing the position of the writer as crossover intellectual.

In the first section, I will trace how, in his approach to theater, Galdós endeavors to rid the Spanish stage of what he sees as its vices, using his already acquired prestige as a novelist to advocate a turn away from melodrama and toward realism. This is a change he promotes both through the contents and staging of his plays, and through the innovative use of their publication to encourage, even demand, a more careful and studied reaction on the part of audiences. Through this process, Galdós goes far in stimulating a transformation in the concepts of the writer, of the nature of the literary text (and of theater as literature), and of the role of the reader or spectator, that will in turn spur a *canonical* conception of Spanish theater. In the second section, I will perform a reading of Galdós's reporting on the subject of crime, specifically of *El crimen de la calle de Fuencarral* [The Crime on Fuencarral Street] in reference to the novel *La incógnita,* to place his attempts at literary renewal in a larger cultural context. His efforts to regenerate theater and the novel are ultimately the cornerstone of a more comprehensive vision that sees Spain as intellectually ailing and actively seeks new paradigms of literature, of social behavior, of knowledge, and of reality itself as interdependent orders. Thus, while Galdós fosters in Spain the creation of a modern, autonomous field of strictly "aesthetic" literature, he also sees that literature in intimate relationship to the forms of understanding that permeate the culture as a whole.

## Benito Pérez Galdós and the Nineteenth-Century Field of Theater

In the introduction to the 1974 special issue of *Estudios escénicos* dedicated to Benito Pérez Galdós's drama, Ricardo Doménech referred to it as a "lost" theater: "[It] has been lost, invisible, for a long time. One can observe this absence . . . in any handbook of literary or theatrical history: because the persistent repetition of a few commonplaces is also an absence, and sometimes the worst of all" ("En busca," 11). Although some significant contributions to its study have been made since then, Galdós's theater is in a sense still lost—especially if one compares critical attention to it with the attention devoted to the theater of other authors like Ramón del Valle-Inclán and Federico García Lorca, or with that devoted to Galdós's other work. Why this neglect, given the critical profession's constant search for unexplored terrain, and given the canonical status of the *author* in the history of Spanish literature? Doménech himself outlines several reasons, among which not the least is the relative scarcity of studies about modern Spanish theater in general—in contrast to other genres—and about nineteenth-century theater in particular.

Nevertheless, another reason for the limited attention dedicated to this theater is the implicit qualitative distinction made between Galdós the playwright and Galdós the novelist. As Doménech himself puts it, "his novelistic *oeuvre*... has overshadowed his dramatic work, being indisputably superior to the latter" (12). If the novelist is basically consecrated as the creator of the modern Spanish novel—the direct descendant of Cervantes—there is much less consensus about the impact of the dramatist on the theater's trajectory. This distinction provokes a reluctance to write about a cultural product considered inferior, an unwillingness to damage Galdós's reputation by having to insist on what many critics consider important defects in his work. Thus, while Galdós the novelist forms part, with Cervantes and García Lorca, of the reigning troika of the Spanish canon, Galdós the playwright is almost relegated, if not to the sphere of the popular, at least to the sphere of the noncanonical.

In a 1981 article, Theodore Sackett points out that criticism of Galdós's theater gradually turned from complete disregard to two antithetical attitudes which he describes in the following manner:

> The distinguished theater historian, Francisco Ruiz Ramón, believes that Galdosian theater has no merit beyond that of closing, with a certain dosage of innovation and high literary quality, the mediocre nineteenth-century theater: in the second volume of his history of theater, he only mentions Galdós twice, without any indication of his work having had any impact on twentieth-century dramaturgy. Conversely, others, like Domingo Pérez Minik ("contemporary theater begins with Galdós") and Juan Guerrero Zamora ("personally, I think that the writer from the Canaries is an undeniable foundation ... of contemporary Spanish drama") offer another critical possibility. ("Galdós dramaturgo," 6)

Opposed to the dismissal of Galdós's theater that subordinates the playwright to the novelist, there emerges the conscious or unconscious impulse to bring the two facets of the writer closer by insisting on the radicalness of his dramatic project, on the innovation it entails with regard to the theatrical horizon of the time, and on its social and aesthetic value in contrast to the rampant mediocrity of other nineteenth-century playwrights.

In this fashion, Sackett himself mentions "a broadening of the hackneyed conventional problems of the theater of his time, . . . formal experimentation, and a variety of unprecedented dramatic resources" (8), against what he calls the "panorama of poverty and mediocrity" of a theater rotating around "the orbit of Echegaray's dramaturgy" (6). He also elaborates on the impact of Galdós's dramaturgy on the later work of, among others, Jacinto Benavente, Valle-Inclán, García Lorca, Rafael Alberti, and Alejandro Casona. Gonzalo Sobejano too—before Sackett, in 1970, and again in 1978—contrasts Galdós's innovations "to the hocus pocus and triviality" prevailing in theater ("Razón y suceso," 46). For Sobejano, these are exemplified by the *género chico* as well as by the theater of José Echegaray and his followers: "the propensity of almost every playwright to yield to Echegaray's affectation." The contributions of these two critics and of others with equal authority have resulted in the construction of another Galdós playwright to set against the figure of the novelist out of place in the theater. Thus the image of the original thinker, of the superior creative genius who rises above the middling dramatists of his time to advance theater with the same resolve as he transformed the novel begins to establish itself. Against the defective author guilty of excessive exposition or poor handling of plastic resources, there appears another whose ostensible problems are precisely his strength: he champions analysis instead of the prevalent supremacy of action, and firmly proposes to revolutionize melodramatic staging.

It is certainly not my intention to refute this image or dispute the talent or the quality of Galdós's theater, both undeniable. Nevertheless, in the short review of criticism above, it is readily observable that the value-laden terms in which critics are accustomed to treating writers determine an all-or-nothing approach to literary history. We either refer to Galdós's dramaturgy tentatively and uncomfortably (or not at all), or opt for categorical praise or rejection. Either he radically renews nineteenth-century theater, or he fails, due either to his recourse to the models he proposed to break with, or to the inability of his contemporaries to understand his design. The first alternative can be inferred from arguments like that made by Isaac Rubio in *Estudios escénicos,* where he remarks that after 1896 Galdós undergoes a crisis "because his plays have for some time contradicted the theatrical theory he had put forward . . . and increasingly approximate the model he had condemned: Echegaray" ("Alma y vida," 176). The second alternative is suggested by research such as that of Roberto Sánchez, who ponders in 1984 why *Realidad* (1892) did not place Galdós among the masters of modern theater, and asks "if perhaps the modernity of the novelist's first drama may not have exceeded the capabilities of the impresario [Emilio Mario] and his actors" (264).

A reexamination of the critical vocabulary used to assess Galdós's theater is extremely helpful in trying to understand better the particular character of his dramatic renovation—which was not limited to textual or staging elements. As Pierre Bourdieu states, it is not sufficient to read and interpret literary works (or, in the case of theater, watch them when they are performed) in order to confirm or not confirm a hypothesis about their meaning and their impact. Instead, one should attempt to (re)construct the field of literary production as it existed when Galdós came to the theater, so as to comprehend both the space of possibles that allowed him to exist as a playwright and the ways in which he contributed to its modification. The assessment of a work through the examination of the network of relations that constitute the field of its production does not constitute a turn away from the author's and the text's individuality and toward the secondary, almost statistical, form of inquiry that literary studies have traditionally seen in "sociology" (a term often derisively applied to contextual analysis). In Bourdieu's words,

> Analysis of the social conditions of the production and reception of a work of art, far from reducing or destroying it, in fact intensifies the literary experience. . . . Such analysis seems to abolish the singularity of the "creator" in favour of the relations which made the work intelligible, only better to rediscover it at the end of the task of reconstructing the space in which the author finds himself encompassed and included as a point. To recognize this point in the literary space, which is also the point from which is formed a singular point of view *on* that space, is to be in a position to understand and to feel, by mental identification with a constructed position, the singularity of that position and of the person who occupies it, and the extraordinary effort which . . . was necessary to make it exist. (*Rules,* xix)

Although Galdós's textual revision of the predominant melodramatic theatrical model is, as I have argued elsewhere, incomplete and hesitant, more clearly appreciable is his decisive contribution to the redefinition of the category of "dramatist" and of the ideal of theatrical value in late nineteenth-century Spain.[1]

According to Bourdieu, few fields rely as much on the cult of the figure of the great individual creator as those of art and literature. For him, the consequent emphasis on "literary hagiography" (*Rules*, xviii) relegates to invisibility the complex structural relationships that constitute the field at any given time and in any given society. Alternatively, Bourdieu configures the literary field as a network of forces and struggles in which each individual—not only authors of all levels of success, but also readers or spectators, directors, agents, impresarios, editors, critics, etc.—carries out a function determined by the existing repertoire of possibilities. The field itself functions according to two fundamental oppositions: the first, the opposition between the consecrated figures and the neophytes, between orthodoxy and heresy; the second, the opposition between a space of large-scale production and a space of restricted production (the strictly "aesthetic" creation of a few and for a few). The field of restricted production is what Bourdieu calls a "bad faith economy" (*Field*, 76), a game of "loser takes all" (*Rules*, 21) characterized by a denial (or deferral) of monetary profit, and aspiring instead to symbolic capital: "the only legitimate accumulation consists in making a name for oneself, a known, recognized name, a capital of consecration implying a power to consecrate objects (with a trademark or signature) or persons (through publication, exhibition, etc.)" (*Field*, 75).

But the field of literary production has not always been configured in the same way, and throughout the nineteenth century different genres advance at different paces toward autonomy from the fields of power and money, and toward the appearance and consolidation of the space of restricted production. Poetry, which is never directed at a large audience, is the first genre to achieve the autonomous dual structure. At the opposite end, theater tends to be the genre to move at the slowest pace, given its greater dependence on a (large) bourgeois audience, and its greater susceptibility to bourgeois modes of legitimation like the recognition of the powerful in their salons or the honors, prizes, and memberships in academies that official organisms might grant.

As the field of restricted production appears, it begins to follow a pattern of permanent revolution, becoming the site of constant, cyclical struggle between new generations of artists—who fight for imposing their aesthetic ideals—and older, consecrated figures. Those who have already acquired a dominant position naturally try to retain it, helped by their previous success in imposing their ideas about art, as well as by the whole apparatus of critics and agents who have a stake in the continuation of the existing order. The neophytes, in contrast, adopt subversive strategies, frequently supporting their artistic production with a corollary corpus of manifestoes and declarations of their views. Their revolutions can nevertheless never be total: new authors must take care to overthrow the hierarchy of the field without disturbing the field itself. At the risk of losing everything they struggle for, they must break with the previous generation they seek to replace, but not with the "rules" of art as a system; thus, one of the preferred strategies is a return to the origins:

> The dominated producers, for their part, in order to gain a foothold in the market, have to resort to subversive strategies which will eventually bring them the disavowed profits only if they succeed in overturning the hierarchy of the field without disturbing the principles on which the field is based. Thus their revolutions are only ever partial ones, which displace the censorships and transgress the conventions but do so in the name of the same underlying principles. This is why the strategy *par excellence* is a "return to the sources" which is the basis of all heretical subversion and all aesthetic revolutions, because it enables the insurgents to turn against the establishment the arms which they use to justify their domination, in particular asceticism, daring, ardour, rigour and disinterestedness. (*Field*, 83–84)

Bourdieu's evolutionary view of the field of literary production can be very illuminating when applied to Galdós's trajectory as a writer and as a playwright. It is well known that he begins to write plays moved by the desire to revitalize Spanish theater, to introduce decisive changes that will make it less artificial and more artistic.[2] As he states in one of the essays collected in *Nuestro teatro* (written throughout the 1880s): "los patrocinadores intransigentes del teatro tal como hoy existe, no han caído en la cuenta de que defienden una forma novísima, de ayer, como quien dice, el teatro de Scribe y su escuela, sistema de artificios para producir efectos de la índole más grosera y vulgar" [the close-minded patrons of theater such at it now exists have not realized they defend an extremely new form—born yesterday, so to speak; the theater of Scribe and his school, a system of tricks to produce effects of the most crude and vulgar sort] (154). In opposition to the mere "habilidad mecánica" [mechanical ability]

(154) that characterizes the theater of the time, Galdós considers it necessary to develop an aesthetics of naturalness, for which he finds a model in the theater of the late eighteenth century: "[es] virtud que en España no ha poseído nadie como la poseyó Moratín" [it is a virtue that no one in Spain has shown like Moratín did] (*NT,* 22).

In order to recover, and improve, the aesthetic ideals of the grandparents—not only Moratín, but also Ramón de la Cruz—Galdós challenges the father, Echegaray, to take the necessary steps: "Echegaray . . . es el llamado a marcar este camino. No le faltarían recursos para ello. Necesitaría únicamente cortarse un poco las alas, abatir el vuelo, atender más a la verdadera expresión de los sentimientos humanos que a los efectos" [It is Echegaray . . . who should point the way. He would not be lacking the necessary resources. All he would have to do is trim down his wings a bit, lower his flight, attend more to the true expression of human feelings than to effect] (*NT,* 142).[3] Perhaps disappointed by Echegaray's failure to take up the challenge—having all the symbolic capital he needed, the future Nobel laureate continued his melodramatic trajectory—and encouraged by the enterprising Emilio Mario, Galdós begins in 1892, with *Realidad,* his own attempt at theatrical renovation. From this moment on and throughout his career, he will struggle, both in his plays and in documents like the prologues to *Los condenados* (1894) and *Alma y vida* (1902), to impose his aesthetic ideal. In his plays, the degree of success in its implementation varies, and Galdós does not always manage to transcend Echegaray's melodramatic paradigm (see note 1 of this chapter). If in works like *Realidad* and *Los condenados* he achieves ethical nuances and staging effects uncommon in Echegarayan melodrama, in others like *La loca de la casa* (1893) or *Electra* (1902) the impulse toward moral and social reform leads him to make use of interpretive resources instituted by Echegaray.

In this specific respect, my assessment of Galdós's theater approximates that of Isaac Rubio (although, while this critic negatively values the playwright's use of the melodramatic model, I take melodrama as a fundamental mode of thought that bears no necessary relation to literary quality).[4] Nevertheless, what is relevant here is that according to the view of the literary field described by Bourdieu, the terms in which we normally value Galdós's theater—as a decisive rupture, observable (as a success or a failure) in the texts—are not the most useful ones to understand it. Rather, it is more helpful to approach late nineteenth-century theater as a field in flux in which there coexist two currents, that of permanence and that of change. There is a gradual move toward a new standard (realism), and it is in this process that Galdós participates. Other playwrights before him, like Enrique Gaspar, had reacted against the melodramatic aesthetic that prevailed in Spanish theater since long before Echegaray arrived on the stage in 1874. For several reasons, however, Galdós's reaction is more visible and more effective in propitiating a change of paradigm.

From his first performed play (*Las circunstancias*, 1867), Enrique Gaspar denounces the overt moralizing and the artificiality he considers prevalent in Spanish theater. He argues for increased realism on the stage, and seeks to implement it both through plots that force the audience to work at drawing its own conclusions and through *didascalia* that challenge conventional expectations.[5] But while Gaspar's plays probably go farther than Galdós's in deploying alternatives to melodramatic staging, his efforts have little success and less impact, and *Realidad* is hailed as the first serious attempt to regenerate the theater. While there are surely many explanations for this complex circumstance, a very simple yet persuasive one stands out: in 1892, Galdós is not only a successful novelist, but he has also become the symbol of a new philosophy of quality and a new image of the writer. When the most prestigious author of the moment describes drama as "en decadencia" [in decline] (*NT*, 151) and applies himself to its reform, the theatrical establishment listens.

In this way, the argument often made by critics (sometimes as an accusation) that Galdós brings the novel to theater is true in more ways than one. It is true about the resources with which he seeks to renew both the textual plot and the mise-en-scène. As Peter Szondi argues, around the end of the nineteenth century Western modern drama goes through a period of crisis and renovation, in which certain authors (he focuses on Ibsen, Chekhov, Strindberg, Maeterlinck, and Hauptmann) question the traditional tenets of the drama begun with the Renaissance: its "absolute" (*Theory*, 8) or "primary" (9) nature, separate from everything external and referring only to itself; the total absence of the dramatist as a conscience; the "complete separation" of the spectator from the play, even if that separation encourages identification; the sealed-off "picture-frame" stage; and the unification of actor and character in a "single personage" (9). Like other important European playwrights, Galdós ruptures the dramatic world with a transgression of its tenets that introduces "an epic *I* which permeates the work" (10). His frequent use of introspective monologue over dialogue, the overt political and social referent of many of his plays, and the rebellion against the *piéce bien faite* (well-made piece) all point to the working of the novelistic mind. And this union of novel and theater is so organic in Galdós's imagination, that he repeatedly resorts to the intermediate, transitional form of the dialogue novel to explore the connections.

But Galdós also brings the novel to the theater in a different way. His plan for theatrical regeneration is evidence of the process by which, according to Bourdieu, genres (and even homologous cultural fields, such as art and literature) do not undergo the development toward the modern dual structure only in reference to their own history, but rather borrow from each other and build on each other's achievements. Novelists and playwrights form part of the same structure of exchange Bourdieu ascribes to writers and painters:

> If the innovations that led to the invention of the modern artist and art are only intelligible at the level of all the fields of cultural production together, this is because artists and writers were able to use the lags between the transformations occurring in the literary field and the artistic field to benefit, as in a relay race, from advances carried out at different moments by their respective avant-gardes. Thus the discoveries made possible by the specific logic of one or another of the two fields could have a cumulative effect and appear retrospectively as the complementary profiles of one and the same historic process. (*Rules*, 132)

Once the field of restricted production appears in the sphere of the novel—which, unlike poetry, already has a large audience—the expectations it creates in a significant segment of the public (and the critics) begin to be transferred to the theater. Consequently, the process of cleavage between the more autonomous space of restricted production and the commercial space of large-scale production within a single genre is accompanied by "a process of unification of the whole set of genres." Each sector of a genre thereby "tends to become closer to the similar sector of other genres . . . than to the opposite pole of the same subfield" (*Rules*, 120). In other words, the division between "artistic" and "mass" production is more determinant of a work's characteristics than its generic tradition.

Like Echegaray before him, Galdós brings to the theater his cumulative prestige, his power to consecrate a text with his mere signature.[6] Even more importantly, he brings a previously disseminated theory about art—novelistic or theatrical—and an audience that already admires him and is already initiated into his realist doctrine. All this paves the way for his success, if not in a radical and immediate renovation perfectly achieved in his plays, at least in impelling a decisive movement toward a new theatrical norm. For Bourdieu, there are authors—in the French novel he mentions Flaubert, and in the theater Zola—who, through both their works and their relations with the artistic milieu, redefine the position of the writer and the prevailing notions about what art is, so that they push genres toward the modern state of the literary field. In Spain, it is without a doubt Benito Pérez Galdós who performs these functions, to a greater degree than other writers (who, of course, also participate in the process). As I suggested in the previous chapter, he does so for the novel, and he also impels the process in the case of the theater. If, by the beginning of the 1890s, audiences and critics already made a distinction between high theater and the *género chico* analogous to the distinction between art and entertainment, it is Galdós who spurs an analogous differentiation *within* the "serious" theater hitherto dominated by melodrama.

I highlighted earlier the importance of statements of poetics as a supplement to "primary" literary works, and their frequent use by writers who seek to reform the artistic field in which they exist. Through his own critical writings, Galdós is the first figure in Spanish theater to introduce and insist on the concept of an intellectual theater. In this context, perhaps it is his prologue to the first edition of *Alma y vida* which best synthesizes his theses about the subject. One of the ideas Galdós asserts in this text is the writer's independence from the (bourgeois) audience's sanction—which is, according to Bourdieu, the chief defining characteristic of the modern artist in the field of cultural production.[7] In a surprising declaration, given the time and place in which he writes, Galdós affirms that

> nunca pensé ganar en este drama el aplauso popular, y que más bien he tratado de esquivarlo. . . . Buscaba, sí, el sufragio de las clases superiores, de ese público selecto que aquí tenemos, compuesto de personas extrañas a la profesión literaria, pero de notoria cultura, sin prejuicios, con el cerebro limpio de las estratificaciones de escuela que a tantos incapacita[n] para el libre goce de las dulzuras del arte. (*OC*, 6:904)

> [I never thought this drama would earn popular acclaim, in fact I've rather tried to avoid it. . . . I sought, of course, the endorsement of the superior classes, of that select audience we have here, composed of individuals alien to the literary profession, but possessed of notable culture, without prejudices, with their minds devoid of the school stratifications that render so many unfit for the free enjoyment of the richness of art.]

This upper class should not be confused with the aristocracy, whose lack of literary sensibility Galdós harshly criticizes: "La presencia del público aristocrático en los teatros españoles . . . no lleva calor, sino frialdad; no entusiasmo, sino indiferencia. Es un personal florido y brillante que entra en la casa de Lope como en visita desigual o de circunstancias, mirando con poca estimación al dueño de la casa" [The presence of the aristocratic public in Spanish theaters does not convey warmth, but coldness; not enthusiasm, but indifference. It is a flamboyant and glittering establishment that enters Lope's house as in a casual or unequal visit, looking down on the master of the house] (910). Nor is this class the high bourgeoisie—Galdós's much proclaimed relationship to the middle class is one of problematic analysis rather than unproblematic representation.

Through the above dictum, Galdós avers the independence of the field of cultural production from the field of power. No longer shall consecration come from the approval or the patronage of those in positions of social and economic authority, but rather from the endorsement of those in possession of the pure gaze. This possibility of perception is another result of the process of autonomization of the literary and artistic fields:

> The eye of the nineteenth-century art-lover is the product of history. From the angle of phylogenesis, the pure gaze capable of apprehending the work of art as it demands to be apprehended (in itself and for itself, as form and not as function) is inseparable from the appearance of producers motivated by a pure artistic intention, itself indissociable from the emergence of an autonomous artistic field capable of posing and imposing its own goals in the face of external demands; and it is also inseparable from the corresponding appearance of a population of "amateurs" or "connoisseurs" capable of applying to the works thus produced the "pure" gaze which they call for. (Bourdieu, *Rules,* 288)

Paradoxically, although the work of art is the final product of the ensemble of agents engaged in its generation—not only the artist, but those who properly recognize the art work as an aesthetic and not a utilitarian object—this collective construction distinguishes only the artist as privileged creator. Correspondingly, Galdós maintains for himself the author's superiority before the audience: "El autor es entidad superior al público, y así debe continuar hasta que se demuestre lo contrario" [The author is an entity superior to the audience, and it must remain so until the opposite is proven] (*OC,* 6:908). His mission is to contribute to the formation of an audience that can increasingly perceive and appreciate art. Thus, neither here nor in the prologue to *Los condenados* does Galdós abstain from lecturing public and critics, instructing them about the positive and negative judgments they might have made about the play (a resounding failure on the stage), and almost literally laughing at the criticism that did circulate, like that of labelling the latter play melodramatic.

Galdós's use of prologues as theatrical documents is quite significant. As a review of early editions of, for example, Echegaray or Eugenio Sellés, will confirm, it was not then common practice for dramatists to write introductions to the published versions of their plays. Among other things, Galdós's prologues seek to offset and respond to the judgment of theatrical critics, whom he considers lacking in both time for reflection and expertise. On the one hand, he warns that it is not acceptable to issue a report about a play the morning after its premiere, without stopping to ponder its design and its techniques. On the other hand, he criticizes the regrettable situation that, while "true" intellectuals concentrate on other matters, "periódicos poderosos mandan al estreno de una producción literaria al revistero de toros" [powerful newspapers send the bullfighting critic to the premiere of a literary production] (prologue to *Los condenados, OC,* 6:704).

For these reasons, Galdos considers it appropriate and necessary for an author to expound on his own work:

> Ningún autor debe abandonar sus obras, aunque el público las oiga con frialdad y el frívolo reporterismo las maltrate. . . . Todo autor que tiene lazos de simpatía y de gratitud con el público está obligado, hasta por cortesía, a decir algo a éste sobre la obra que no fue de su agrado, a defenderla si puede, a explicarla si es obscura, a declarar sus errores, si los ve; a trazar, en fin, una línea divisoria entre la crítica formal y la garrulería impertinente. (706)

> [No author should abandon his works, even if the audience hears them coldly and frivolous journalism abuses them. . . . Any author who has ties of sympathy and gratitude with the audience is obligated, even as a courtesy, to tell it something about the work it did not like, to defend the work if he can, to explain it if it is unclear, to state its faults, if he sees them; to mark out, in summary, a boundary between formal criticism and impertinent chatter.]

It is implied that Galdós confers upon the publication of his plays an importance that goes beyond the market strategy by which even nowadays the scripts of successful plays or films, or even the novels on which they were based, are published. From the outset, the work is written not (or not only) to run for the maximum number of days possible, but also to yield its substance through reading, and to form part of a theatrical and literary canon.

While the dominant theater of the time sought to *move* spectators through its treatment of popular themes and its straining-after-effect—Echegaray aspired especially to provoking a "sublime horror trágico" [sublime tragic horror] (*Teatro escogido*, 447)—Galdós reformulates the goal to that of stimulating thought and spiritual enlightening. Such is the argument with which he defends *Los condenados*, in whose prologue he attacks the emotion-seeking audience who would tell the playwright: "Yo vengo aquí en busca de emociones fáciles, de ideas claras, de accidentes alegres o patéticos, . . . y tus filosofías me aburren" [I come here in search of easy emotions, clear ideas, cheerful or pathetic adventures, . . . and your philosophizing bores me] (*OC*, 6:700). It is precisely *filosofías* as well as "lo espiritual" [spiritualness] that Galdós chooses to present to this public in need of tutoring on the new "rules" of art. In opposition to sentimentality, Galdós champions intellectual rigor both intratextually—in the presentation of characters and subjects he terms "analytical"—and extratextually, through the plays' system of distribution (in reading and criticism).

In effect, Galdós is proposing a new aesthetic ideal to replace the melodramatic bent that has prevailed in Spanish drama since the early nineteenth century, and which Echegaray has made into the standard of cultured, "high" theater. His institution of the realist model is certainly not definitive: Echegaray, the symbol of melodramatic theater, continues to write through 1916, and is awarded Spain's first Nobel Prize for literature in 1905. Even Galdós himself will often take advantage of melodramatic resources in his works, and sometimes heed his predecessor's personal advice about specific staging problems. Nevertheless, his views on theater and his textual example are influential enough to sway Echegaray himself. After the premiere of *Realidad*, the elder playwright will generally attempt to approximate Galdós's dramaturgy through the frequent use of female protagonists (following in the wake of *Realidad*'s Augusta), a higher emphasis on contemporary settings and problems, and a more muted tone of action and diction.

Both the realist and the melodramatic model of theater will coexist into the twentieth century, and Galdós's drift away from the dominant standards is only the first significant step in the turn toward the modern, autonomous state of the theatrical field. While the project of renovation for both genres has been the same, in nineteenth-century Spain theater could not accommodate such change in the same way as the novel, a relatively new form with a limited history and few established rules. In general, among the cultural fields of restricted production, the case of theater, a collective spectacle, stands apart for its notorious precariousness. Dependent on popular or insitutional support for its very access to the stage, contemporary experimental theater is always in danger of not existing, and is forced to negotiate much more than poetry—the genre with the smallest audience—with official sanction (in the form of subsidies, for example) and audience acceptance.

In this context, Galdós's break with existing theatrical norms is not as evident as his separation from the pre-realist novel. Nevertheless, the model of theater he proposes will eventually triumph in terms of cultural prestige, and functions to begin a process of partition in the genre that will already be a fact of life for the generation immediately following him. Thus, at the turn of the century, the mass phenomenon of Jacinto Benavente's theater will share the field, if not the stage, with the radical dramaturgy of Valle-Inclán, now more openly directed at reading than at performance. In this convoluted way, Valle-Inclán owes much to *Don Benito el Garbancero*, including not only the realist aesthetic that serves as the positive or negative point of origin for self-reflexive twentieth-century literary forms, but also the invention, in the context of the Spanish literary field, of the social position of the writer that he will occupy with such zeal. In addition, Galdós's (witting or unwitting) success in replacing Echegaray, now almost forgotten, as the most important figure of nineteenth-century Spanish theatrical history—whereas his immediate successors will not achieve his own displacement—attests to the power and the consequence of his reform project.

In the end, I have returned to the idea of the singular creator who effects an essential regeneration in the theater of late nineteenth-century Spain. Galdós brings drama closer to the modern configuration of artistic fields—to the distinction between "high" and "low" that had already emerged, through his influence, in the novel, and to the constitution of a canon clearly distinguishable from nonaesthetic theatrical production. My return to this topic of literary history seeks, however, to avoid value judgments, or at least either total admiration or objection: if, on the one hand, Galdós accomplishes more, and more visibly, than any other nineteenth-century writer, on the other any critic concerned with the relativity of the canon must certainly work against the massive evaluative apparatus to whose entrenchment he contributed. Nonetheless, one must bow to the fact that if any writer deserves inclusion in the canon of Spanish literature—with all the revisions that should be made to the idea of the canon in itself, and especially to its lack of permeability—it is that writer who most advanced the processes that would lead to its solidification. Processes which, it is important to stress, Galdós himself firmly grounded, not only on textual contents, but on historical developments: "Cuando el gusto cambia, muchos lo atribuyen a influencias de este o el otro autor, de esta o la otra escuela, y no ven la lógica profunda a que el fenómeno obedece" [When taste changes, many attribute it to the influence of this or that author, of this or that school, and don't see the deep logic the phenomenon follows] (Galdós, *NT,* 139).

## Canon and Knowledge:
### Galdós's "Criminal" Pursuits

In chapter 1, I attributed Benito Pérez Galdós's transcendence of the serial novel archetype to the successful reformulation of the notion of quality, as well as of the figures of the reader and the writer. Such a revision of cultural paradigms is not limited to the sphere of the novel, but, as we have seen above, extends to theater. It is, in fact, part of a comprehensive project that links theater, fiction, and journalism; as I will now argue, Galdós's public writing in all its manifestations entails a far-reaching refashioning of the concept of the artistic, of the cultural position of the intellectual, and of knowledge itself.[8] In promoting the modern specialization of the aesthetic and intellectual fields, and their increasing differentiation from previously accepted models of understanding and production, Galdós constitutes an essential link in the transition from nineteenth-century positivistic ideals to twentieth-century critiques of perception (reality) and communication (writing) in Spanish culture.

If the great nineteenth-century cultural theme was adultery—involving, as it did, issues of modern class and gender construction—there is another theme that explodes at this time as never before. In late-century European societies the subject of crime—its definition, its detection, and its punishment—is the locus for the convergence of numerous discourses. As Marie-Christine Leps points out, during this period crime becomes a subject for the scientist, the legislator, the journalist, and the writer alike:

> The emergence of criminology as a human science established the criminal as an object of scientific investigation, thereby aligning criminality with other social problems like poverty or disease, which, according to the positivistic belief in progress, *could be grasped, contained, and ameliorated by scientific advances.* The rise of mass journalism turned crime stories into ordinary commodities made for daily consumption as news items. Finally, an ever-expanding mass of crime literature began to move from mysterious and faraway crimes to familiar, local situations; specialized products such as the detective novel or the French . . . *roman policier* emerged as extremely popular genres, and the study of crime became fashionable as "high literature material." (*Apprehending*, 2)

Crime groups together many of the current cultural anxieties, and its treatment in fictional and factual writing is thus extremely revealing of the way in which key social questions take shape.

Between July of 1888 and May of 1889, Galdós writes for the Argentinian newspaper *La prensa* a succession of articles detailing developments in the investigation and trial of the sensational Madrid crime that came to be known as *de la calle de Fuencarral*. Although not considered "literary" (by the author or subsequent criticism), this series is extremely significant in the context of Galdós's writing project, of his criticism of prevailing narrative and intellectual patterns, and his effort to replace these with new categories. As such, *El crimen de la calle de Fuencarral* is most fruitfully read in intertextual relation to Galdós's novels, and in particular to *La incógnita*, written simultaneously (1888–89) and especially concerned with the topics of crime and detection.[9] The two narratives are also in dialogue with the multiplicity of discourses about crime spreading through Europe at that historical moment: on the one hand, the scientific approaches deriving from Cesare Lombroso's criminological studies; on the other hand, the use of the subject in fiction, and especially in the detective narratives of which Arthur Conan Doyle's Sherlock Holmes stories are the chief contemporary example.

Against this background, *El crimen de la calle de Fuencarral* showcases the author's interest in a shift of paradigm with significant consequences for the evolution of Spanish culture. Just as in literature and theater Galdós advocates a change in the figure of the writer (from inspired romantic or commercial producer to dedicated artist) and in the character of the text (from series to book, from mass to specialized product, from entertainment to intellectual engagement), he also champions an analogous redefinition of widely held convictions and ways of thinking. The act of covering a gruesome murder, informing of its investigation, and interpreting facts for an audience of presumed outsiders affords Galdós the opportunity to reflect on the topics of deviance and normalcy. The way in which these are treated in both *El crimen* and *La incógnita* posits sharp questions about how individuals are classified within a society, whether there are absolute standards of innocence or guilt, and to what extent truth is accessible to reason. Galdós's journalism on the subject of crime, read in the light of his other production, helps to identify the tenets of a far-reaching project for the reconceptualization of reality, truth, and knowledge.

Ultimately, for Galdós, the criminal subject does not stand apart from the "normal" subject—as nineteenth-century science assumed. Rather, they both exist in a continuum in which character and motives are never readily apparent—even to the keenest observer—but lie beneath the surface, awaiting not just observation, but *analysis*. This writer, so concerned with reality in his fiction, nevertheless holds a relativist view of what it means, problematizing the relationship between that reality and truth, between a manifest and an authentic reality distinguishable only to the analytical mind. In this fashion, Galdós once again sets an intellectual mandate for Spanish culture that foreshadows the rigorous thinking of turn-of-the-century writers like Angel Ganivet and Miguel de Unamuno. In a larger European context, Galdós also distances himself from the positivistic thought of the nineteenth century, and prefigures the kind of understanding of the individual that Sigmund Freud will pioneer years later.

On 2 July 1888, an old widow, Doña Luciana Varela, was found dead in her home on Madrid's *calle de Fuencarral*, stabbed to death and her body set on fire. The ensuing inquest and trial, in which suspects included the woman's own son and her ultimately convicted and executed maid, Higinia Balaguer, created much public stir.[10] For almost a year, the public faithfully followed each new development and the press's treatment of it with obsessive interest. The case was also related to larger social issues, becoming symbolic of Spain's cultural problems. Declarations, for example, that the son, who was in jail when the murder occurred, had repeatedly been allowed out with the warden's permission prompted widespread discussion of the troubled Spanish penal system; the offer of prominent conservative politicians to defend the maid pro bono caused great reaction against political opportunism; and so on. A section of the public insisted on attributing the final authorship of the crime to a mysterious, politically important character, thereby charging it with strong political undertones.

Generations of *galdosistas* have studied how in his fiction the author first establishes and utilizes the resources of realism—such as the presentation of a "natural" chronology or the free indirect style—to create fictional texts that give readers the illusion of reality, and then how he subverts these very resources by exposing them as literary techniques, thereby creating a metafictional hyperrealism. *El crimen* is a text set apart from this context: here Galdós assumes the role of a journalist reporting on a true and current event—specifically, a crime. While, from a narratological point of view, such a distinction is of course tenuous and not grounded on any qualitative differences between fictional and factual narrative, it is nevertheless important: the generic claim to journalism and the material element of publication in the news (as opposed to the literary) section of a paper are already determinant of reception. In the context of Galdós's novelistic project, it is interesting to contrast the language of his journalism to that of his fictions. If realist discourse seeks to create a fictional yet verisimilar image of reality, how does it compare to the language of fact journalism purports to be, a language that claims truth and objectivity in bringing to the reader "all the news that's fit to print"?

Perhaps the most striking feature of *El crimen de la calle de Fuencarral* is the "literary" quality of its prose. In *Fiction and Diction,* Gérard Genette alludes to certain "indexes" (58) or markers that signal to the reader that he or she is in the presence of either fictional or factual writing. Guided by previous experience of such conventions, the reader will then be able to apply the appropriate strategies (including belief or disbelief) to the text and its contents.[11] Despite its identity as a journalistic text, however, *El crimen* consistently points to literature as a central matrix through a mixing up of the pertinent signs. In the first place, the narrator repeatedly refers to the events as fiction, or, most frequently, theater. He tells us how journalists feverishly collect information with which "construyen luego la historia más o menos fantaseada y novelesca del espantoso drama" [they later construct the more or less fantasized and novelesque plot of the frightful drama] (*El crimen* 5), but it is the Judge who handles "todos los hilos de la trama" [all the threads of the netting] (13).

Toward the end of indictment proceedings, matters appear nebulous, and "todo se vuelve conjeturas más o menos razonables, cálculos y estudios psicológicos de los personajes del drama, sin llegar nunca a desentrañar el argumento" [everything becomes more or less reasonable speculation, calculations and psychological studies of the play's characters, without ever getting to the bottom of the plot] (26). And during the trial the courthouse literally turns into a theater house, with Higinia Balaguer as the leading lady:

> Damas elegantes ocupan las primeras filas, y no vacilan en soportar los estrujones y el calor, por ver de cerca la cara de la tremenda Higinia, oír su voz empañada y admirar la soltura de su mímica, digna de una consumada actriz. Las emociones del juicio interesan a las damas tanto como una buena ópera bien cantada. . . . Gentes hay que se estacionan, desde las primeras horas de la mañana, a la puerta de la sala, formando cola, para conseguir un puesto, y se lo ganan con la larga espera, y lo defienden luego como si de cosa mayor se tratase. (35)

> [Elegant ladies occupy the front rows, and do not hesitate to bear the crushing and the heat, in order to look from up close at the face of the tremendous Higinia, to hear her faint voice and admire the ease of her gesticulation, worthy of a consummate actress. The trial's emotions absorb the ladies as much as a well-sung opera. . . . There are people who station themselves, from the earliest hours of the morning, at the gate of the courtroom, standing in line to get a space, earning it with their long wait, and later defending it as if it were something major.]

Similar literary allusions are present all over *El crimen,* but what is most surprising about them is not their mere presence, but the *kind* of literary model to which Galdós relates this factual narrative about crime. For this is not the measured language of his realist fiction; it is a sensationalist language that points to yellow journalism and harks back to the literary styles of melodrama and the serial novel.

Nineteenth-century melodrama's most essential property is its division of the world into polar moral opposites. Absolutely virtuous heroes or heroines (such as Gaspar Media-Noche in *Los desheredados* or María in *María, o la hija de un jornalero;* see chapter 1) battle authentic villains, whose evil nature is revealed in every detail of their physique and their personality. Nevertheless, this battle is one of signs—signs that get scrambled, obscuring virtue. Melodrama progresses, not merely toward the final *reward* of virtue, but toward its *recognition*—the moment of virtue triumphant in all its splendor

(Brooks, *Melodramatic Imagination,* 27). In this infinitely repeated formula the metaphor of darkness giving way to light is perhaps the most frequent cliché and reappears in a great number of individual works. The melodramatic outlook is readily apparent in *El crimen*'s (in)quest for truth.

From the narrative's origin in a series of questions—which of the suspects, Higinia or José Vázquez Varela, committed the crime? was it committed by only one person, or were there accomplices? was robbery of the money Mrs. Varela kept on her own person the motive, as was widely believed, or were there others? could such a violent murder have been committed by women alone?—the tone remits to that of melodrama. In searching for answers, the narrator insistently employs images that come directly from the world of melodramatic theater and fiction. Near the beginning of the first report, Galdós refers to the need for the "esclarecimiento de la verdad oscura" [elucidation of the obscured truth] (*El crimen,* 6), and variations of the image reappear innumerable times. Thus, further on, "cuando parecía que iba a resplandecer la verdad, ésta se obscurece más" [when it looked like truth would shine through, it became hazier] (10). Galdós criticizes sensationalist reporters because, "lejos de dar luz . . . lo que hacen es . . . aumentar las tinieblas" [far from shedding light . . . what they do is . . . increase the darkness] (17). At a more optimistic point (early on in the narrative) he predicts that "cuando la causa pase al juicio oral, la verdad resplandecerá limpia de toda duda" [when the trial gets to its oral phase, truth will gleam free from all doubt] (18). The metaphorical counterposition between light and darkness is sustained through the end of the narrative, giving it unity and becoming its emblem. Metonymically, it is a substitution for the dichotomy of good and evil, and the need for the clear assignment of these moral qualities seems to guide the articles' narrative.

In the same way, the descriptions of characters remind readers of the melodramatic model. There is, of course, no heroine in this story (or rather, only a dead heroine); the villains, on the other side, assume their fullest, most horrible form. As in theatrical melodramas and serial novels, there is a frequent correspondence between physical appearance and moral nature. Dolores Avila—presumed to be Higinia's accomplice once the theory of the maid's guilt becomes predominant—therefore resembles the archetypal wicked witch: "es biliosa, pequeña de cuerpo, grosera y desfachatada" [she is bilious, dwarfish, rude, and brazen] (38); additionally, "su figura es de las más vulgares, y su condición moral y física la coloca en las capas más bajas y degradadas de la sociedad" [her figure is among the most vulgar, and her moral and physical condition places her in the lowest and most degraded layers of society] (34). But the characterization of evil goes further, and gets more vivid and unnatural when it refers to the actual murderer.

Throughout *El crimen de la calle de Fuencarral,* the narrator, following and summarizing the sway of public opinion, alternates between ascribing guilt to José Vázquez Varela or to Higinia Balaguer. According to collective moral categorization, only a monster could have committed such a crime. Correspondingly, when it appears possible that the son killed the mother, he is referred to as "un monstruo sin ejemplo ni precedente" [a monster without model or precedent] (8). In contrast, at the trial, when Higinia's culpability is the most likely prospect (though one should emphasize that Galdós's narrative voice never speaks without the shadow of a doubt, a fact to which I will return later on), the narrator dwells on her macabre aspect:

> Si moralmente es Higinia un tipo extraño y monstruoso, en lo físico no lo es menos. Creen los que no la han visto que es una mujer corpulenta y forzuda, de tipo ordinario y basto.
> No hay nada de esto: es de complexión delicada, estatura airosa, tez finísima, manos bonitas, pies pequeños, color blanco pálido, pelo negro. Su semblante es digno del mayor estudio. De frente recuerda la expresión fríamente estupefacta de las máscaras griegas que representan la tragedia. El perfil resulta siniestro, pues siendo los ojos hermosos, la nariz perfecta con el corte ideal de la estatuaria clásica, el desarrollo excesivo de la mandíbula inferior destruye el buen efecto de las demás facciones. La frente es pequeña y abovedada, la cabeza de admirable configuración. Vista de perfil y aun de frente, resulta repulsiva. La boca, pequeña y fruncida, que al cerrarse parece oprimida por la elevación de la quijada, no tiene ninguna de las gracias propias del bello sexo. Estas gracias hállanse en la cabeza, de configuración perfecta; en las sienes y el entrecejo, en los parietales mal cubiertos por delicados rizos negros. El frontal corresponde, por su desarrollo, a la mandíbula inferior, y los ojos, hundidos, negros, vivísimos cuando observa atenta, dormilones cuando está distraída, tienen algo del mirar del ave de rapiña. (32–33)

> [If, morally, Higinia is a strange and monstrous type, she is not less so physically. Those who have not seen her believe she is a burly and brawny woman. Not at all: she has a delicate countenance, graceful stature, the smoothest skin, pretty hands, small feet, pale complexion, black hair. Her visage deserves thorough study. Seen from the front, she recalls the cold,

benumbed expression of those masks representing tragedy. Her profile appears sinister, for, though the eyes are beautiful, and the nose perfect, with the ideal shape of classic statuary, the excessive development of the lower jaw destroys the good effect of the other features. Her forehead is small and arched, the head has a striking contour. Seen in profile, and even from the front, she looks repulsive. Her mouth, small and furrowed, which, when closed, seems squashed by the rise of the jaw, has none of the gracefulness of the beautiful sex. This grace is found in the head, perfectly shaped, in the temples, barely covered by dark curls. The frontal bone corresponds, in its development, to the lower jaw, and the eyes, sunken, black, most lively when she observes intently, sleepy when she is distracted, have something of the look of the bird of prey.]

In this detailed description, the features of an ordinary, even pleasant-looking woman (fine complexion, hands, and skin and dark curls) are defined as an object of study and treated with an almost forensic tone: her face cleaves into the forehead and the jaw bones; her temples become "parietals." The clinical gaze is nevertheless caught in the trap of a perfectly monstrous, grotesque silhouette. If the frontal view of the face suggests the stylized mask of tragedy, the profile shows a repulsive amalgam of opposites, classical sculpture gone awry. In the end, science gives way to the uncanny. Higinia's *black* hair and eyes literally take over, as she transfigures into the quintessential figure of evil and death, Poe's mysterious dark raven.

The two allusions to the frustration of high art forms (tragedy and sculpture) bring us back to the territory of convention. Galdós reminds us that the story of the murdered widow does not belong to the lofty realm of literature, but to the world of melodrama and the Gothic populated by freaks and fiends rife with horror and vice, such as "aquella diabólica mujer" [that diabolical woman] (30). If characterization and the use of emblematic images are not enough to point to the body of writing whose perception as popular or "low" Galdós has fostered for almost twenty years, the reader need only pay attention to the structure of *El crimen*—a *series* of articles relying on suspense to entice the reader to follow the next installment. Accordingly, every section ends with the reiteration of a question or enigma whose solution is promised for the next one. The first article, for example, states that "aguardaremos con impaciencia el desarrollo de este grave proceso en la nueva fase que ha tomado ahora" [we will await impatiently the development of this serious process in the new phase it has just entered] (13). The final sentence of the third one announces that "el juicio oral que ... se celebrará el mes próximo, lo aclarará todo, seguramente" [the oral trial ... to be celebrated next month will clear everything up, for sure] (30).

For the reader still unable to identify the intertext, Galdós repeatedly makes it explicit. It is the serial novel, "la novela folletinesca" [the *feuilleton* novel] (45). *El crimen de la calle de Fuencarral* both replicates and names the model. We also see it used analogically to describe the burning interest with which the public approaches the investigation: "el secreto que guardan los encargados de la sumaria es causa de que se forjen novelas dignas de la fantasía enfermiza de Ponson du Terrail o de Montepin" [the secret maintained by those in charge of the indictment generates the concoction of novels worthy of the morbid fantasy of Ponson du Terrail or Montepin] (23). For Galdós, the fantasizing encouraged by the serial novel has spilled over from the domain of the literary to the larger social domain, so that people apply to reality inappropriate strategies of understanding. The public finds entertainment in the murder of Mrs. Varela, it demands in life the same processes of revelation and restitution it finds in fiction, and most of all, it applies to this very real crime the extravagant interpretive habits to which such fanciful narratives have accustomed it. In this way, the journalistic reports on the Fuencarral crime provide Galdós with an always welcome opportunity to decry the corpus of serial fiction. More importantly, though, he shows that fiction in relation to a corrupted collective character—perhaps its cause, perhaps its effect.

Galdós portrays the audience as an army of ineffectual amateur detectives, incapable of putting two and two together, mistaking what is externally conspicuous for what is fundamental, slave to facile frameworks. The work of Justice is hindered by the press's appropriation of its role: "La diligencia de los periodistas para cazar noticias es febril. ... En cuanto se indica que tal o cual persona va a ser interrogada por el juez, los periodistas buscan su domicilio, le encuentran, se encuentran con la persona, y no vuelven a la Redacción sin un caudal más o menos auténtico de noticias" [Journalists' assiduity in searching for news is feverish. ... As soon as it is revealed that this or that person will be interrogated by the judge, they look for the address, find it, meet with the person, and do not return to the office without a more, or less, genuine wealth of news] (20). Such probes are nevertheless of no value, since each newspaper has decided from the start on a certain version of the events, disregarding all evidence to the contrary. In this respect, the press leads the people, who search frantically for one more new lead that will confirm one more theory, each one more preposterous than the other.

Consequently, as we read, "hay personas en quienes la sugestión obra prodigios . . . [y] llegan a creerse también testigos, sueñan que han visto algo y concluyen por creérselo" [there are people on whom self-suggestion works wonders . . . and they get to believe themselves witnesses, they dream they have seen something and end up believing it] (44). Circumstances border on the farcical, and, constantly asked by obsessed friends and acquaintances if he himself might not be the culprit (in a situation reminiscent of "La novela en el tranvía"), Galdós passes judgment on this state of affairs. His judgment is a social diagnosis: "Reconozco, y lo reconozco como un mal, que esas estupendas y maravillosas máquinas gozan, por su propia falta de lógica, de todo el favor de las imaginaciones *de esta raza*. Creo que es deber de todos corregir ese amor a lo inverosímil en vez de fomentarlo" [I recognize, and I recognize it as an evil, that those stupendous and marvelous machinations enjoy, due to their very lack of logic, the absolute favor of *this race's* fancy] (43, my emphasis). This crime and the ensuing investigation say something not only about themselves and the individuals involved, but also about the national character. The author's criticism thus intimately links the realms of the literary and the journalistic to the larger realm of cultural identity. Unbridled imagination is a Spanish malady, and fiction, as well as all kinds of public writing, are part of the fundamental responsibility to help correct it.

It is precisely in the collective social sphere that the subject of crime acquires all its contemporary magnitude. If crime literature, *causes célèbres* (famous trials), and the topic in general explode in the late nineteenth century, it is because the birth of the bourgeois, industrial, urban world provides the grounds for it to become a full-fledged social problem. As suggested in the passage by Marie-Christine Leps quoted at the beginning of this chapter, the perception of crime as a social problem, on par with poverty or disease, especially encourages a particular kind of response: the institutional effort to grasp, contain, and ameliorate it "according to the positivistic belief in progress." At this historical moment, the various discourses on crime approximate and rely on each other as intertexts increasing reader recognition of "facts" and providing each other with support and verification. According to Leps, this intertextual relationship typically serves to establish and strengthen hegemonic truth. In other words, discourses about crime reinforced the perception of criminals as predetermined subjects to be controlled by those who already had the power of science, the law, or the printed word in their hands.

Above all else, nineteenth-century discourses on crime affirm the possibility of knowledge. Criminology posits the existence of an identifiable "criminal man"; police investigation follows in criminology's footsteps with new techniques like fingerprinting and Alphonse Bertillon's anthropometrical system of identification. For Galdós to write a crime report in 1888 is, then, to engage in a dialogue with the variety of contemporary arguments about crime. Nevertheless, rather than working as one more discourse in support of the hegemonic belief in knowledge and control, Galdós's articles question these possibilities and the very conception of reality that governs them. One may find in *El crimen de la calle de Fuencarral* implicit views on the possibility of accessing and relaying truth, and on the legitimacy of existing power relations.

I noted earlier how Galdós's lengthy description of Higinia Balaguer remits readers to the territory of popular fiction. A contemporary reader would nevertheless also have detected a second intertextual relationship, this time to the current debate over criminal anthropology. Luis Maristany documents the rapid diffusion of Cesare Lombroso's ideas, and the role of the Madrid *Ateneo* as a forum for their dissemination and discussion:

> El papel desempeñado por el Ateneo madrileño en la difusión de las ideas de los italianos . . . debe ser subrayado. . . . No es casual que dicha institución sea el escenario en que tuvo lugar la conferencia pronunciada por Salillas en 1888 sobre *La antropología en el derecho penal,* primera exposición de interés en España de las teorías lombrosianas. ("Lombroso y España," 368)

> [The role performed by the Madrid Athenaeum in the dissemination of the Italians' ideas . . . must be emphasized. . . . It is not fortuitous that this institution was the stage of the lecture read by Salillas in 1888 on *Anthropology in Penal Law,* the first exposition of Lombrosian theories of any interest in Spain.]

The subject immediately generates a lively controversy, and the association's journal, *El Ateneo,* soon publishes (between January and April of 1889) both Rafael Salillas's lecture and a second lecture on Italian criminology (F. de Llanos y Torriglia's *Ferri y su escuela*), each together with excerpts from the discussion that followed. The exact period when Galdós writes *El crimen de la calle de Fuencarral* thus sees the eruption of a polemic on the subject of criminality and science that will last throughout the 1890s.

In secular positivistic fashion, criminology, or criminal anthropology, especially in its Lombrosian version, believed in the biological disposition to criminality, and sought to establish the possibility of identifying the criminal man (or woman) on the basis of physical traits:

> Cesare Lombroso (1835–1909), criminologist and professor of psychiatry at the University of Turin, used the methods of physiognomy to promote the idea of the "born criminal." ... Lombroso maintained that he could identify degenerate types by facial peculiarities such as low brows and eyes set closely together.
> 
> Using the evolutionary theory of Charles Darwin, Lombroso argued that criminals could be identified through malformations of their skeletons, especially their skulls. Signs of criminal tendency also included such features as big ears, excessively long arms, projecting or receding jaw, high cheekbones, and red hair. ... Criminals have the physical features of primeval man. (Kellogg, "Born Criminal," 143)

Despite raging debates about the plausibility of this theory, and about its legal and even religious implications (such as its effect on the belief in free will), the presumed features of the criminal are rapidly divulged by Spanish authors in books and in the press.

Even at the end of the century, when Lombrosian criminal anthropology has lost much of its prestige all throughout Europe, there is intellectual discussion about the role it should have in Spanish penal law. In his 1899 *Estudio de antropología criminal espiritualista* [Study on Spiritualist Criminal Anthropology], Benito Mariano Andrade still attempts to balance traditional religious doctrine with the teachings of criminology: "Es posible ... formar una ciencia penal en la que, con los principios y fundamentos espiritualistas que integran su parte jurídica, coexistan casi todas las consecuencias hijas de las modernas experimentaciones antropológicas (que no son fatalistas *per se,* sino *per accidens,* ó sea porque sus principales apóstoles lo son)" [It is possible ... to create a penal science in which, along with the spiritualist principles and foundations that constitute its juridical part, there coexist almost all the consequences deriving from modern anthropological experimentation (which is not fatalist *per se,* but *per accidens,* that is, because its principal apostles are so)] (42). Beyond all qualms about the moral and philosophical tenets that may be extrapolated from the principles of criminal anthropology, at this point, in Spain, there is still a basic acceptance of its most fundamental observations about criminals. Thus, Andrade still spends considerable time listing the features of the thief, of the rapist, and of the murderer: "Los homicidas, mirada vidriosa, fría, inyectada y sanguinosa; la nariz aguileña á menudo y voluminosa, la mandíbula fuerte, las orejas largas, cigomas pronunciados, obscuro el cabello, labios delgados, dientes caninos fuertes" [Murderers, [have a] glassy stare, cold, bloodshot and bloodthirsty; an often hawkish and large nose, a strong jaw, long ears, prominent browbones, dark hair, fine lips, strong canines] (115).[12]

Although Andrade himself rejects it, he also points to the common belief that women approached the atavistic form of the criminal more than men:

> Dice Lombroso que la mujer presenta mucha analogía con el hombre primitivo y, por tanto, con el malhechor.
> Parece á los antropólogos que la mujer tiene el prognatismo más acentuado que el hombre, . . . el cráneo más voluminoso y el cerebro menos pesado; es más frecuentemente zurda ó ambidextra, más débil de músculos, y carece en absoluto de barba, teniendo muy larga y poblada la cabellera; es vanidosa é imprevisora (señales indelebles del criminal, según Ferri) y muy dada á la imitación. (79)

> [Lombroso tells us that woman exhibits great similarity with primitive man, and, therefore, with the criminal.
> It seems to anthropologists that she is more conspicuously prognathic than man, . . . her craneum is more voluminous and her brain lighter; she is more frequently left-handed or ambidextrous, her muscles are weaker, and she completely lacks a beard, while the hair on her head is longer and thicker; she is vain and improvident (ineffaceable signs of the criminal, according to Ferri), and quite given to imitation.]

Despite the obvious fact, noted by Andrade, that women committed less crimes than men (being more religious and moral, in his opinion), the fact that these theories were being expounded and discussed as the latest European scientific developments at the very same time that Higinia Balaguer was being tried for murder is certainly significant. One of the most contested points throughout the entire process was, as Galdós tells us, the question of whether a woman (or two women, if Dolores Avila was her accomplice) could have possibly commited that particular crime. For that segment of the audience acquainted with current scientific discussions, the point was not gratuitous. The case was in this and many other ways a practical test of concepts they were learning about.

Awareness of these debates thus reveals a second intertext in *El crimen de la calle de Fuencarral*, particularly visible in the description of Higinia quoted earlier. Such detained inspection does not merely point to the monstrous countenance of a melodramatic villain, nor is it there solely to make the narrated scene come alive in the eyes of readers. Galdós is also providing his audience with *clues* they may analyze according to what they know of current "scientific" practice — much like the DNA tests of our day—in order to come to a conclusion about her guilt or innocence. There, for all to see, are the (obvious) scarcity of facial hair, the dark mane, the sharp nose, the cold expression, the protruding jaw. Also obvious is the conceit of a woman basking in public attention: "con . . . afabilidad se presta a contestar a cuantas preguntas se le hacen . . . [y] no abandona un momento su sonrisa complaciente y bondadosa" [she . . . politely agrees to answer all questions asked . . . and does not drop for a moment her kind and obliging smile] (27). So what are we to make of all this? The positivistic, experimental method dictates a guilty verdict—the verdict rendered in actuality by the court—but Galdós's narration, open to two very different readings, stays away from such a clear-cut resolution.[13]

The attentive reader cannot ignore the *mixed* description of Higinia: the black hair is shaped in attractive soft curls; the distortion of the skull is offset by the mention of the perfect, graceful, shape of the head; the rapacious look contrasts with the affable smile, the delicate complexion. This hesitation—the shadow of doubt I mentioned earlier—reappears in Galdós's consistent verbal restraint. Grammatically, the text is dominated by the presence of "if" clauses, statements of doubt, and cautious assertions: "dícese" [it is said], "según parece" [as it seems] (15), "si esto es cierto" [if this is true] (16), "la última apreciación con visos de exactitud" [the latest plausible judgment] (20), "tal es el estado de la cuestión" [such is the state of the matter] (30), "queda la gran duda" [there remains great doubt] (38). In the last article, dated 30 May 1889, Galdós reports on the judge's resolution: Higinia has been convicted and sentenced to death (on the evidence of her eventual confession), and her presumed accomplice Dolores Avila has been sentenced to eighteen years in prison. But in Galdós's narration the judgment, and the end of the narrative, convey no absolute certainty.

On the one hand, the author questions the fairness of a decision that sentences the confessed criminal to death while allowing the one who denied everything (Dolores) to live.[14] On the other, he doubts Higinia's confession and refrains from declaring closure or finality. He expresses his own suspicion: "el juicio no ha hecho luz completa sobre todos los pormenores del crimen" [the trial has not thrown complete light on all of the crime's details] (46). He expresses the public's suspicion: "he aquí un veredicto que no satisface a nadie" [here is a verdict that satisfies no one] (47). And most revealing of his tone are the narration's final words: "Veremos si el Supremo confirma la sentencia. Aún hay quien dice que este proceso dará mucho que hablar todavía; que ofrecerá nuevas peripecias; que ha de abrirse un nuevo período de prueba; que Higinia o Dolores, o las dos juntas, han de hacer, cuando menos se piense, nuevas e importantes revelaciones" [It remains to be seen if the Supreme Court will confirm the sentence. There are yet some who say that these proceedings will still make for much talk; that it will offer new adventures; that another period of proof will be opened; that Higinia, or Dolores, or both, will make new and important revelations when it is least expected] (47). The passage evidently remits, once again, to the world of serial fiction, which often ended with the promise of continuation in a future work (as in, for example, the ending of *Los desheredados* announcing its second part, *Los hijos perdidos*). We also find, however, an implicitly critical view of the tendency to understand reality—to construct it— in terms of conventional schemes, especially those imported from serial and melodramatic fiction. The idea of a clearly identifiable monstrous villain who can be put to death and exorcized shows an unproblematic concept of right and wrong, as well as a naive reliance on the possibility of a protected society.

Galdós's refusal to accept completely that all the pieces of the puzzle may have already fit together according to the rules of evidence also throws into question the entire notion of the identifiable "born" criminal. Higinia's jaw may protrude and her countenance may be cold, but we cannot know through her features what lies at the bottom of her soul. Like the consummate actress that she is, she might lie; but, furthermore, so might her body, which is not an immediately readable text. It cannot be opened like a serial novel, approached from previous knowledge of a set of conventions, categorized or classified in terms of biology or natural history. However far it may go in the quest for knowledge, the positivistic scientific gaze is finally insufficient, as it becomes trapped in the folds of physical and spiritual forces not accessible through observation, but rather (if at all) through discerning analysis of the unseen as well as the visible. On the one hand, Galdós's invocation of the world of criminology places his writing in the context of naturalism as Henry Céard defined it in 1885: "Naturalism is the transposition into literature and art of the means of investigation employed by science for the study of earthly phenomena" (qtd. in Baguley, "Nature of Naturalism," 16). On the other hand, however, Galdós turns away from the particular scientific paradigm the naturalist novel had taken as a frame of reference. As I will argue further on, he takes a definitive step from the empirical domain of positivism toward the epistemological grounds of hermeneutics.

It is evident from my discussion of *El crimen de la calle de Fuencarral* that it is a text in open dialogue with other texts, from "popular" fiction to science and philosophy. In addition, this journalistic piece stands in a unique intertextual relationship to a work of fiction written by the same author at the same time, and which clearly echoes and develops the ideas it proposes. Such is the case of *La incógnita*, an epistolary novel that both quotes and thematizes the events narrated in *El crimen* through an utterly modern metafictional structure.[15] The novel is composed of a collection of letters written by Manuel Infante to "Equis," his correspondent in the provincial city of Orbajosa. Infante's attempt to "contar la historia de mi vida en Madrid" [tell the story of my life in Madrid] (*OC*, 5:686) focuses on a series of mysteries either he or the other characters he writes about are attempting to solve. In the background is the murder of *la calle del Baño*, strongly reminiscent of the murder on Fuencarral Street: "De lo que más se habla . . . es de ese misterioso crimen de la calle del Baño. . . . Una señora joven, madre, cuyo estado se ignora, apareció asesinada en su lecho y medio quemada, juntamente con su hijo, niño de pocos años. En la casa no había más persona, al descubrirse el crimen, que un sirviente, Segundo Cuadrado" [The most talked-about matter . . . is that mysterious crime on Bath Street. . . . A young lady, a mother, of unknown status, turned up murdered on her bed, half-burned, together with her son, a very young boy. When the crime was discovered, there was no one else in the house except for a servant, Segundo Cuadrado] (737).

Before discussing the two foregrounded enigmas in which Infante himself is involved, it is worthwhile to review the many points of coincidence between this fictional crime and the real crime on which Galdós was reporting around the same dates. Not only do the incidents share many features; they also give rise to the same kind of investigative frenzy. Newspapers lead the way in the frantic search for witnesses, accounts, and evidence, and individuals contribute to the proliferation of theories and clues that may prove them, so that Infante fears "que tantas pistas acaben por despistar a la Justicia" [that so many clues will leave Justice clueless] (737). They do, of course, and "la Justicia [anda] embarullada, dando palos de ciego, prendiendo y soltando gente" [the authorities are confused, striking out blindly, arresting and releasing people]. As in the case of the Fuencarral crime, the frame of conventions through which the public approaches such a serious event comes from the fiction Galdós blames for the intellectual atrophy of the Spanish race: "La imaginación de esta raza fabrica toda clase de extravagancias novelescas.... Las noticias más frescas [son] siempre estrambóticas, y al parecer tomadas de un folletín de Ponson du Terrail" [Our people's imagination fabricates all sorts of novelesque nonsense. . . . The latest news is always outlandish, and seemingly taken from a Ponson du Terrail serial] (737–38).

Infante implicitly looks down on these armchair detectives that never get anywhere (readers of *La incógnita* do not eventually learn the outcome of the criminal investigation). Explicitly, he looks down on the narrative form that shapes their consciousness, and which he satirizes many times in the course of his own story. At one point, for example, he announces: "Si esto fuera novela pondría: *Aparición de un nuevo personaje*" [if this were a novel it would say: *Enter a new character*] (702). At other times he borrows the serial novel's language in the same way Galdós does in *El crimen:* "La casualidad, una voz, una cita, un nombre, son el rayo de luz que esclarece todos los misterios" [Chance, a voice, a rendezvous, a name, are the shaft of light that illuminates all mysteries] (733). He also parodies the structure of installment fiction, as when he writes "la contestación, *en el próximo número*" [the answer, *in the next issue*] (734). Or he humorously welcomes Equis's presumed observation about the novelesque extravagance of everything around him: "¿Te resulta esto divertido, o te parece extravagante, empalagoso, digno sólo de figurar en el folletín de *El Impulsor Orbajosense?*" [Do you find all this amusing, or do you find it extravagant, cloying, worthy only of inclusion in the *feuilleton* of *The Driving Force of Orbajosa*] (734).

To Infante, the murder on Baño Street is clearly inferior in seriousness and transcendence to the first of the foregrounded mysteries that concern him: the identity of the lover he is sure that his cousin Augusta Cisneros keeps. And yet the background invades the foreground as his own discourse jumps from one level to another, using one as a point of comparison for the other: "Mientras los demás roen el crimen, yo mastico mi enigma . . . y trato de dilucidar el arduo punto de quién será su cómplice. Mi sumaria está tan embrollada como la del hecho de la calle del Baño, y a cada hora veo una pista nueva. La sigo, y nada.... ¿Dónde está el criminal que busco?" [While others gnaw at the crime, I chew on my enigma . . . and try to clear up the arduous point of who might be her accomplice. My investigation is as tangled up as that of the events on Bath Street, and at every moment I see a new clue. I follow it, and nothing. . . . Where is the criminal I pursue?] (738). He may chew while others gnaw, but his presumed superiority is undermined by the many ways in which he mirrors the would-be private eyes that fail to discover the murderer of the unfortunate mother. Not only do both their stories fit into the mold of serial fiction, but they are equally ineffective in getting to the truth they seek, constantly derailed by the prejudice of their own theories, and by a failure to gain a comprehensive understanding of the situations in question.

The two spheres that Infante would keep separate—the murder on Baño Street and his own inquiry into Augusta's intimacy—join together in the second enigma foregrounded in *La incógnita*. Thus the mystery of the murdered mother and the mystery of the secret lover meet in the mystery of the murdered lover, when Federico Viera turns up dead in a dunghill. Infante is plunged into a new inquest without having learned of the solution to the first crime, and without having himself discovered the name of Augusta's lover (his earlier assessment of Federico as the possible lover is as provisional as all the previous ones). He assumes the role of detective (looking for footsteps, interrogating suspects and witnesses), and even of forensic pathologist: "Asistí a la autopsia. . . . El cadáver tenía varias contusiones y dos heridas de revólver. . . . Además, se observó una fuerte erosión en el brazo izquierdo, y los dedos de ambas manos desollados. Hubo, pues, lucha" [I attended the autopsy. . . . The body had several bruises and two pistol wounds. . . . In addition, one could observe a severe abrasion on the left arm, and the fingers on both hands were torn to shreds] (754). In his investigations, Infante once again remits to the quasi-scientific scientific discourse of criminology, but his observation is tainted by the always pervasive sensationalistic approach. Thus, all his efforts lead nowhere, and this third mystery is also left without an explanation.

In this way, near the end of the novel, Infante is at a point of "interpretive crisis," a crisis that "prompts Equis to participate in the deciphering of the unresolved enigmas by transforming Infante's letters (the text of *La incógnita*) into the dialogue-novel, *Realidad*"

(Tsuchiya "Enigma of Writing," 349). Several critics have performed incisive readings of the ways in which the two novels supplement each other, but whatever answers to the mysteries in *La incógnita Realidad* may yield (and we never learn all the details, either in the second novel or in *Realidad,* the play), it is also productive to separate them: they are, after all, *two* texts. And reading *La incógnita* by itself, we find an extremely original and intriguing conclusion to the multilevel enigma. We read that there is discovery and closure, that the fragmented narrative of Infante's letters to Equis has been magically transformed inside the garlic box into the (at least slightly) more cohesive shape of a "diálogo dramático" communicating, not *incógnitas,* but reality itself. Rather than learning the solutions to the mysteries in *La incógnita,* the reader is *told of* a solution that turns "los datos aparentes y públicos" [manifest and public data] into "la verdad de un caso" [the truth of a case] (784).

Throughout *La incógnita,* Infante has been concerned with discovering material reality. Against the "pura novela" [pure novel] (739), he seeks positive, verifiable facts that will reveal objective truth: "Yo no me aferro a las opiniones, ni tengo la estúpida vanidad de la consecuencia del juicio. Observo lealmente, rectifico cuando hay que rectificar, quito y pongo lo que me manda quitar y poner la realidad, descubriéndose por grados, y persigo la verdad objetiva, sacrificándole la subjetiva" [I do not hold on to opinions, nor do I have stupid vanities about the consistency of my judgment. I observe loyally, I rectify when one should rectify, I say one thing or the other as reality dictates, revealing itself by degrees, and I pursue objective truth, sacrifying subjective truth to it] (717). He pays obsessive attention to every detail of the other characters' speech, of their demeanor, of their dress, of their homes, in hopes of finding firm answers to the questions that trouble him. In his quest to put aside "una realidad verosímil" [a plausible reality] and uncover "la realidad auténtica" [the authentic reality] (760), Infante ignores the advice of his uncle Cisneros, a mouthpiece for interesting and radical ideas that have otherwise variously seduced him all through the novel: "La santa verdad, hijo de mi alma, no la encontrarás nunca, si no bajas tras ella al infierno de las conciencias, y esto es imposible. Conténtate con la verdad *relativa y aparente*" [The holy truth, my dear son, you will never find, unless you follow it into the hell of individual consciences, and this is impossible. Content yourself with the relative and manifest truth] (763). Nevertheless, this is a piece of advice Infante would have done well to follow, since in the world depicted in *La incógnita,* observable facts do not lead to objective truth, and both are questioned.

Within this novel, readers never learn beyond any doubt who committed the Bath Street murders, who had the adulterous affair with Augusta, who killed Federico Viera. Yet, as I mentioned before, it does not end on a note of uncertainty. As Linda Willem points out, "within the context of the novelistic world, the manuscript of *Realidad* does provide the truth that has eluded Infante . . . and he is grateful for Equis's cooperation in bringing his investigation to a close" ("Turning," 388). As in melodramatic fiction, recognition and revelation ("light") take place, but their final nature is not the one the narrative had been leading us to expect. In this respect, it is useful to acknowledge Willem's suggestion about another intertextual relationship that underlies both *El crimen de la calle de Fuencarral* and *La incógnita:*

> At the time of *La incógnita*'s composition in the late 1880's detective fiction was just entering its boom period of popularity, and Galdós capitalized on the reading public's familiarity with this type of novel. . . . Together the detective and the reader assign guilt or innocence by following the clues and assessing the evidence. Indeed, reader expectation demands that a solution can be found for the mystery through the systematic application of logic and order. (386)

As a point of contact between the melodramatism and sensationalism of popular fiction and the goals of the positivistic search for knowledge, the detective novel of the late 1880s certainly provides a remarkable point of contrast for the operations Galdós performs in his fictional and "factual" narratives.

Although Galdós read some English (Ortiz Armengol, "Galdós y Valle-Inclán," 193), there is no evidence to suggest that in 1889 he would have already read Arthur Conan Doyle's *A Study in Scarlet* (1887), the novel that first introduced to the public the character of Sherlock Holmes (the second Holmes text was "The Sign of Four," of 1889). With his knowledge of English and European literature, however, it is likely that he would soon be aware of the character's incredible popularity, which would prevent Doyle from killing him off in 1893 and force him to continue the Holmes series through 1919. It is also known that by the 1860s Galdós had already read Poe, and would thus be aware of Holmes's literary precedents. But aside from any question of direct influence, the contemporary paradigm of Holmes is there to provide a point of reference as to the qualities assigned to the ideal detective and his pursuit in late nineteenth-century Europe. And those qualities are expressed in terms of a very specific paradigm of knowledge and of the nature of reality.

As has been widely acknowledged, Holmes's method is the incarnation of positivist empiricism—he is a scientific machine (first shown in the chemical laboratory) whose customary use of narcotics does not prevent him from constructing foolproof theories from minutely observed facts. Observation and experimentation are thus his instruments, and complete impassibility his trademark. As a friend describes him to Watson before the two meet,

> Holmes is a little too scientific for my tastes—it approaches to cold-bloodedness. I could imagine his giving a friend a little pinch of the latest vegetable alkaloid, not out of malevolence, you understand, but simply out of a spirit of inquiry in order to have an accurate idea of the effects. To do him justice, I think that he would take it himself with the same readiness. He appears to have a passion for definite and exact knowledge. (Doyle, *Study in Scarlet,* chap. 1)

Holmes applies current positivistic ideals specifically to the study of crime—he knows nothing of philosophy or literature (though he has read Poe and Gaboriau), or even about Copernican astronomy. Nonetheless, his approach to crime is thoroughly scientific, indeed very close to the perspective of actual criminology. At the beginning of *A Study in Scarlet* he has already devised a "medico-legal" test of blood hemoglobin that will correctly identify stains on suspects' clothes. He is also the author of an article on "the Science of Deduction and Analysis," in which he expounds on how to infer "the history of a man, and the trade or profession to which he belongs" through observation of his appearance: "By a man's finger-nails, by his coat-sleeve, by his boots, by his trouser-knees, by the callosities of his forefinger and thumb, by his expression, by his shirt-cuffs—by each of these things a man's calling is plainly revealed" (chap. 2). There is no detail too trivial for Holmes, whose biggest talent is identifying and selecting relevant facts and integrating them into coherent explanatory narratives, unique in their truth-value. Reality is univocal, and it is an open text, if only one knows how to read it.

What a poor match for Holmes, this Infante who is distracted by art and has barely endured the time he had to spend in Orbajosa putting his financial affairs in order. This fickle Infante, who pays no attention to his professional obligations as a parliamentary deputy, among which is the discussion of the "proyecto de ley de Enjuiciamiento criminal" [criminal prosecution bill] (*La incógnita*, 736), feels driven to assess and uncover private crimes. In contrast to the steadfast Holmes, Infante is absolutely ruled by his feelings, as mutable as his theories, which preclude any rational analysis of incoming information. But it is not only Infante who fails in his emulation of the archetypal detective. No other character in *La incógnita*, nor, for that matter, any "real" person involved with *El crimen de la calle de Fuencarral*, including the magistrate, succeeds in applying a rigorous criminological, scientific, inductive, or deductive method to arrive at the unquestionable face of truth. Unable to know "la realidad auténtica" [authentic reality], they must all be content with partial, artificial versions that will satisfy them differently according to their expectations. In fact, only Cisneros in *La incógnita* overtly embraces what others take as limitations, assuming an active role in constructing and manipulating the truth or the reality that he will live by (as shown, for example, in his arbitrary attribution of works of art in his collection to certain artists, or in his efforts to curtail any rumors about Augusta's possible connection to Federico's death). And only Augusta's husband, Tomás Orozco, will arrive at a true knowledge of deep-seated reality, through both profound analysis and spiritual openness.

Galdós's negative invocation of the detective archetype, a figure conspicuously absent from both his narratives, is, in part, a national self-critique. It is "the imaginations of this race" that fall short of the necessary discipline and sangfroid to produce a Sherlock Holmes. Beyond this criticism, however, it is also possible to detect a sense that the very endeavor to ameliorate and contain crime, as well as the very possibilities of knowing a person's character and motives, and of apprehending "authentic reality" are, as Cisneros says, unattainable. Holmes's science of deduction and analysis placed absolute trust in observation as a way to infer a man's "calling" and circumstances, and totally relied on their truth-value. In contrast, throughout Galdós's novels, observation fails to yield any real knowledge:

> Nuestra época de uniformidades y de nivelación física y moral . . . nos ha traído una gran confusión en materia de tipos. . . . Hombres hallamos bien vestidos, y hasta elegantes, de trato amenísimo y un cierto ángel, que dan un chasco al lucero del alba, porque uno los cree paseantes en corte, y son usureros empedernidos. Es frecuente ver un mocetón como un

castillo, con aire de domador de potros, y resulta farmacéutico o catedrático de derecho canónico. (*Torquemada en el purgatorio, OC,* 5:1038)

[This era of uniformity, of physical and moral leveling ... has brought us great confusion as regards (human) types.... We find well-dressed, even elegant, men, of most agreeable manner and a certain charisma, who fool the morning star itself, because you think they are court idlers, when they are actually hardhearted usurers. It is frequent to see a burly youth, who looks like a horse-breaker, but turns out to be a pharmacist, or a professor of canonical law.]

In this world where appearance and identity no longer coincide, the reader gets the impression that the languages of criminology and detective fiction (as of naturalism) are disabled, because the questions they ask and the mode of knowledge they posit are obsolete. In place of the positivistic paradigm, which locates truth in external observable facts, Galdós seems to propose, through the words of Cisneros and the actions of Orozco in *La incógnita,* the hidden and *relative* truth of inner consciousness. In other words, we are moving from the domain of positivism toward that of hermeneutics: "Hermeneutics is ... the route to philosophical reflection, to reflection premissed on the assumption that by following the indication of symbolic meaning one will arrive at a deeper understanding of human existence" (Thompson, "Editor's Introduction," 6).

Within the field of hermeneutics, Paul Ricoeur gives Freud's psychoanalysis a privileged standing "as an interpretative discipline concerned with relations of meaning between representative symbols and primordial instincts" (Thompson, "Editor's Introduction," 7). Hermeneutical thought has traditionally been opposed to positivistic thought chiefly in terms of its attitude toward the existence of external, verifiable facts preceding perception or interpretation. In that context, psychoanalysis has been under attack from very early on in its history, for its claims to be scientific were not obviously backed by a system of verification identical to that of the natural sciences. In assessing the issue of proof in psychoanalysis, Ricoeur argues that it pays attention to a particular kind of fact arising specifically in the analytic relationship. Working from this assumption, he proceeds to outline four criteria through which psychoanalysis defines and selects relevant facts. First, "there enters into the field of investigation and treatment only that part of experience which is capable of *being said*" (*Hermeneutics,* 248). Second, "the analytic situation singles out not only what is sayable, but what is said *to another person.*" Third, psychoanalysis distinguishes between material reality and psychical reality, a term that designates "certain productions which fall under the opposition of the imaginary and the real" (251). Quite importantly, "the criterion for this reality is no longer that it is observable, but that it presents a coherence and a resistance comparable to that of material reality." And fourth, psychoanalysis selects as relevant fact "what is capable of entering into a story or narrative" (253). It is in working through the events of a life and integrating them into a meaningful story that the "case history" is constituted and the therapeutic process set under way. In psychoanalysis, in fact, "*the psyche [exists] as a text to be deciphered*" (256).

Ricoeur goes on to defend the truth-value of psychoanalysis as analogous (though not identical) to truth-value in the natural sciences, even if it is "extremely complex, very difficult to handle, and highly problematical" (273). Rather than following his line of argumentation, what interests us here is the late nineteenth-century ideological shift of which Freudian psychoanalysis will be an example, and the close relationship between this new thinking about reality and knowledge and the thinking expressed in Galdós's 1888–89 texts. What is suggested in *El crimen de la calle de Fuencarral* and *La incógnita* is the surpassing of epistemological and ontological paradigms that posit reality as a unitary, material order, and knowledge as the result of observation and experimentation on the part of the trained eye. For Galdós the subject of crime—joined in *La incógnita* to the subject of desire—is not merely comprehensible as a social problem for which objective science will provide a weapon in the mutual nourishment of hegemonic discourses. It is, like desire, a matter of probing into the human psyche to unveil mysteries much greater than the identity of the murderer in a whodunit.

It is in this light that we can best read Infante's letters and their final metamorphosis into a revelatory text. *La incógnita* is a fragmentary novel, not only because it is composed of the series of letters, but also because it is fractured into two incongruous segments marked by different epistemological aims. The first segment searches, in positivistic (and sensationalistic) fashion, for the clarification of the three mysteries; the second posits an answer that does not fit the questions asked in the first. Elucidating this final answer requires first and foremost that we look at the circumstances of its production. At the most immediate level, it is the product of a sudden magical transformation inside the garlic box: "¡puf!" (784). At another level, it is the product of a months-long exchange that closely prefigures the Freudian relationship between analyst and analysand.

Infante singles out those events in his life that are sayable to another person, articulates the particulars of his psychical reality (which transcends the division between the imaginary and the material), and these particulars are finally integrated into a coherent story from which understanding is derived. In this regard it is important to remember that the new text, though a *novela dialogada,* is printed in Infante's own handwriting, as Equis points out at the end: "pero ven acá, tonto, ¿es posible que no reconozcas tu letra?" [But come here, you fool, is it possible that you don't recognize your own handwriting?] (784). As in psychoanalysis, the interlocutor prompts and facilitates discourse, but it is ultimately the patient who makes sense of the relevant facts: "the patient is both the actor and the critic of a history which he is at first unable to recount. The problem of recognising oneself is the problem of recovering the ability to recount one's own history, to continue endlessly to give the form of a story to reflections on oneself" (Ricoeur, *Hermeneutics,* 268).

The final answer of *La incógnita* is, then, the metamorphosis that forces Infante, as well as readers, to relinquish the questions that had moved them and to see their ultimate irrelevance. The epistemological shift carries an ontological shift to a notion of reality as a multifarious mosaic comprising perception of the material and experience of the psychical, the visible and the invisible, the conscious and the unconscious. As a subjective construct, it cannot be grasped in its totality, and must be sought in "the hell of individual consciences." Ultimately, it cannot even be arrived at once and for all, even through the analytical relationship Infante and Equis have worked through—Galdós very tellingly returns to the same story again and again, not only in the dialogue novel *Realidad* (1889), but also in the play of the same title (1892) and in the many other novels in which the characters we have gotten to know here make an appearance. Such a reconceptualization of reality gives an interesting twist to Galdós's position as the "creator" of Spanish realism. Realism now has less to do with the attempt, however ironically assumed, to create the illusion of reality through the urge for comprehensiveness, the device of omniscient impersonality, or the painstaking craftsmanship that recreates existing places and character types; it has more to do with evoking the incompleteness and fluidity of human life, its multifaceted intricacy.

*La incógnita* complements the propositions of *El crimen de la calle de Fuencarral*. Both narratives reject prevailing notions of crime, detection, and punishment, and use this rejection to structure larger cultural schemes. First, the two texts come together with Galdós's other writings on the serial novel to champion a new type of narrative stressing complexity and depth of meaning over convention and emphasis on plot. The melodramatic urge for truth to shine and virtue to triumph, its conception of life as a contest, are replaced with the power to shape existence and the obligation to shape it through thought and work. This movement, analogous to the one Galdós undertakes in the theater, will begin to succeed in reeducating writers and readers to leave behind old models and venture into new territory. In both cases, narrative and theater, it leads to the definitive split between a field of limited aesthetic production and a field of large-scale, "popular" production. Thus, Galdós reformulates the image of the writer as an intellectual and places on the reader greater demands than ever before.

But Galdós's initiative goes further, becoming a critique of existing forms of understanding and patterns of reality. Some years before Freud, he posits a conscious and an unconscious mind, and a relational interpretive process as the way to bridge them.[16] He proposes a textual model of reality, but it is no longer an open text just waiting for an attentive reader. It must be approached symbolically, semiotically, critically; it must be actively construed and constructed. The reading strategies that Galdós's fiction and theater help readers build are the same ones they need to use in a renewed relationship with the world around them. In this way, his influence on the literary field and on the canon can be understood only in the context of a larger cultural influence. Galdós forms part of a new breed of thinkers who will propel Europe into the philosophical preoccupations of the twentieth century.

Through all of his public writing, Galdós in fact builds a new relationship to the bourgeoisie that grounds the modern literary and cultural fields. From his early "Observaciones sobre la novela contemporánea en España" [Observations on the Contemporary Novel in Spain] (1870) through his 1897 speech "La sociedad presente como materia novelable" [Present-Day Society as Novelistic Matter], the author refers to the novel's need to abandon outdated or idealized models of the Spanish nation and focus on this new class that now shapes Spanish social life—or blurs its shape, to be more exact. Since then his novel has been known as the novel of the middle class, but the subtleties of this relationship have hardly been analyzed. Close attention to the serial novel plot archetype reveals that there was in fact a previous novel of the middle class, which took on the ideological task of securing its ascendancy. What has changed in the second half of the century is the relationship of the writer to the bourgeoisie. Whereas earlier novelists were concerned with defining the class and its rituals—assuming it could be as homogeneous and recognizable as the aristocracy or the lower classes—Galdós sees it as structurally composite, socially ambiguous, and morally complex. He is utterly conscious of the bourgeoisie's unprecedented need to *signify* and *represent* itself, and of the many paradoxes this entails. In this new circumstance, the writer's relationship to his class will now be one of interpretation and critique.

Angel Ganivet writes in *Idearium español* (1897) that a work of art "encierra un sentido, que pudiera llamarse histórico, concordante con la historia nacional: una interpretación del espíritu de esta historia" [contains a sense, which one could call historical, consistent with national history: an interpretation of the spirit of that history] (153). For Ganivet, the writer needs to come close to this historical spirit, for "cuanto más estrecha sea la concordancia, el mérito de la obra será mayor" [the closer the concordance, the higher the merit of the work]. For both the nation and the work of art to be healthy, however, "hay que infundir nueva vida espiritual en los individuos y por ellos en la ciudad y en el Estado" [new spiritual life must be infused into individuals and, through them, into the city and the State] (155). More than a decade before Ganivet's regenerationist manifesto, Galdós makes a stern judgment about the intellectual and moral state of Spain, and he focuses on literature as both cause and symptom, as the centerpiece of cultural reform. As his contemporary scholars are busy building a national canon, Galdós advocates nothing less than canonical thought: literature moving away from entertainment, and becoming an intellectual system closely implicated in the (re)building of the nation. Nevertheless, as a binomial structure, the canon can never exist without its Other, and Galdós's work is always in dynamic relationship with melodrama, the serial novel, popular theater. Literature and the canon do not exist in a vacuum, but rather form part of a comprehensive network of cultural forces and institutions. Galdós will always be preoccupied with the circulation of ideas and energies throughout that network, and the relationship thus established by him and, very shortly, by his contemporaries will set the stage for the understanding of literature throughout the twentieth century. The same consciousness of exchange will remain operational for the writers and intellectuals discussed in the following chapters, either as an anxiety or as a productive challenge.

# II
# The Twentieth Century

# 3
# Literature and Propaganda: Agustín de Foxá's and Ramón J. Sender's Novels of the Civil War

As one enters the territory of twentieth-century Spanish literary history, the separation between high and low is already firm, and the processes of categorization that assign works to one or another field are becoming increasingly entrenched. One of the most interesting cases of critical evaluation (or its absence) leading to widespread neglect takes place with regard to the novels of the Spanish Civil War—texts that, though perhaps qualitatively indistinguishable from others that made it into the narrative of literary history, have been all but lost. The definition of a war novel is here to be understood narrowly: although there are many Spanish novels that deal with the topic of the Civil War, relatively few of those were actually written or published during war time, and those are precisely the ones which, as a class, have remained outside the modern Spanish canon.[1] The few novels that exist have hardly received any critical attention, and if criticism is any index of reading—or at least of reading in curricular contexts—they are probably rarely read. In an article about Spanish war novels, José-Carlos Mainer states and explains this fact in the following manner:

> In the three years it lasted, the Spanish Civil War did not produce a single literary work of great magnitude. It gave rise to them later, when the experience turned into memory, when passions turned into repentance or obstinacy, when the blurring of the past fruitfully checked itself against the present its vicissitudes engendered: a certain distance is not only necessary in order to heed a greater number of historical ingredients and behavior triggers, but also grants a convenient aesthetic dimension, an amount of reflection and emotion that it is not easy to find in the immediacy of the events sung or narrated. ("Retórica," 73)

While Mainer's wording appears to state a fact, it also contains an implicit evaluative judgment about the expressive and artistic possibilities of works written in the midst of overwhelming conflict. War novels written during the hostilities, he tells us, are generally not—perhaps cannot be—of great magnitude, because they lack the distance necessary for lucid analysis and aesthetic visualization.

A second layer of scrutiny reveals within Mainer's assertion automatic assumptions about the novel in particular and about literature in general. Most obviously, both depend on a crescendo of antitheses, metonymically related: experience versus remembrance (or invention), immediacy versus aesthetic reflection and emotion, engagement (with a proximate present, particularly a political one) versus literary quality (a logical inference about what he means by *magnitude*). Further, Mainer's argument about war novels written from either side of the conflict is, as the title of his article indicates, that they are caught within the limitation of a "rhetoric of obviousness" (73), of a certain relationship with reality—and, presumably, a certain use of realism. A philosophy of narrative thus shows through, one which aligns the literary with a strictly "aesthetic" stylization, understood as a detachment from historical events that translates into or is accompanied by a specifically artistic kind of rhetoric. We are two steps beyond Galdós, whose problematization of reality and its relationship to writing has been superseded. Literature is no longer chiefly concerned with "representing," however complex that notion had already become, but has developed into an almost intransitive language. Already in twentieth-century territory, whether in content or in form, it is the text that looks chiefly to itself that is considered more unmistakably literary.

The previous considerations are, of course, arbitrarily focused on Mainer, not only extrapolating from extrapolations, but also locating specifically in his writing ideas that are widely shared by literary scholars of different persuasions, even in our poststructuralist, postmodern times. In her remarkable study of the *roman à thèse*, to which I will return further on, Susan Suleiman makes a similar observation:

> Modern criticism has been tremendously wary of any literary work that "means to say something" (that has a "message"), and of any critic or reader who reads literature as an "attempt to say something"—who reads it for its "message." The Sartrian dream of transparent language . . . has been replaced, in contemporary avant-garde criticism, by Mallarmé's dream of language as a mirror of itself. . . . This substitution (where the

pertinent opposition is not between prose and poetry, but between "literary" language and "ordinary" language, or between literature and communication) has had as one of its consequences the devalorization of a whole vast field of literature—a field that includes not only . . . the *roman à thèse*, but all the realist genres founded on the aesthetic (or as some of its attackers say, on the ideology) of verisimilar representation. (*Authoritarian fictions*, 18)

While these (and other) ideas about what fits within the category of literature—and consequently of the discipline of literary study—are often explicitly acknowledged, just as often they are held at the level of presupposition. As such, they can remain unconfronted even as they dictate apparently "natural" choices of texts and formulations of arguments, leading to processes of canonization that leave behind some works for reasons that may not stand up to critical questioning, or worse, that are never categorically given form to.

If literature is taken to be language that is not merely communicative, then the discourses that it is opposed to are those that serve chiefly to communicate, to describe, to refer to, or to change a reality that is considered external to language itself. From this perspective, narrative that appears too close to a local situation, whatever its gravity, or perhaps even seeks—or is perceived as seeking—to elicit a specific response from the reader (whether it "asks for" a practical, contemporary action, as in "join the war effort," or a receptive, more timeless action, as in "espouse these views") will logically appear by necessity less literary than narrative that exhibits—or is perceived as exhibiting—an undoubted predominance of the "aesthetic" impulse. The lack of attention on the part of literary critics to the novels of the Spanish Civil War would thus be grounded on the basic premise of their not being (at least mainly) literature, but rather some other kind of discourse, perhaps of more interest to the historian, the sociologist, or the journalist.

Something interesting happens, however, if one takes a step back to examine, not which works (or kinds of utterances) belong to the class of literature, but the very distinction between literary language and other types of language, and specifically the "ordinary" language to which Suleiman alludes. Stanley Fish has disputed this opposition in his essay "How Ordinary Is Ordinary Language?," in which he argues that there is no such thing as a transparent language that relays external truth, innocent of interpretation, evaluation, or even creation of the fact that it purports to communicate as well as of the logical and verbal structures that allow it to be conceptualized or articulated at all. The main difference is that when a text is considered literary the interpretive processes are conscious, whereas with ordinary language they work automatically to constitute comprehension in itself. If one cannot isolate the formal properties of "ordinary" language as purely communicative or propositional, it follows that one cannot define literary language through the opposite formal properties, and the distinction between the two becomes diffused. His conclusion is that all discourse is literary, or potentially literary, depending on how it is perceived by a human agent and of the consensus that agent is able to obtain from others.[2]

There is a consequent relativization of the criteria according to which we delimit the literary word in opposition to other kinds of discourse. For Fish, literature "is language around which we have drawn a frame, a frame that indicates a decision to regard with particular self-consciousness the resources language has always possessed" (*Text*, 108–9), or, again: "Literature is the product of a way of reading, of a community agreement about what will count as literature, which leads the members of the community to pay a certain kind of attention and thereby to *create* literature" (97). The literary is, then, a category constructed historically on the basis of the partialities, prejudices, values, and beliefs of certain human communities. Shared systems of conventions determine what a text is, what kinds of texts are literature, and what features make them so; and to the extent that we find and foreground those features (and ignore others) in any particular work, that work will be considered literary.

Nevertheless, the relativity of literature does not invalidate it as a category. There are obviously texts that are considered literary, some by a consensus that is almost absolute across a very widely defined community (high modernist poetry, for example). In this sense, literature "exists," and it remains possible to say things about it; such is the function of literary criticism.[3] The acceptance of its relativity is significant, however, to avoid confusing consensus with essence, and (particularly where there is little consensus or negative consensus) to problematize assertions about whether this or that particular work "possesses" artistic quality. If literariness is not an essence, then one must probe into the evaluative implications of apparently constative statements, and imagine, for all texts, the possibility that things might be otherwise—that the agreement of interpretive communities might evolve or be broken, with the productive "danger" that texts we now value might lose their ascendancy, or that texts we have forgotten might be made the ground of fertile readings. And while the two prospects are theoretically possible, it is the second that offers the most potential for critical relativism. Relativist theories do not work so much to destroy literature as to create it, to question (from many different positions, overtly political or not) the unquestioned premises of exclusion and examine whether a literary canon—to the extent that this cultural construction also "exists"—might not be differently configured.

From this position, it is my purpose here to reconsider the literary history of the novels of the Spanish Civil War—those novels by Spanish authors dealing with the war, as well as written or published between 1936 and 1939—paying particular attention to the possible motives for their virtual elimination from critical attention.[4] To do this, I will concentrate specifically on two novels, one written from each ideological side of the war. One is *Madrid de corte a checa* [Madrid from Court to Jail], a fascist novel written by Count Agustín de Foxá, and published in Madrid in 1938. The other is Ramón J. Sender's *Contraataque* [Counter-Attack in Spain], a testimonial novel of the first months of the war, sympathetic to the Republican side and also published in Spain in 1938. What this inquiry shows may indicate useful ways in which "the devalorization of a whole vast field of literature" pointed out by Suleiman may be sidestepped, and such texts successfully integrated into a more comprehensive view (or construction) of the Spanish tradition.

Naturally, one may always attribute the lack of critical studies and the scarcity of readings of the war novels to the unavailability of editions throughout the twentieth century, and this is certainly a fact to be considered. *Contraataque*, for example, was first published in Spanish by the Communist Party's *Ediciones Nuestro Pueblo* in the middle of the war (1938)—with the consequent accidents of preservation presumably inherent to an extremely "unofficial" distribution system at a time of armed conflict.[5] It was not reprinted until (or since) the 1978 Aymar edition, and, as Mary S. Vásquez has previously pointed out, Sender "claims in his 1978 foreword that he himself had no copy of the original edition" for a long time ("Narrative Voice," 112). Nevertheless, both novels have been deposited, for many years, in libraries in Spain, the U.S., and elsewhere, where other equally rare texts were found and studied by critics; the dearth of modern editions is not often an obstacle to scholars in search of new material to study. The texts' canonical fortune cannot be totally explained by the number of accessible copies and has to be located in the combination of this factor with other phenomena of critical reception. The fact that the studies about either novel can be counted with the fingers of one hand remains significant as an implicit statement about which works have not been considered appropriate ground for literary inquiry.

In this context, it is worth dwelling some more on the "philosophy" of literature (or literary narrative) that I extrapolated from José-Carlos Mainer's statement. Reading such a prominent structuralist critic as Gérard Genette, one finds a summary of these assumptions. As he argued in *Fiction and Diction,* theories of literature have historically been of two types: essentialist or constitutive, and conditionalist. The more traditional essentialist approaches, in turn, had been divided into those that defined literature according to its content, fiction (the Aristotelian line), or according to its particular, self-conscious and autonomous, use of language (the formalist line).[6] Conditionalist theories emerged because both essentialist currents failed to account for a sizeable body of works that were considered literary by many, especially those that might be named "nonfictional prose literature: history, oratory, the essay, and autobiography, for instance" (16). From his structuralist position, Genette does not consider the political (or other) possibilities of conditionalist poetics, but defines it rather as a subjectivization of the essentialist formal approach. In other words, "a text is literary . . . for someone who is more concerned with its form than with its content—for someone, for example, who appreciates the way it is written even while rejecting or ignoring its meaning" (17). Conditionalist poetics cannot replace, or even relativize, essentialist poetics, because the former define literature according to observable inherent features—such as fictionality or poetic form (a conditionalist, for Genette, could not argue that a fictional story or a sonnet, even "bad" ones, are not literary). But it can supplement it, allowing literary study to include literature in all its possible manifestations: "Literariness, being a plural phenomenon, requires a pluralist theory that takes into account the various means at the disposal of language for *escaping and outliving its practical function* and for producing texts capable of being received and appreciated as aesthetic objects" (20–21, my emphasis).

In the resulting scheme, essentialist and conditionalist approaches would coexist, each dedicated to its own field of governance. The former would deal with poetry and fiction, whereas the latter would be involved with the possible literariness of the nonfictional prose genres, or, as Genette also labels them, "the literature of diction" (21).

As quoted above, in both cases the literariness of the text would depend on someone appreciating "the way it is written even while rejecting or ignoring its meaning," or on its language "escaping and outliving its practical function." The practical function is conceived as the purposes ascribed to ordinary language, and "the ordinary sphere of language . . . [is] marked by the concerns for truth or persuasiveness" (9–10). What unites poetry, fiction, and diction, and therefore constitutes the larger category of literature, is, for Genette, "the character of *intransitivity*" (25), inherent or perceived.

Insofar as the attribute of intransitivity—the privileging of representation over expression—was also a requirement of the essentialist (both thematic and formalist) and conditionalist (he mentions Barthes) theories of literature that Genette traces, writing in 1991, its importance in twentieth-century criticism beyond his own—New Criticism, formalism, structuralism, poststructuralism—can be inferred. The important consequence for this study is that what has long been one of the chief ways of thinking about literature—as an intransitive language distanced from communication—has determined a priori the lack of literariness of, and consequent lack of critical attention to, works such as the novels that concern us, to which the character of intransitivity could be attributed only with difficulty. It is interesting to note the almost automatic inclusion of poetry within the essentialist field, which partly explains the different canonical history of Civil War poetry and novels. From Miguel Hernández to anonymous *romances,* critics have paid much more attention to verse texts from this period, even when those texts were originally conceived as direct calls to action. Evidently, linguistic form has conditioned reception, since poetry's foregrounding of composition makes it more likely to be perceived as intransitive. As time goes by, poetry's aesthetic "nature" is consolidated, while it is easier for novels to become dated documents.

Admittedly, some theoretical and critical approaches, such as Marxist and post-Marxist, feminist, queer, ethnic, and generally cultural studies, have been increasingly concerned with the *transitivity* of all kinds of texts. They have already staged the "rescue" of many works previously considered outside the domain of literature, or at least of high literature. One must nevertheless note the degree—not absolute, of course, but high—to which the new approaches are often applied either to texts already recognized as literary, or to texts read through the same interpretive strategies as traditionally literary texts—questioning the category of "canon" only in terms of social representation. These approaches also tend to be applied very often to recent works, so that the change in the configuration of traditional literary history has been limited. Notably in the case of texts that cannot be immediately associated to certain current political interests, there has been little confrontation of the reasons why critical practice ignores them, a confrontation that might prove very useful both for the contextualization of these works and for the development of critical practice.

In fact, the interpretive method itself, at the foundation of literary and cultural studies, encourages structuralist readings even on the part of readers who have abandoned structuralist theoretical views. The form of an academic article or of a class invites one to dissect a text, going beyond "what it says," and searching for its deep structure. Critics impose a given order on the works they study, often paying attention to them to the degree that they construe them as double-voiced or polyphonic (dialogic). Even readings that recognize texts as transitive—as containing a critique of the society in which they are produced, for instance—might focus on the rhetoric used to convey that message (opposed perhaps to other non-artistic ways of conveying the same contents), on the network of supratextual discourses that converge on that author and that text, producing that particular meaning, or on the way in which the meaning is the result of the interplay of voices and forces perceived within the text, as molded by the unifying conscience of the reader (critic).

Why, one might finally ask, this prejudice of literary criticism against texts that are seen as primarily concerned with "truth and persuasiveness" (*as* truthful or persuasive texts, and not necessarily as texts that are truthful or persuasive in a certain "aesthetic" way)? There might be many answers to this question, but an interesting one to consider has to do with the relationship of the reader to the work. As critics, we are accustomed to a particular hierarchy in which the text is the object and we are the subjects. Even the more traditional theories that understood the text as the issuing source of meaning, or those that saw meaning as concretized in the meeting of text and reader, imagined an ideal reader, the *informed* reader, the reader as *interpreter* (the heir of Galdós's desired reader). The vantage point of interpretation implies a power over the text, the power to accept or reject its premises, to determine and proclaim its form, its message, and its place within the field of culture. "Ordinary" language might drive us to buy something or vote for a certain candidate; literature can never be imperative. If it has any effect upon the reader, it can only be a liberating effect, produced by its opening up of our horizons. This, I would argue, is the second great literary prejudice of our time: literature is language that liberates us.

A text that we understand as imposing a certain view on us (particularly one with which we do not agree) violates the principle of our readerly freedom, and thus invites rejection. Such is the case with the *roman à thèse*, one of the most reviled and least studied narrative genres of modernity. The most basic definition of the *roman à thèse*, according to Susan Suleiman, is "*a novel written in the realistic mode (that is, based on an aesthetic of verisimilitude and representation), which signals itself to the reader as primarily didactic in intent, seeking to demonstrate the validity of a political, philosophical, or religious doctrine*" (*Authoritarian fictions,* 7), or, more succinctly, "an authoritarian genre" (8).[7] Such a genre is centered on truth and persuasiveness—it attempts to transmit to the reader an ideology considered "true"—and thus infringes the law of intransitivity as well as the principle of reader supremacy and freedom. As this description suggests, the *roman à thèse* is the genre with which *Madrid de corte a checa* can be most closely identified, and certainly one whose canonical destiny it has shared.[8]

Through the progression of its plot as well as through its verbal formulations, *Madrid de corte a checa* conforms almost point by point to the features of the *roman à thèse* as Suleiman outlines them. Foxá's novel is the story of José Félix Carrillo, a rich Madrid youth seduced by the morbid, intellectualist liberal "underground," and reneging the traditionalist values of the monarchy, Catholicism, and the aristocracy with which he is identified (though he belongs in fact to the upper bourgeoisie). Through the fall of the king, the advent of the Second Republic, the increasing political unrest, and the beginning of the war, he remains confused between his degenerating sensibility and his desire for regeneration, until he meets José Antonio Primo de Rivera. Fascism provides him with the enlightenment he needs to put his life into perspective, and with his newly found energy he joins the Nationalist forces. At the end of the novel, he is a soldier looking over Madrid, and reflecting on the imminence of its taking under the heroic command of General Francisco Franco. This story line is already in itself one of the classic archetypal plots of the *roman à thèse,* the structure of apprenticeship, defined by Suleiman "as two parallel transformations undergone by the protagonist: first, a transformation from *ignorance* (of self) to *knowledge* (of self); second, a transformation from *passivity* to *action*. . . . A story of apprenticeship ends on the threshold of a 'new life' for the hero" (65).

The structure of apprenticeship is at the service of the one element that defines the novel generically: the thesis. The *roman à thèse* is first and foremost distinguished by the presence of a proposition it seeks to demonstrate. The correct interpretation "imposes itself" over any other possible one not only through direct statement by the narrator or another authoritative voice within the novel, but additionally through the fundamental device of redundancy: "the rhetoric of the *roman à thèse* consists in multiplying redundancies on every level, in order to reduce the 'openings' that might make a plural reading possible" (55). Curiously, despite its favorable view of fascism and the protagonist's identification with it, *Madrid de corte a checa* does not expressly expound its doctrine or propose it as the thesis to be demonstrated. The thesis is another. Either through the narrator's impersonal voice or through the free indirect style that allows us to enter José Félix's consciousness, the novel repeats again and again one basic sentiment: that Republicans are savage beings impelled by centuries of deprivation (the result of their natural social inferiority) to destroy the highest representatives of civilization.

Although the idea is suggested through images, descriptions, and anecdotes from the beginning through the end of the novel, it is first clearly stated in a portrayal of Manuel Azaña that ends up being a portrayal of his entire ideological party:

> Era el símbolo de los mediocres en la hora gloriosa de la revancha. Un mundo gris y rencoroso de pedagogos y funcionarios de Correos, de abogadetes y tertulianos mal vestidos, triunfaban con su exaltación. Era el vengador de los cocidos modestos y los pisos de cuarenta duros de los Gutiérrez y los González anónimos, cargados de hijos y de envidia, paseando con sus mujeres gordas por el Parque del Oeste, de los boticarios que hablan de la humanidad, con h mayúscula, de los cafés lóbregos, de los archivos sin luz, de los opositores sin novia, de los fracasados, de los jefes de negociado veraneantes en Cercedilla, de todo un mundo sin paisaje ni *sport,* que olía a brasero, a *Heraldo de Madrid* y a contrato de inquilinato. (130)

> [He was the symbol of the mediocre in the glorious hour of revenge. A gray and resentful world of teachers and postal workers, of second-rate lawyers and badly dressed bar-dwellers, triumphed in its exaltation. He was the avenger of the humble stews and 200–*peseta* apartments of the anony-

mous Gutierrezes and Gonzalezes, laden with children and envy, walking with their fat wives along the West Park, of the apothecaries who speak of humanity, with a capital h, of the gloomy cafés, the badly lit archives, the job hunters without girlfriends, the failures, the department supervisors who vacationed in Cercedilla, of a whole world without landscape or *sport*, that smelled of brazier, of *Madrid Herald* and tenancy agreements.]

Some examples of the many restatements of the thesis warrant citation. At another point, describing the jubilant reaction of the populace at the Republican subjugation of the rebels in Madrid's Cuartel de la Montaña, the narrator observes: "Dejaron de ser menestrales, obreros de Madrid, carpinteros, panaderos, chóferes, cerrajeros. Un sueño milenario les arrebataba. Les resucitaba una sangre viejísima, dormida durante siglos: ¡alegría de la caza y de la matanza! Eran peor que salvajes porque habían pasado por el borde de la civilización" [They ceased to be artisans, Madrid workers, carpenters, bakers, chauffeurs, locksmiths. A millennial dream enraptured them. An ancient blood, asleep for centuries, resuscitated them: joy of the hunt and the killing! They were worse than savages because they had been to the edge of civilization] (259). Describing the authoritative attitude of the militiamen who searched homes presumed suspicious, he tells us that "eran la autoridad los limpiabotas, los que arreglan las letrinas, los mozos de estación y los carboneros. Siglos y siglos de esclavitud acumulada latían en ellos con una fuerza indomable" [the authorities were the shoe shiners, the latrine repairmen, the porters, and the coal merchants. Centuries and centuries of cumulative slavery throbbed in them like an indomitable force] (262). Those who staff the *checas*—improvised popular courts where suspected nationalists were summarily and (according to Foxá) arbitrarily judged, imprisoned, and executed—are described in similar terms: "Era el gran día de la revancha, de los débiles contra los fuertes, de los enfermos contra los sanos, de los brutos contra los listos. . . . En las checas triunfaban los jorobados, los bizcos, los raquíticos y las mujerzuelas sin amor, de pechos fláccidos" [It was the great day of revenge, of the weak against the strong, of the sick against the healthy, of the ignorant against the smart. It was the hunchbacks, the cross-eyed, the stunted, and the loveless whores who triumphed in the *checas*.] (286).[9]

The thesis is reiterated explicitly many times, and it is also supported through a system of characterization that reinforces its premises, and which Susan Suleiman terms "amalgam" (*Authoritarian fic-*

*tions,* 98). Amalgams take place when a character aligned with the corrupt ideological pole is also an example of other traits endowed with negative value in the society within which the novel operates: "a character is constructed in such a way that his or her culturally negative qualities are redundant with qualities whose pertinence is specifically ideological—understandable in reference to a specific ideology or doctrine. The result is that the character is doubly damned: the culturally negative traits and the ideologically negative traits reinforce each other" (190). In this type of characterization, a perceived physical or spiritual aberration seems to coexist logically with an ideological aberration.

In *Madrid de corte a checa,* characters identified with the Republican side and its ascribed values are depicted as repulsive not only in their ideology, but also in their personality and their appearance. At many points it seems like fixing latrines, being cross-eyed, or having saggy breasts would automatically make someone a communist or an anarchist. The Russian ambassador in Madrid, in concrete, is "un judío jorobado, pálido, de espíritu agudo" [a hunchbacked, pale Jew, of shrewd nature] (321). Since Nationalists sympathized with the Nazi regime, the representative of the nation they regarded as the puppetmaster behind the Republican government (and its effort to "Sovietize" Spain) is, naturally, Jewish (or that is a trait to be highlighted), but also, *logically,* a pale (sickly) hunchback, physically and spiritually jagged. Similarly, Azaña appears with his "cara ancha, exangüe, con tres verrugas en el carrillo" [wide, spent visage, with three warts on the cheek] (130). Left-wing politics are the domain of the imperfect, the unsatisfied, and the unfulfilled, of those whose intelligence and physical limitations do not allow them access to the higher realms.

Most of the negative characterizations, however, have to do with sexual depravity, and especially homosexuality. Thus, some characters identified as inanely bourgeois speak admiringly of Gregorio Marañon: "Este Marañón tiene un talento macho—doblaba la hoja sobre el capítulo 'La sexualidad reprimida, el donjuanismo y las glándulas de secreción interna'" [This Marañon has a virile talent—(as they) earmarked the page on the chapter "Repressed Sexuality, Womanizing, and the Glands of Internal Secretion"] (57). Before his political awakening, José Félix goes around with "hombres y mujeres asexuados" [asexual men and women] (150), and the Republic is praised by "enfermizos intelectuales de sexualidad mal definida" [sickly intellectuals of ill-defined sexuality] (78) who talk with "voz atiplada" [high-pitched voice] (9). Sexual excess is directly related to Republican politics, whose emblems signal both the social doctrine and the accompanying sensual indulgence. In this way, the Republic is incarnated by naked cabaret dancers driving around Madrid in grotesque tableaux, while "los carteles de izquierdas . . . tenían una preocupación, poco viril, por el torso desnudo de los obreros" [leftist posters . . . showed a scarcely virile preoccupation with the naked torso of the workers] (236). The message is stated clearly as an addition to the novel's basic thesis: "No se trataba únicamente de una lucha de ideas. Eran el crimen, el odio y el instinto sexual, andando por la calle" [This was not simply a contest of ideas. It was crime, hate, and sexual instinct, walking the streets] (287).[10]

It is interesting that when the narrator wants to treat a character scornfully, he often does it by merely stressing his or her (proletarian) occupation, as can be appreciated in the passages I quoted before to illustrate the novel's thesis, and in many others. But much more than against blue-collar workers or clerks, his attacks seem directed against left-leaning intellectuals. Ramón del Valle-Inclán is "sucio, traslúcido y mordaz" [dirty, transparent, and scathing] (9); Ramón Gómez de la Serna is "rechoncho" [short and fat] and with a "voz chillona" [shrill voice] (115); Rafael Alberti "resultaba un mal poeta" [was a bad poet] (149); Luis Buñuel is an "hombre de aire abrutado y encrespado cabello" [a man of brutish demeanor and wild hair] (167); and José Bergamín is "era un hombre agudo y retorcido" [a harsh and devious man] (338). Most tellingly, Foxá describes how the Chilean ambassador to the Spanish Republic (Pablo Neruda) is busy translating Oscar Wilde, famous among conservative sectors as an example of the sexual decadence and anarchy of the fin-de-siècle (110). The narrator rejects these men because of their perceived politics, but also, and perhaps most importantly, for the aesthetic (and, inextricably, moral) position they exemplify.

To the antithesis between the timeless traditions of the Monarchy *(corte)* and the destructive imposture of the Republic *(checa),* the narrative voice juxtaposes the antithesis between the time-honored conventions of classic art and the iconoclastic impulse of modern art:

> Todo conspiraba contra la vieja cultura; Picasso quebraba las líneas intangibles de la pintura con una anarquía de volúmenes y colores. Negros de *smoking* en los escenarios y los intelectuales tomaban partido por Jose-

fina Baker y su falda de plátanos, en su lucha contra la dulzura del vals de Viena.

Todo arte exótico, fuera negro, indio o malayo, se admitía con fruición con tal de quebrar la claridad clásica y católica de los viejos museos. (147)

[Everything conspired against the old culture; Picasso broke the intangible lines of painting with an anarchy of measure and color. Blacks wearing tuxedos on the stage and intellectuals took sides for Josephine Baker and her banana skirt, in their fight against the sweetness of Viennese waltz.

Every exotic art, be it Black, Indian, or Malaysian, was embraced with delight provided it break the classical and Catholic clarity of the old museums.]

Classicism and Catholicism are equated, and the opposition between "old" and "new" art is verbalized in the same terms as the political conflict: anarchy, position taking, fight. The presumed absurdness of it all is evident in the very images chosen: whoever would "take a position" for a banana skirt is obviously misguided or deceived. Lastly, the passage emphasizes the correlation between this silly aesthetic delusion and the "exotic" (the foreign); in contrast, everything that is good (classic) in art or in people is distinctively Spanish.

José Félix echoes the contrast between classic beauty and avant-garde decadentism and degeneration in one of his first epiphanies. He has joined the Pombo *tertulia*, where Gómez de la Serna pontificates to an audience of second-rate clerk-artists ("el médico-poeta" [the doctor-poet], etc.) who feel themselves "escritores malditos, terror de la burguesía, e imitaban la acritud de Verlaine y el coñac malo de Baudelaire" [cursed writers, terror of the bourgeoisie, and imitated Verlaine's acrimony and Baudelaire's bad cognac] (116). After listening all night to Ramón's nonsensical *greguerías*—"Morir es dormir sin narices" [To die is to sleep without a nose] (117)—José Félix walks out on the street and literally gets a breath of fresh air: "Sobre las azoteas brillaba la luna. La miró José Félix. —Mira la luna. La luna; sencillamente, sin literatura, sin greguerías, sin metáforas" [Above the roofs there shone the moon. José Félix looked at it. –Look at the moon. The moon; simply, without literature, without aphorisms, without metaphors] (117). *Madrid de corte a checa* ridicules the "dehumanized" art theorized by Ortega y Gasset and practiced by the Spanish avant-garde, and directly attributes to its practitioners the responsibility for corrupting taste, and with it social responsibility and respect for the national tradition.

In place of this annihilative art, the narrator advocates its opposite: most obviously, the art of realism as bequeathed by the nineteenth century, and exemplified in his own writing. Despite Antonio Varela's claim that the novel's fascist outlook is incompatible with realism, as well as Susan Suleiman's contention that the *roman à thèse*'s morally simplistic characters are necessarily not verisimilar (and are thus in conflict with the novel's aesthetic), the narration aims for the essentially realist, verisimilar—and politically *engagé*—recreation of a Madrid that its readers will recognize, and with whose destiny they will feel involved. The narrative also clearly mentions the writers who typify this superior aesthetic (most of them, curiously, playwrights). Pedro Muñoz Seca appears resigned, serene, and brave on the November 1936 night when he and many others are taken away from the San Antón school-turned-prison to their death in Paracuellos del Jarama (376–77).[11] There is also an indirect reference to Jacinto Benavente, in a passage in which the people of Madrid laugh at the propagandistic posters everywhere, while Marxism and masonry secretly infiltrate the country: "Porque aún reía la ciudad confiada. Mientras tanto, por la oscuridad de los campos, los trenes conducían hombres rubios, redactores de *Izvestia* y de *Pravda*, que se alojaban en las pensiones modestas. Y se movían las logias. Y entraba el marxismo hasta la aldea más abandonada" [Because the trusting city still laughed. In the meantime, through the darkness of the fields, trains carried blond men, writers for *Izvestia* and *Pravda*, who stayed at modest boarding houses. And the lodges moved. And Marxism entered even the most forlorn village] (237). The wording alludes to the title of Benavente's 1916 success, *La ciudad alegre y confiada* [the Happy and Trusting City], which had, since its premiere, been taken as an allegory of his sympathy for the Germans during the First World War.[12] In a more specifically literary anecdote, a character comments on the more than two hundred performances of José María Pemán's *El divino impaciente*, "porque aprovechaban aquella obra, que tenía unos actos delicados y sutiles, como mentís a la frase de Azaña de que España había dejado de ser católica" [because they took that play, which had some delicate and subtle acts, as a denial of Azaña's phrase that Spain had ceased to be Catholic] (158). Interestingly, another writer pictured favorably is Agustín Foxá, who appears with other intellectuals, collaborating with José Antonio on the lyrics of Falange Española's hymn—it is he who comes up with the stanza about the fallen: "*Si caigo aquí tengo otros compañeros / que montan ya la guardia en los luceros / impasible el ademán*" [If I fall here I have companions / who already stand guard in the stars / their expression imperturbable] (230). All of these writers are placed in direct relationship to a heroic national literary tradition, among references to *Guzmán el Bueno* and *El cerco de Numancia*.[13]

As we have seen in this review of *Madrid de corte a checa*'s structure and characterization, the novel's thesis is not stated as a doctrinal principle, but as a contrast between morally charged extremes: the Nationalists who stand for everything that is good or elevated (including high culture), and the Republicans who stand for everything that is evil or low. This opposition corresponds to what Suleiman considers the second archetypal plot of the *roman à thèse*, the structure of confrontation. But this structure is not merely an alternative narrative design: "The structure of confrontation, with its stark dichotomies that admit no middle term and its organization of events into antagonistic patterns, can be considered as the generic deep structure of the *roman à thèse*. In effect, this structure underlies stories of apprenticeship as well as stories of confrontation" (*Authoritarian fictions*, 133). The thesis of the *roman à thèse* is not, then, merely any "truth" of which an author might want to convince a reader, but one envisioned in terms of a moral conflict—evident, in the case of *Madrid de corte a checa*, from the title through almost every sentence.[14]

The mention of the structure of confrontation provides an excellent ground from which to consider how Ramón J. Sender's *Contraataque* also functions as a *roman à thèse*. At first reading, this text might seem very different from *Madrid de corte a checa*, partly, of course, because of its politics, and partly because it does not take the shape of a bildungsroman, but that of the memoirs of a mature individual (named Sender) committed from the beginning to the Republican cause. This form, and the fact that many of the narrated events happened to Sender, might even lead one to doubt its very identity as a novel, and to read it perhaps as the autobiographical war chronicle of an intellectual in combat—and there is little doubt that the difficulty of placing *Contraataque* within a single recognizable mode of writing has been partly to blame for the critical silence that surrounds it. But in the case of this novel, I believe that the uncertainty about its fictional or truth value supports its reading as a *roman à thèse*, a novelistic form always on the edge of fictionality (and thus very close, in the narrative spectrum, to autobiography and testimonial literature).[15] Apart from the insights that reading it as a document of the Civil War might lead to, it is easy to find in *Contraataque* the basic features of the *roman à thèse*: a story that contains a conspicuous ideological argument, and an assemblage of textual devices designed to make readers accept that argument, most notably those of redundancy and polarized characterization.

*Contraataque* is the first-person account of a narrator who relates his experiences beginning in May of 1936. After the uprising of the *nacionales,* he joins the Republican effort first as a member of Cultura Popular, a group that takes literature and propaganda pamphlets to the soldiers throughout the country, and later as the captain of a company that participates in at least two military offensives. The story ends after December of 1936, when he learns of the October assassination of his wife and leaves the front to procure a safe place for his children, hoping nevertheless to return soon to the fight. The novel was first published in England, France, and the United States (see note 5 of this chapter), in the hopes that it would generate foreign support for the Republican cause, and it consequently has a very clear thesis. Everything in it seeks to demonstrate that Republican warfare is the justifiable defensive action (the counterattack) of a legitimate government and of the workers and peasants it was in the process of redeeming, against the brutal force exercised by those who want the return of injustice and oppression—the rich, supported by the Church. The latter are led by a puppet general, Franco, pushed by the interests of international Nazism (Germany) and fascism (Italy). Thus, the victory of Republican Spain is of vital importance for the world: "Si nosotros no ganáramos (que ganaremos, y en ello va la vida de España y la paz del mundo), tampoco ganarían ellos" [Were we not to win (which we will, and the life of Spain and world peace depend on it), neither would they] (237). As stated elsewhere, "El espíritu de nuestra democracia se nos presentaba como espíritu de paz, de convivencia. Un espíritu civilizado y culto. La barbarie de la guerra estaba con nuestros enemigos, cuyo espíritu era el del *gangster,* consagrado por Hitler y Mussolini y adobado con la tradicional crueldad por los altos cuadros eclesiásticos" [The spirit of our democracy seemed to us a spirit of peace, of coexistence. A civilized and cultured spirit. The barbarism of war was with our enemy, whose spirit was that of the gangster, anointed by Hitler and Mussolini and seasoned with the traditional cruelty by top ecclesiastical authorities] (146).

The thesis is substantiated by a great deal of information (often statistical, giving numbers of the dead, etc.) organized to characterize the Nationals as barbarous and antipatriotic, and the Republicans as connected at once with the primeval emotion of the land and with the highest refinements of civilization. Through the narrator's account of his journeys with the traveling libraries of Cultura Popular we see the integration between Republican intellectuals and soldiers. We also see the story of a humble sublieutenant who only has one book, which he has read eighteen times—the serial novel *El hijo de la noche, o la ilusión del bien perdido* [The Son of the Night, or the Illusion of Lost Joy], about a single mother defended by the valorous Rochebrune from the viscount of Beauchamp, who had seduced and abandoned her. In addition to internally duplicating the class conflict at the root of Sender's novel (and of the war), the episode serves to confirm the instinctive desire of the workers for a culture they would be able to understand, and even advance, if they had not always been "fed" fantastic and inferior fictions: "¿Qué sería España . . . si estos hombres, limpios de atavismos de casta, fuertes, de cabeza virgen, se instruyeran y pasaran al primer plano? ¡Qué sorpresas nos reservarían en el arte, en la política, en la ciencia [*sic*]?" [What would Spain be . . . if these men, free of caste atavisms, strong, of virgin minds, were given instruction and stepped into the spotlight? What surprises they would hold for us in art, in politics, in science!] (262–63). These intuitively intelligent though rough men are also linked positively with the forces of nature. The earth itself grants them the rights to its fruit and its glory: "¡Llévate la tierra de España entre las uñas, camarada! Es tu gloria. Para ti esa tierra. . . . Frente a esos derechos tuyos, divinos sobre la tierra, ¿qué pueden las trampas sucias y vulgares de Franco, tratando de empeñarla a los prestamistas alemanes e italianos?" [Take the dirt of Spain with you under your nails, comrade! It is your glory. For you that earth. . . . Before those rights of yours, divine on earth, what power have the dirty and vulgar tricks of Franco, trying to pawn it to German and Italian moneylenders?] (144).

In its portrayal of antithetic characters, *Contraataque* uses many of the same techniques as *Madrid de corte a checa*. Sometimes it resorts to almost identical descriptions, although reversing their valuation. One example is the portrayal of the men in Sender's infantry division:

> Allí estaban los obreros, los campesinos, los artesanos, los Pérez y los Martínez, el vendedor de fruta y el escardador de cebollas, el gran maestre de los pozos negros de Madrid y el primogénito del cobrador del tranvía C-22 haciendo correr, con su inteligencia y su arrojo, a los elegantes caballeros de Santiago, a los maestres de Alcántara, a los linajudos nietos de Gonzalo de Córdoba, educados en las mejores academias, con el mejor armamento, y aconsejados por los más sabios guerreros de la "inmortal Germania" y del "invicto Lacio." (197–98)

[There were the workers, the peasants, the artisans, the Perezes and the Martinezes, the fruit merchant and the onion raker, the grand master of Madrid's cesspools and the C-22 streetcar collector's firstborn, driving away, with their intelligence and their bravery, the elegant knights of Santiago, the masters of Alcántara, the pedigreed grandsons of Gonzalo de Córdoba, educated in the best academies, with the best weapons, and advised by the wisest warriors of "immortal Germania" and "undefeated Latium."]

The minimal description seen in the first lines of this quote, where the mere reference to a man's occupation is supposed to provoke a positive reaction in the reader, underscores how much characterization depends, in this novel as in *Madrid de corte a checa*, on the doctrinal apparatus (and on the extent to which the reader shares it, either because he/she always did, or has been persuaded to). If one goes back to Foxá's words—for example, "the authorities were the shoe shiners, the latrine repairmen, the porters, and the coal merchants"—it is clear that they could just as well be found in Sender's text, and that they acquire their force only through the contextual and intertextual relationships informing each of the works.

As in *Madrid de corte a checa*, here culturally negative traits—often the same ones—connect their owners with the censured ideological pole, and vice versa. Such is the case with (National) effeminacy versus (Republican) virility. While a Falange youth speaks "con una voz atiplada, alzando el bracito cubierto con un lindo jersey de seda" [with a high-pitched voice, raising his little arm covered with a pretty silk sweater] (28), the Republican men of Madrid lift their "brazos viriles" [manly arms] (215) against the bomber planes that kill their children. For them, even the weakness of emotion turns into an affirmation of manliness: "por primera vez las lágrimas eran una amenaza y una afirmación viril" [for the first time, tears were a threat and a virile assertion] (216). The amalgamation between beliefs and masculinity, or lack thereof, is in fact explicitly stated:

> El fascista gira alrededor de dos ideas adquiridas: la personalidad y el poder. Todo lo sacrifica a ellas. Niega todo aquello que puede afirmar calidades humanas con fines en sí mismas. Nosotros andamos, pensamos, luchamos alrededor no de ideas adquiridas, sino de sentimientos innatos: la hombría y la relación social en pie de igualdad.... La *personalidad* del fascista puede ser una enfermedad de la hombría—y lo es casi siempre—y su idea del poder es una enfermedad del sentimiento de solidaridad humana. (274)

[The fascist revolves around two acquired ideas: personality and power. He sacrifices everything to them. He denies anything that can uphold human qualities as ends in themselves. We walk, think, fight, not around acquired ideas, but innate feelings: manly vigor and social relations of equality. . . . The fascist's personality can be—and almost always is—a diseased form of manliness, and his idea of power is a disease of the feeling of human solidarity.]

Effeminacy is of course associated with lack of courage, and the *nacionales* are criticized repeatedly for hiding behind their superior armaments and their foreign protectors. Against the depersonalized strength of their tanks and their planes, the Republican soldiers express their frustration in gendered terms: "Queremos luchar contra hombres. . . . Quizá no hubiera hombres bastantes para nosotros" [We want to fight against men. . . . Perhaps there weren't enough men for us] (142).

Some individual characterizations strengthen the novel's structure of confrontation. Nevertheless, few concrete characters associated with the *nacionales* emerge. Two deserve special note, even though their appearances are very brief: the unnamed fascist with whom the narrator's female friend seems to have some kind of affair, and Ceferino, a young soldier made prisoner by Republican militiamen, who leaves a letter addressed to his parents. Both are described as deranged, and express themselves in delirious ravings, proving the point that Nationalist politics is an illness. The fascist is surrounded by mysterious circumstances—we do not find out exactly who he is, or exactly what relationship he had with the narrator's friend. In fact, as a historical or autobiographical character he does not seem believable, because his existence is not well "documented" within a text otherwise adamant about proof and documentation. His function ends up being that of restating the narrator's contention about the Republicans' righteousness in war: "Lo que les pasa a ustedes es que están empachados de dulzura humanitaria. Si no fuera por eso, nos hubieran ganado ya" [The matter with you is that you're stuffed with humanitarian sweetness. If it weren't for that, you would have already beaten us] (156). On the other hand Ceferino, who has lost his mind, writes incoherently, and his letter ends with a juxtaposition of phrases that also helps to describe the National side as mercenary and fanatical: "Siempre el maldito interés. ¡Arriba España! ¡Viva el Caudillo!" [Always one's own damn interest. Hail Spain! Long live the *Caudillo!*]

## 3: LITERATURE AND PROPAGANDA 141

(244). The two characters serve to strengthen the novel's thesis, confirmed especially by the fact that it is intentionally or unintentionally upheld by the enemy itself. Their own words and deeds identify the triteness of their cause.

Historical figures from the band of the *nacionales* are also portrayed negatively. General Queipo de Llano's radio addresses are "mitad de bufón, mitad de verdugo" [half a clown's, half an executioner's] (22). Speaking about General Mola, the narrator affirms that "se puede tener prestigio militar y ser imbécil" [it is possible to both have military prestige and be an imbecile] (31). Millán Astray is described as "un general siniestro, . . . más siniestro en su estupidez y en su ojo vacío—y en su brazo ausente" [a sinister general, . . . more sinister in his stupidity and his empty eye socket—and his missing arm] (147), so that his many war injuries become a metaphor not of his heroism but of his intellectual and moral vacuity.[16] Franco, above all, is "un militar mediocre, ambicioso y fantástico, pero . . . tonto" [a mediocre soldier, ambitious and fanciful, but . . . dumb] (269–70); "Franco era la muerte" [Franco was death] (253). These men serve mostly as referents rather than active characters within the novel, and are not, in consequence, fully developed as individuals. Surely, and perhaps because of its presumed audience and specific purpose, *Contraataque* tends toward a greater level of abstraction in its development of character than *Madrid de corte a checa*.

The most vivid characterizations in the novel are collective. One example is the depiction of the Moor batallions:

> Yo recordaba a aquellos moros de los aduares de Marruecos, casos humanos desviados antes de alcanzar la plenitud, casos de humanidad incompleta, intermedios entre el hombre y el cerdo. Se les cultivaba en la miseria física y moral, y luego se utilizaban esas mismas condiciones, en España, como "elementos de salvación de la patria." Era preciso otro degenerado, como Franco, para que fuera posible que esos medios seres de las Cabilas marroquíes del interior, vinieran a violar a nuestras mujeres y a robar la luz de los ojos a nuestros niños. (116)

> [I remembered the Moors of the outskirts of Morocco, human cases warped before reaching plenitude, cases of incomplete humanity, halfway between men and pigs. They were raised in physical and moral misery, and then those same conditions were used, in Spain, as "elements for the salvation of the fatherland." It took another degenerate, like Franco, to make it possible for those half-beings from inland moroccan villages to come rape our women and steal the light from the eyes of our children.]

As much as the expendable Moroccan fighters they willingly sacrifice, the *nacionales,* led by a scarecrow general, are barely human, approaching the status of animals. In order to substantiate this proposition, the narrator chooses to construct a very meticulous system of impersonal characterization that carries the same image from the realm of the natural to the realm of the fabulous.

Thus, the depiction of the Nationals as animals expands until it reaches the mythic image of the apocalyptic Beast. Throughout the text, the rebels are pictured as "el monstruo que rugía [a] pocos metros" [the monster that roared a few meters away] (33), or "el monstruo asomando por todas las bocacalles" [the monster coming out of every corner] (214). The monster takes form as a phantasmagoric bull-like creature stalking Madrid: "Los colmillos de la Bestia asomaban por las primeras bocacalles, por las ventanas y las puertas de las últimas casas de Madrid abiertas al campo. La Bestia enviaba su acero sobre los tejados y mugía, de noche, sobre las chimeneas" [The Beast's canines showed through the first street corners, through the windows and doors of the last houses of Madrid, open to the fields. The Beast sent its steel over the roofs and bellowed, at night, over the chimneys] (247). Within this framework, one literary figure emerges strikingly: that of personification. Finally the monster's steel itself materializes and acquires the faculty of speech. Enemy planes fly over Madrid, roaring with "la voz de la Bestia" [the voice of the beast] (217), a threat directed at the besieged city: "Destruiremos, destruiremos, destruiremos. . . . Cuantos menos de vosotros (los débiles) quedéis, mejor" [We will destroy, destroy, destroy. . . . The less of you (the weak) there are left, the better] (218).

One must admit that, although there are more Republican than Nationalist characters, their portrayal is not much more detailed or differentiating. To a much higher degree than the characters in *Madrid de corte a checa,* the brave peasants and workers who people *Contraataque*'s pages are types rather than individuals. The residents of Madrid are heroic in their resistance, communists are courageous and effective, anarchists are vigorous though ineffective, the improvised military leaders are bold despite their inexperience, and no one is ever overcome by horror or lack of morale.[17] Only once, after the Republic decides to professionalize its militiae and allow those volunteers who wish to leave to do so, does a group of men from Sender's company surrender to their fear and decide to return home. But they return immediately, newly excited by the prospect of participating in an offensive action. The presentation of all these characters is usually exemplary, working mainly to illustrate a point about Republican integrity.

The preference for collective, impersonal characterization and personification has to do with an attitude that Susan Suleiman deems peculiar to stories of confrontation and the "holy wars" (*Authoritarian fictions*, 102) they textually stage. Any individual in such a story, including the protagonist, exists as member and representative of a group defined by its values: "individual destiny tends to merge with a collective one; it is as the representative and spokesman of a group that the hero elicits our interest" (106). The narrator exalts this total identification with and commitment to the group, exempt from any personal interest, as a particularly Republican virtue: "Había una fusión tal entre el *derecho* individual y el común, y una limpieza de objetivos . . . que no aparecía jamás el individuo ni lo individual" [There was such a fusion between individual and common *rights,* and such clarity of objectives . . . that the individual never appeared] (*Contraataque,* 42). From this quote it is also evident, however, that the disappearance of the individual into an abstract entity is not limited to the members of the privileged ideological faction. It is, rather, one method for the unqualified moral categorization of each side. The more distinct characters appear with their personal idiosyncrasies and interests, the less absolutely good or evil each side will seem.

There is one figure who nevertheless separates *Contraataque* from the prototypical *roman à thèse:* that of Sender himself. As suggested above, even the protagonist is customarily submerged within his or her ideological group. In other words, "the antagonistic hero . . . is barely an individual, if by an individual one means a character whose destiny is important because it is the destiny of that *particular character* and not of someone else" (Suleiman, *Authoritarian fictions,* 106). I would argue that this feature is precluded or qualified in most cases when the protagonist narrates in the first person, since it would be extremely hard to construct oneself in nonidiosyncratic terms. It is only natural that readers will come into contact with the narrator-protagonist's ideas, doubts, and feelings, and that those will distinguish him from his ideological community, even when that community makes him what he is. This would probably occur in any *roman à thèse* written in the first person, but Sender the narrator goes beyond self-description, and beyond the role of centralizing personality. Often he seems to assert his preeminence over the world narrated, to the point that it is his particular destiny that appears to give meaning to the cause, and not the other way around.

From the first pages of the novel, Sender alerts the reader to his influence and his superior vision. A captain of the Foreign Legion comes to Madrid from Morocco, looking to forewarn someone in a position of authority within the Republic of the plans for military insurrection that are taking shape. He comes to the narrator, but neither he nor the government officials to whom he eventually sends the captain pay much attention at this point—a fact he will justify as an indication of good faith, rather than as carelessness. Nevertheless, he has already shown himself as the first one contacted, the first one with privileged information. By this point, his centrality in regard to impending events is established, and this protagonism will manifest itself at every future stage. Whatever group he is in, he feels singled out in a way that suggests not isolation, but an implicit power: "Entre los camaradas de esta Organización [Cultura Popular] era 'el soldado.' Entre los soldados, quisiéralo o no, el escritor" [Among the comrades of this Organization (Cultura Popular) I was the "soldier." Among the soldiers, whether I liked it or not, the writer] (103). To each component of the Republican side—the fighters or the intellectuals—he supplies what it lacks, either the authenticity of risking life for the cause, or the totalizing vision of the reasons for the war.

Likewise, the narrator often assumes the task of "advisor" to other characters (usually anarchists), making them see clearly circumstances that they did not previously understand. At one point, for example, he confronts three militiamen who arrest him in the belief that he is impersonating the "real" Sender—whom they claim to know well. He argues with them, "conociendo la simplicidad de reacciones de algunos de esos anarquistas 'de base'" [knowing the simplicity of reaction of some of these rank and file anarchists] (76), until he finally induces them to let him go. But he finds it almost impossible to resist driving home the point of their stupidity:

En fin, los persuadí, y serían las cinco de la mañana, cuando me dijeron ... que si quería podía marcharme. Otra vez les hice ver que era estúpido dejarme marchar después de haber pensado en fusilarme, sin que las circunstancias se hubieran modificado en lo mas mínimo. Pero, antes de que se complicara más el debate, decidí marcharme. (77)

[In the end, I persuaded them, and it was probably five in the morning when they told me ... that I could go if I wanted to. Again I made them see that it was stupid to let me go after having thought of shooting me, without circumstances having changed in the least. But, before the discussion became more complicated, I decided to leave.]

This is not, by far, the only time he undertakes the function of convincing: *hacer ver* or *persuadir*. While travelling the country with Cultura Popular, he manages to talk an orator from the Confederación Nacional de Trabajadores into not using the term "dictadura roja" [red dictatorship] (105) by manipulating his insecurities, accusing him of falling back on "un clisé hecho" [a ready-made cliché] (106). Another time, as he is being transported to the outskirts of Madrid to participate in the city's defense, he enters into a polemic with a young poet who has also joined the militia: "Ese muchacho sentía cierta simpatía por los anarquistas, y, con mi tendencia a discutir con los argumentos de mi interlocutor, con sus mismas palabras vueltas del revés, íbamos hablando por el camino" [That kid felt some affinity with the anarchists and, with my tendency to debate with my interlocutor's arguments, with his own words turned upside down, we were talking along the way] (225). He argues for the superior commitment of the Communists, until "mi amigo tuvo que darme la razón" [my friend had to concede I was right] (226).

Sender's central role is confirmed everywhere, not the least when a lead Republican commander insists that he leave his company and join him as a member of the army's staff—an offer he refuses because "si algún trabajo me ha gustado es el de capitán" [if there's any job I've liked it's that of captain] (175). From this position he can maintain the prerogative of rising above the soldiers to lead and judge them, or allowing himself to feel like one of them. Both attitudes surface in the incident of the men who decide to leave the company. When they tell him of their decision, his reaction could not be harsher:

En el fondo, comprendía que la campaña era muy dura. Llevaban más de dos meses en primera línea, sin relevos. No comían, apenas. Iban, hasta que yo llegué, semidesnudos. Lo comprendía yo todo, menos una cosa: que se marcharan ... La actitud general hacia aquello era: es imposible, pero es necesario. A esa síntesis, ellos no podían llegar. Lo impedía su falta de educación política. (179)

[Deep inside, I understood the campaign was very hard. They had been at the frontline more than two months, without backup. They barely ate. Until I got there, they were half-naked. I understood everything, except one thing: for them to leave. . . . The general attitude toward the situation was: it is impossible, but it is necessary. They could not arrive at that synthesis. Their lack of political education prevented it.]

Despite his claim to understanding, and furious at their lack of vision, he severely reprehends them and sends them off without the protection of a safe-conduct. Nonetheless, when they return bearing no grudge, he interprets this as a sign of discernment, as evidence that they have come to see things as he does and consider him a brother: "Me impresionaba el hecho de que, habiéndoles llamado el día anterior 'cobardes y traidores,' lo hubieran olvidado todos. Este hecho lo interpretaba yo en el sentido de que me consideraban, al mismo tiempo que su jefe, su camarada fraternal" [I was impressed by the fact that, though I had called them "cowards and traitors" the previous day, they had all forgotten it. I interpreted from this that they considered me, as well as their chief, their brotherly comrade] (190). He has satisfied his need both to prevail over and identify with these men, because despite their ostensible lack of political education, they are the group through which he fixes his identity.

The ultimate demonstration of the importance of the narrator's personal experience is the place that the murder of his wife assumes in the story. This incident acts as a meaningful silence throughout the text, because even though it will not be related until the very end, it looms over the entire narration. The matter of telling us or not telling us is, for Sender, inseparable from the matter of why he writes these pages: "Ya he eludido hablar de mi vida familiar, que pensaba dejar en la sombra de mi intimidad. He huido siempre, además, de lo autobiográfico en mis escritos. . . . Pero quizá no me es lícito. . . . Si he dado a la defensa de las libertades populares algunas cosas substanciales, no tengo derecho a restarle una verdad, aunque sea tan cruel" [I have already avoided talking about my family life, which I was planning to leave in the shadows of my privacy. In addition, I have always shunned the autobiographical in my writings. . . . But perhaps this is not licit. . . . If I have given the defense of popular liberties some substantial things, I do not have the right to deny it a truth, even such a cruel one] (150–51). At the chronological point where he inserts this reflection—the first mention of his family of any kind—he will not (intradiegetically) find out about his wife's death for another two months, and thus, despite the novel's retrospective point of view, readers will have to wait another 150 pages for the concrete account of the circumstances that resulted in her execution.[18] Nevertheless, a second reading of the novel will show that, through phrases like this one, the narrative thread is constantly leading up to this final "truth," offered as the supreme testimony of the Beast's cruelty, and as a sacrificial confession that will sanctify the fight for popular freedom.

The particulars of his wife's death permeate every page, and can be deemed the fundamental explanation for many apparently unrelated statements. One instance occurs in a section about the defense of Madrid. As he talks about the people's resistance, he surprises us with the observation that "la verdad es que la mujer no sirve para lo extraordinario. Se comporta de una manera extraordinaria también, y eso no se debe hacer. Hay que acoger lo excepcional con el aire de cada día" [the truth is that woman is no good for the extraordinary. She behaves in a way that is also extraordinary, and that must not be done. One has to receive the exceptional with an everyday air] (277). The comment is all the more surprising because elsewhere he has described women in very different terms, for example: "Bajo la nube de acero, no eran ya mujeres. Se transfiguraban en hermosas fieras de Dios" [Under the cloud of steel, they were no longer women. They were transfigured into beautiful beasts of God] (215). It remains a negligible incongruity, until we find out—almost a hundred pages later—that, after his wife arrived at her hometown of Zamora, she attracted attention to herself by acting exceptionally, out of fear for her life and her children's:

> Al llegar allí supieron que uno de los hermanos de mi mujer había sido también asesinado.... Mi mujer fue al Gobierno civil a solicitar un pasaporte para marchar a Francia con los niños. No sólo no había pertenecido ella a ningún partido político, sino que su familia había sido considerada en la ciudad como "gente de orden," burgueses liberales. Pero el hecho de solicitar un pasaporte, después de haber sido asesinada su familia ... fue sin duda muy sospechoso.... La detuvieron en el mismo Gobierno civil. (304)

[When they got there they learned that one of my wife's brothers had also been murdered.... My wife went to the Civil Government to apply for a passport in order to leave for France with the kids. Not only had she herself not belonged to a political party, but her family had always been considered in the city like "orderly people," bourgeois liberals. But the act of applying for a passport, after having her family assassinated ... undoubtedly seemed very suspicious. They arrested her right at the Civil Government.]

The way the affair is related brings up the issue of responsibility. In fact, the narrator seems almost obsessed with accountability, whether the enemy's—"son crímenes que pertenecen al *debe* de la Bestia" [these are crimes that belong in the Beast's debits] (302)—or his sister's: "como la vileza es contagiosa entre ciertos espíritus, mi hermana y su marido marcharon a Burgos, dejando a mi mujer sola con mis niños" [since vileness is contagious among certain spirits, my sister and her husband left for Burgos, leaving my wife alone with my children] (304). Even his wife's guilt seems implicit in his words, as if by acting irregularly she had brought her own murder onto herself.

Equally obsessive is his self-justification.[19] He emphasizes that these events took place "mientras yo luchaba al lado de los míos en Guadarrama" [while I was fighting among my own in Guadarrama] (303), pointing back to the early passage in which he recounts how he decided, on impulse, to join the first militiae in the Guadarrama range. He does not take responsibility for having left his wife alone even before his sister and brother-in-law did, but legitimates his choices through a maxim stated earlier in the narration: "Cuando tenemos zonas oscuras en nuestra ansiedad, en nuestros presentimientos, no hay manera de abstraerse. Algo nos llama, no sabemos para qué ni desde dónde" [When there are dark zones in our anxiety, in our premonitions, there is no way to withdraw. Something calls us, we know not what for or where from] (18). A higher order calls him to action and dictates his trajectory, making it as incontrovertible as Republican warfare itself. Before this higher order, the sacrifice of self and family is the hero's tragic choice, impossible but necessary.

In the narrator's eyes, this personal tragedy brings him closer to the war's true victims: "Este crimen me liga más, y de una manera permanente y eterna, a mi pueblo y a las fecundas pasiones de los trabajadores" [This crime binds me even more, and in a permanent and eternal way, to my people and to the fertile passions of the workers] (305). His immediate reaction to his wife's murder is to bring his children to safety and return to the front to win the war. At the same time, the experience seems to give him a new perspective, stated precisely in opposite terms: "Lo único que se deshumaniza ahora, a veces, es lo que me rodea" [The only thing dehumanized now, sometimes, is what surrounds me]. Her death introduces between him and his surroundings a distance—the same one perceivable throughout the novel, narrated retrospectively—that contradicts his own observations about the merging of the individual into the collective. His claim about the absence of personal interest or investment dissipates behind the definitive personalization of the war: "Pronto os podré contar cómo fue el triunfo, aunque para mí, en el círculo de mis alegrías o mis dolores privados, ya no será un triunfo, sino una compensación" [Soon I will be able to tell you what triumph was like, although for me, in the circle of my private joys and sufferings, it will no longer be a triumph, but a compensation]. The strategic placement of the episode at the end (and zenith) of the novel, as well as the final statement just quoted, ultimately work so that the individual engulfs the collective, and both the novel and the military enterprise can be understood as a very specific counterattack, a search for retribution.

In the end, the most powerful figure with which the narrator identifies is that of the artist, who not only portrays reality, but actually confers unity onto it through his totalizing vision. He likens himself to Goya, and to the blunt expression of the captions that underline the *Disasters of War,* as in "Yo lo vi" [I saw it].[20] As he tells us, "Goya es de mi región, y esas frases secas, llenas, rebosantes de una densa efusión, nos son familiares a los aragoneses, nos chocan menos que a los de otras regiones, porque son la expresión misma de nuestra tierra" [Goya came from my region, and those dry phrases, full, brimming with a dense effusiveness, are familiar to us Aragonese, they shock us less than they shock those from other regions, because they are the very expression of our land] (280). Like Goya in the *Disasters,* he is a personally implicated yet privileged observer, expressing himself through a paradoxically laconic yet powerful *efusión*—a word that means "effusiveness" or "outpouring," but also "bloodshed," thus linking tragic experience with narration. In this way he is ideally suited to communicate to the world the horror of an otherwise impersonal, and cyclical, violence: "Aquellos pasajes Goya los había visto, ya en su vejez, manchados de sangre, temblorosos bajo los estampidos de los pelotones de ejecución. Los 'Horrores de la guerra' salieron, en su mayor parte, de allí. Y allí volvían un siglo después [The elder Goya had already seen those landscapes, stained with blood, trembling at the thunder of the execution squads. The "Horrors of War" came mostly from there. And there they returned a century later]. Despite the apparent departure from the conventions of the *roman à thèse* that the narrator's all-powerful presence implies, its testimonial authority ultimately works effectively to carry out the highest function of any such novel: that of demonstrating the thesis in the most striking terms possible. The artist's shaping of the events grants them conclusive significance, renders them legible, and assigns them their moral import.

As we have seen, and as the novel's title confirms, the thesis of *Contraataque* (like the thesis of *Madrid de corte a checa*) hinges on the confrontation between two strongly characterized, aggressive moral extremes. This contraposition brings the *roman à thèse* close to a modern literary mode, melodrama—a term used to designate initially any play and eventually any creative piece that stages a battle between good and evil, leading to the clarification and justification of the signs of good, with its tangible or intangible victory at the end.[21] In confirming this, however, we run into another problem of critical reception. Melodrama, in theater and in narrative, has probably been both the mode of widest modern appeal and the one most condemned by critics, to the extent that statements about works are very frequently underlied by the equation "melodramatic = bad, nonliterary." Often, some text or element of a text will be immediately criticized by virtue of being considered melodramatic, thus precluding any further evaluation.

Melodramatic discourse, on the one hand, permits easy comprehension. It is immediately identified as monologic and obvious, rendering the tools of the interpretive method purposeless. On the other hand, in its Manichaean rhetoric it is seen as simplifying the problems of history. Melodrama allows us to divide the world into heroes and villains, to identify with the former, and to exorcize the latter. It is the writing of self-confirmation and self-absolution. These characteristics make it the entertainment of the masses, opposed to the art of the intellectuals (whether they are interested in transitive or intransitive texts). And this association is immediately linked to other negative associations, such as that of melodramatism with commercialism. Whether because of its rhetoric or because of the world views it allows, the melodramatic stands in opposition to everything that is ordinarily valued by those who practice criticism.

Nevertheless, melodrama, though berated, is still considered feasibly literary or artistic; it is a mode, if lowbrow, of creation. There is, however, one way in which the *roman à thèse* exceeds even the bounds of melodrama. As it is usually defined, this mode has as its object the fulfillment of a false, or simplified, catharsis. The method of operation is that of identification: readers or audiences identify with the heroes, and share with them in the purification of the world through the extermination of evil. This extermination, effected again and again in every new melodramatic work—because evil is always waiting to return—constitutes in fact a cycle of spiritual purgation. The nature of this cleansing is, I insist, spiritual and archetypal, a fact which most often makes melodramatic plots fantastic and implausible, contrary to all verisimilitude. In its insistence, conversely, on the factuality of its stories as well as on the need to persuade readers of certain concrete and material principles, the *roman à thèse* squarely enters the territory of propaganda—a territory generally considered outside that of the literary.

The two novels with which this chapter is concerned are, rather obviously, propagandistic—that is to say, much in existing contexts of reception allows them to be read in this way, and even encourages this interpretation. They attempt to convince their audience of a proposition that might affect its real-life conduct, especially in the case of contemporaneous readers, but also in the case of present-day ones (insofar as the conflicting values are still, at least partly, attendant in Spanish politics in particular, or in Western politics in general). Both novels were intentionally written in support of distinct doctrines, and are consequently founded on biased presentation. Their depiction of war does not seem geared, as it might be in other texts, to eliciting an abstract feeling of horror, but rather a repugnance for the very determinate systems of ideas in the name of which specific people commit specific acts, and a desire for the eradication of those systems. In this sense, they both come close to what Jacques Ellul has termed political agitation propaganda, with which a governmental or otherwise ideological group attempts to move an audience to a reaction of opposition or subversion.[22]

*Contraataque*, in particular, sought to move the English, the Americans, and the French to support Republicans with men, money, and arms. Its seventh chapter, "Primera de acero," was distributed separately to militiamen, also seeking to motivate them with its repeated cries of "Ra, ra, ra" (82, 83, 86, 89, etc.). Through the device of personification, death itself appropriates the narrative voice of this chapter, urging the men to fight bravely: "Adelante con los zapatos puestos. No me temáis" [Come forward with your shoes on. Do not fear me]. (87) The novel's proselytism is, of course, evident throughout, and makes the narrator insist on some blatantly false, or at least erroneous facts, such as the supposed extraordinary efficacy (284) of Republican militiae. He stresses the unity of all the factions grouped under the Republic: "Todos veíamos a cada paso cómo el comunista cede en algunos puntos básicos para ponerse de acuerdo con un republicano. Todos vemos a éste aceptar formas de socialización que antes no hubiera tolerado, y al anarquista tolerar la idea del poder y de la autoridad" [At every step we all saw how the communist yielded on some basic points so as to reach agreement with a republican. We all see the latter accept forms of socialization he would not have tolerated before, as the anarchist tolerates the idea of power and authority] (101). And he considers this harmony the reason for the so far successful defense of Madrid: "El milagro de Madrid . . . consistió en esa unidad" [The miracle of Madrid . . . lay in that unity] (286).[23]

Mary Vásquez has ascribed *Contraataque*'s disappearance from the canon of Spanish literature precisely to this propagandistic character and to critical attitudes with regard to propaganda: "An anti-propaganda bias has in all likelihood dissuaded those readers who have heard of the obscure *Contraataque* from an attempt to gain direct knowledge of the text" ("Narrative Voice," 113). Whether or not *Madrid de corte a checa*'s publication and distribution were equally aimed at rallying support for the Nationalist cause (which they were, but in a different way, because the *nacionales* were on the offensive, not the defensive), it too works, as we have seen, in ways traditionally known as propagandistic. This quality has been singled out by what little criticism of the novel there is: "It is, in part, propaganda. This pejorative term, however, does not explain the complete human impulse operating within a text" (Varela, "Foxá's *Madrid,*" 107). In both cases the "diagnosis" of propagandism has been quick to appear, and has severely limited critical attention to the novels. As for the genre they belong to, it is precisely its propagandistic value that has often been cited as its most unartistic property. In Suleiman's words, "in ordinary critical usage, the term *roman à thèse* has a strongly negative connotation; it designates works that are too close to propaganda to be artistically valid" (*Authoritarian fictions,* 3). And, as in the case of melodramatism, once the offending discourse has been ascertained, critical impulse stops.

Common formulations distinguish literature and propaganda as, once again, two different functions of language. If literature, or the literary, has traditionally been seen as a case of extreme intransitivity, propaganda has been characterized, at the opposite end of the spectrum, as a case of extreme transitivity. In fact, many definitions of propaganda approach it as a linguistic phenomenon, as opposed to a sociological one. As Peter Foulkes outlines, propaganda is customarily described as a system for the transmission of a message from an issuing source—the "active participation of a propagandist" (*Litera-*

*ture and Propaganda,* 9) is usually assumed—to a receiver. The message itself is usually taken to be false, biased, or otherwise perverted, to the extent that works whose belief system is attractive to the reader are often not seen, and therefore rejected, as propaganda, even if they are ideologically didactic (take, for example, patriotic legends, or children's stories).

Additionally, the message's reception is ostensibly facilitated through the suppresion of the receiver's usual interpretive freedom. In Charles Morris's semiotic theory, for example, an interpreter's comprehension of signs would be limited by the interpretant, that is, "the disposition to respond, because of the sign, by response sequences of some behavior-family" (qtd. in Foulkes, *Literature and Propaganda,* 23). In normal communication the interpretant would not be absolutely determinant, because any interpreter is able to think and evaluate the options available and the consequences of his or her actions. Other situations, such as advertising, propaganda, or hypnosis, "seem to cut down the intervening sign-processes of which the individual is capable, and thus allow the interpretants ... to take overt form more directly and quickly" (24). According to this view, propaganda artificially manipulates the message and the interpretant in order to produce a given reaction, and it is thus a prescriptive and systemic discourse: "Prescriptors are 'signs which signify to their interpreters the required performance of a specific response to some object or situation,' while in the systemic use of signs 'the aim is simply to organize sign-produced behavior, that is, to organize the interpretants of other signs'" (24).

According to Foulkes, propaganda and literature are, or can be, antipodal because the latter can channel perception in precisely the opposite way.[24] If propaganda integrates the reader into its system, making interpretants invisible and automatic, literature can reverse this process, generating higher forms of awareness. Literature is capable of demystifying, a concept related to Formalist "defamiliarization" but which Foulkes locates more precisely in Marxist thought: "Demystification is commonly held to be a Marxist strategy which permits us to observe the origins and nature of 'false consciousness.' ... Although we have immediate access only to a world of appearances and phenomena, certain conceptual systems will illuminate the real relationship between phenomena and underlying reality" (55). Where propaganda hides, then, literature can reveal. It can fulfill its liberatory function not only by restoring to the reader his or her interpretive freedom with regard to the particular text, but also by producing a heightened critical sensitivity with regard to apparently innocent concepts and contexts imperceptibly diluted throughout the culture. At its subversive "best," literature isn't merely not propagandistic; it can also function as antipropaganda, and this is certainly the way it is viewed by many critics concerned with its political and ideological transitivity.

It is obvious that this type of approach to propaganda invests it with precisely the opposite properties commonly accorded to literature. It is the ultimate transitive discourse, since it exists only in order to persuade of a "truth"—that is, its contents are supposed to be accepted as true by the receiver, even if they are not necessarily so for the propagandist. It is the least autonomous of all discourses, since it cannot be conceived of apart from intentionality. It assumes no ideal informed reader, because any act of interpretation might deprive it of its force. In fact, it immobilizes readers, making them unable to discern and evaluate the message, let alone ignore it in order to pay attention to style. The relationship of the reader to the work is inverted, so that he or she can exercise no power of explication, classification, or dissection—the work has a single voice, speaking loudly and clearly. Finally, it is in no way a liberating discourse, but rather operates to enslave those who approach it. It is not, according to everything most critics believe, literature, and thus no business of ours. And we could not even play the role of its audience, because we could never read in the way that propaganda requires. Propaganda is a product for the "rank and file" of nonspecialist readers, and can only "work" on them—rejecting any contact with texts identified as such is, thus, one more way in which intellectuals separate themselves from the masses.

The problem with such a view of propaganda is, of course, that it is untenable. Like literature, propaganda is not a particular function of language, but an institutional fact. Only those readers who are in a social place to receive something as propaganda and to respond with the "appropriate" sign-induced behavior can encounter it—and one could say the same thing about literature, with the distinction that this tends to be a more desirable experience. No matter how distrustful as readers we are, there is always a level at which certain things are presupposed, and at which interpretation seems merely cognitive. This is the point at which we can become "objects" of propaganda, since presuppositions, as Suleiman comments, "are a way of 'slipping in' the doctrine without its being contested by the reader"

(*Authoritarian fictions*, 75). It is when shared knowledge is assumed as natural and used as a "logical" foundation of the advocated doctrine that the propagandistic *situation* can take place.

If, in fact, some text is operating on us as propaganda, we will probably not know it, and not the least because we might agree with the text's premises, and thus find it merely illuminating. A text classified as propaganda is, in a way, invalidated as such, whereas the texts we do not classify in this manner might affect us precisely that way. Literary critics are more likely to experience criticism and theory, rather than a novel or a play, as propaganda—and these discourses do indeed attempt not only to convince others to read certain texts in certain ways, but also to disseminate and consolidate ideological values considered positive.[25] Identifying a novel—a *roman à thèse*, for example—as propagandistic, and consequently putting it aside, does not insulate us from the institutional fact of propaganda, nor does it confine our experience to that of texts that work in sophisticated ways to defamiliarize, demystify, or liberate. Neither does it automatically exclude the text in question from our field of study, exhausting its possibilities, both because it might be read in a different way and because the monological, propagandistic relationship with the reader might in itself be of interest.

As Fish observed about literature, propaganda is "language around which we have drawn a frame." Labelling any work propaganda implies identifying and isolating the features associated with political persuasion, making them count as the relevant facts that give unity to the work. Other features, especially contradictory ones, are ignored at the same time, so that, once again, paying a certain kind of attention contributes to creating the observed phenomenon. Here I depart from the position Suleiman states in *Authoritarian fictions*, that the *roman à thèse* is not merely a matter of perception—she detaches herself from any "theory of interpretation that puts all the emphasis on the reader" (10)—but one of codification: "the role of the reader in the *roman à thèse*. . . is strongly 'programmed'" (141). The recognition of the importance of perspective, and of the relativity of the categories of literature and propaganda, warrants, at the very least, a second look at texts dismissed because of their presumably propagandistic quality.

What can we do, then, with novels like *Madrid de corte a checa* and *Contraataque*? How do we integrate them into our research and our classrooms, when they seem to counter everything we hold as sacred? When we hardly know how to vary our reading techniques and our vocabulary in order to get anything out of them? I have proposed, throughout this chapter, one possibility, perhaps the one most likely to be overlooked, especially by relativist or perspectivist critics: to read them in the way they apparently invite us to, as "monological" attempts to prove a thesis. It is true that critics can never totally recuperate an original context, or occupy the place of readers who might have actually been persuaded of the thesis in its immediate circumstance. This is why Suleiman affirms that the *roman à thèse* is a dated genre: "the more closely it is tied to a specific circumstance— the more perishable the novel is" (148). Nevertheless, this type of reading, the least specialized, can help us approach a rarely experienced domain of reception. Putting aside the taboo of reading a text for its message, there is much cultural insight to be gained from assessing the way in which ideology was transmitted at a very concrete moment, and the way in which novelists dealt with a presumed audience that was not necessarily their usual one.

The concrete moment when the novels I refer to were written is that of the Spanish Civil War. The time frame is not irrelevant to their canonical fortune, for it makes them censurable not only for being so strongly *à thèse*, propagandistic, but for being anachronistic. The *roman à thèse* is, in terms of aesthetic developments, a nineteenth-century form (albeit one that will have a continuity in the *novela social* of the Francoist period), so that in a sense these novels were already "old" at the time when they were written. As relevant as the time frame is the message, the referent of war. In acknowledging these novels (at least provisionally, for my purposes) as a "genre" to observe, I have used this message as a constitutive factor, defining them as a literary form (the war novel) in relation to what they are about. And it is not accidental that their subject is war, because the topic in itself generates conventions and expectations that are at odds with the usual attributes ascribed to literature. Evelyn J. Hinz enumerates

> a number of current perspectives on the war/literature connection: the view that first-hand experience is an essential requirement for those who write about war and that biographical background is necessary to interpret such texts; that the facts must speak for themselves and that the less sophisticated the writer the more accurate will be the account; that diaries and journalistic accounts are the most appropriate literary forms for capturing the realities of war; that war literature calls for a different mode of evaluation than that used to assess traditional literary

## 3: LITERATURE AND PROPAGANDA 157

works; that, as a rational mode of discourse, literature invariably distorts and domesticates the violent and irrational nature of war and that herein the historian of war and the war novelist go hand in hand. ("War and Literature," vi)

While it is impossible in the context of this chapter to explore the many avenues for the analysis of *Contraataque* and *Madrid de corte a checa* that the topic suggests, one can think of possibilities such as the way in which the texts obey what must have been their authors' assumptions about war writing. In the case of Sender, particularly, a detailed reading contrasting *Contraataque* with his much better known *Requiem por un campesino español* [Requiem for a Spanish Peasant]— the fictional account of a priest's experience of the Civil War—would show much about how the chosen conventions signal one text as more "literary," and the other one as more "authentic."

What Hinz's inventory of attitudes of reception toward war literature makes clear is the difficult relationship between the subject matter and the issues of value and evaluation. Critics can easily be at a loss when it comes to judging the literariness of war narratives, because they challenge existing assumptions about aesthetic writing and historical fact:

> Of all types of literature, war literature seems the most resistant to the notion that literary texts are autonomous constructs without any referential status or grounding in reality. Equally, of all types of autobiographical literature, war memoirs most resist being viewed as solipsistic exercises, and the more they tend to be self-reflexive and private the more they tend to lose their status. (Hinz, "War and Literature," vii)

The case of war narratives is an interesting example of how a work's message is not merely a variable, subordinate to whatever other features make the text "aesthetic" (or not so). On the contrary, it affects the perception of the text and the determination of its quality as well as its place in the canon. War writing emphasizes as authentic and therefore valuable a manner of presentation very distant from that usually valued as literary; in it, indexes of fictionality as well as rhetorical play are inversely related to quality.

One area in which war—not only as a topic but as a context of production—causes an immediate change is that of readership. As Brigitte Magnien remarks, in relation specifically to the Spanish Civil War,

Another fundamental change intervenes, that of the public: for the engaged writer on the side of the republicans, war created a new obligation, he could no longer be content with being read by a few initiates; the irruption of a mass audience, that of the crowd of combatants, to which the writer will from now on address himself, profoundly changes the conditions of communication. ("Le roman," 97–98)

Whether or not the implied readers were specifically the fighters, the importance the mass acquires during war, and the new relationship that the novelist establishes with it—in the European intellectual climate of the 1930s—is a largely unexplored phenomenon. Moreover, war represents a sudden, drastic change in the literary field—in the identity and the attitude of writers and readers, as well as in the systems of distribution, the organization of criticism, the determination of value, and the processes of consecration.[26] Going back to the works of the moment is an opportunity to perceive the most immediate effects of that change, and understand the ways in which the disruption of civil "normalcy" also generates an anomaly in literary production, creating texts that will afterwards be very difficult to recuperate.

On a related note, one may observe how *Madrid de corte a checa* and *Contraataque* illustrate diegetically the association between an ideological conflict—the Civil War—and an aesthetic one. At the same time as the novels allude to the rival political views at issue in the war, they allude to the competition between rival aesthetic projects that structures the literary field. As Pierre Bourdieu has outlined, the fields of art and literature are in a constant state of strife, in which the advocates of new definitions of what constitutes "good" or "high" production struggle with the older, already consecrated proponents of established definitions. It is remarkable that both Foxá and Sender, though to different degrees, infiltrate aesthetic doctrines into their narratives of war. Their advocacy of a political position is inextricably linked to the advocacy of an aesthetic position, presented as opposing other existing definitions of literature or art.

Sender, perhaps the more subtle in this regard, implicitly condemns the division of literature between high and low—one product for the upper classes, one for the masses—and the concept of art as a privilege. The narrator of *Contraataque* praises the model of the politically engaged intellectual who contributes to the denunciation of injustice, and understands his writing as part of the war effort against the high bourgeoisie and the aristocracy seeking to maintain their supremacy. Through the episode of *El hijo de la noche,* he rejects the culture of the *folletines* that approximates literature to industrial production and affects workers as propaganda, limiting the development of their awareness. This is somewhat paradoxical, since the *folletines* represent an "open" art, of evasion and entertainment, to which the workers effectively related more easily than to the more "sophisticated" or "closed" art traditionally embraced by the upper classes and the intelligentsia. The model of literary experience Sender advocates in *Contraataque* shares in the contradiction Manuel Vázquez Montalbán has observed in Marxist literary theory. Vázquez Montalbán comments about Marx and Engels that

> [as] offspring of the cultured bourgeoisie's good taste in reading, . . . they were in a position to sample *good literature,* aside from the historical goodness or badness of what they read. Marx and Engels always preferred Heine, with all his political contradictions, to any resolute minor revolutionary poet, and they chose the good bourgeois narrators of the XIXth century, disdaining the cheap populism of an Eugène Sue. (*La literatura*, 164–65)

Ultimately, the tacit view of literature in *Contraataque* remains contradictory, because it does not reconcile historical, social perspective with aesthetic beliefs about what constitutes quality in a work of art. One can extrapolate from the novel convictions about the writing craft that are not necessarily opposed to the concept of art as privilege, and that might, furthermore, keep it from the audience its political views require.

For his part, Foxá could not stress more the rejection of any sort of avant-garde artistic attitude, and explicitly criticizes any writer that he even remotely associates with such a current. Aesthetically, his narrator pronounces himself for classicism, understood as the traditional search for beauty in line and expression, and identified as distinctively Spanish. Ideologically, he defends a conventional art that reflects rather than challenges existing class structures (hence his conspicuous admiration for bourgeois theater, even in its comic version), working as a vehicle for the promotion of "eternal" values such as beauty, fatherland, love, decency, or respect. In fact, this claim also harbors a contradiction, for as Mainer has accurately observed, *Madrid de corte a checa* sometimes achieves a style of expression that strongly reminds the reader of the most radical Valle-Inclán: "What is most surprising about a tale built from such conventional plots is the quality of its descriptive excipient: Foxá has learned very well the lesson of Valle-Inclán in *El ruedo ibérico,* he knows how to break up the action into efficacious scenes, and each of these into almost nominal phrases" ("La retórica," 75). The episodic, concise nature of many of the novel's passages, as well as other features—like the interest, even if distrustful, in modern urban technology (see note 9 of this chapter)—bring it closer to some twentieth-century narrative developments than the narrator would care to admit.[27] And this literary modernity is, in fact, one of the reasons given for the novel's reediting in the 1990s.

The fact that there is inconsistency in each novel's exposition of its aesthetic stance does not invalidate the attendant position taking. Instead, it points to the very nature of artistic self-definition; each artist is always caught between the tradition he or she acknowledges and the desire to make an original statement, to distinguish him or herself from the norm. The struggles between competing aesthetic options are not unequivocally incarnated in rival artists or groups of artists, but may also appear as tension (however minimal) in a single producer's work. This approximates what Suleiman calls the "overflow effect": when "it appears that the meaning of an event is not exhausted by the 'right' interpretation according to the thesis of the novel . . . [and] this surplus of meaning can even contradict the 'right' interpretation" (*Authoritarian fictions,* 216). While a "dialogical" reading can certainly make much of internal contradictions, the "monological" reading I have been concerned with throughout this chapter notes them only as a "'local' perturbation" (Suleiman, *Authoritarian fictions,* 139).

As I have suggested, to the extent that monological redundancy succeeds in seducing and convincing the reader, it can lead the text to fail as literature. I already alluded to the failure implicit in the structure itself—the novels are not considered literary because they are not read as ideologically complex or polyphonic in their discourse. In the case of *Madrid de corte a checa* and *Contraataque,* the "defeat" extends to the fact that the aesthetic models they propose have little continuation. If, as Bourdieu argues, "the field of cultural production is the site of struggles in which what is at stake is the power to impose the dominant definition of the writer" (*Field,* 42), neither Foxá nor the Sender of *Contraataque* were successful in that struggle, because neither stylistically conservative realism nor politically engaged testimonial writing became the models of literature most widely accepted or valued throughout the twentieth century. In this sense, the novels' fall off the territory of the canonical and, more generally, of the literary is also related to their distance from the models of literature and the writer that became most culturally viable in the contexts either of Francoist Spain or of the Spanish exile. If, politically, only one of these novels "won" the war conflict, aesthetically, they both "lost" the war for literary legitimacy.

The "monological" reading allows us to renew contact with largely forgotten forms—the *roman à thèse,* melodrama—and to confront the reasons for their rejection, as well as to review the relationship of literature with forms of discourse to which it is normally opposed—"ordinary" language, propaganda. It provides a concrete axis around which to pose questions about our beliefs as critics, and re-examine our assumptions about the texts we pay attention to and why. It yields an understanding of how presumably "noncritical" readers experience texts, and of the different possible phenomena that might come under the rubric of "literature." It permits a rethinking of the narrative of literary history to which we have become accustomed, encouraging us to imagine a different conformation of the literary canon or, what would be preferable, a conception of the canon as a dynamic institutional process, always susceptible to new, and not necessarily incompatible, configurations. Finally, such a reading also stimulates thought about the places that current revisionary critical practices are not reaching—because canonical change has been undertaken chiefly from the provinces of feminism, queer studies, and ethnic studies, and largely as a matter of political representation. If it is true that the demarcation of the literary and the process of canonization always obey some interest, it is not always (or not only) the interest of groups of power as presently construed by politically engaged criticism concerned with representation.

Nevertheless, as it is generally agreed, a text's meaning is not limited to the one it most overtly appears to propose. Even the attempt outlined above to adhere to a univocal reading of *Madrid de corte a checa* and *Contraataque* and to the immediate theoretical consequences of that reading points to the many ways in which the novels exceed their "monologism." One may choose, for example, not to ignore the contradictions in the novels' presentation of an aesthetic model. One may explore their ideological incongruities, paying attention especially to the ruptures in the novels' persuasive apparatuses. *Contraataque,* for instance, allows readers to see the disorganization that it denies Republicans had. It presents a narrator that ultimately some readers might find, at best, an overwhelming and contradictory presence, and, at worst, morally suspicious. *Madrid de corte a checa* treats one liberal intellectual more ambiguously than all the others: Federico García Lorca, precisely the writer who became the Republic's martyr, and who had already died when the novel was first published. While it does suggest his homosexuality, it also describes him with a mixture of hostility and admiration: "Era moreno, aceitunado, de grandes pómulos, gran calavera y cara redonda; tenía una gordura de redondeces y un busto combado; presumía de gitano. Era un magnífico poeta. Había sacudido y vareado el romance castellano como un olivo, sacándole frutas nuevas y maravillosas" [He was dark, olive-skinned, with prominent cheekbones, a large skull, and a round face; he had a rounded corpulence and bulging bust; he thought himself a gypsy. He was a magnificent poet. He had shaken and stirred up the Castilian *romance* like an olive tree, knocking down new and marvelous fruit] (173). Through its inclusion of Agustín de Foxá among the characters, the novel also suggests a play between reality and writing that inevitably remits us to modern metafiction. These and many other details permit critical readings that find in these novels, if not the quality of intransitivity or the politics of liberation, at least the complexity that has been denied them and their genre.[28]

Ultimately, no text is completely sealed, constrained, authoritarian, because the structure of language is always open and constructed. The singleness of purpose of the *roman à thèse* or, more generally, of propaganda, cannot withstand non-synthetic readings, a possibility that Susan Suleiman concedes at the end of her study, despite her repeated claims to the contrary:

> Fortunately for the reader, neither the postmodernist text nor the *roman à thèse* is totally successful in realizing its aims: despite its yearning for a kind of total "unreadability," the postmodernist text becomes, willy-nilly, readable—and even, on occasion, conventionalized; despite its yearning for a repressive readability, the *roman à thèse* gets caught up in the play of writing and finally designates the arbitrariness of its own authority. By evoking, however indirectly or unwittingly, the possibility of "other readings" and the relative status of all interpretation (and consequently of all "absolute" truths), the *roman à these* allows the reader to become aware of his or her own freedom. (237–38)

The fruitful paradox of these propagandistic, manichaeistic war novels is that, although they have been rejected for presumably telling us how to read, how to act, and what to believe, they work ideally to allow us to problematize our relationship with texts, our individual position as interpreters, and our collective place as members of the institutions of the university, the cultural field, etc. We, as readers and critics, acknowledge the novels' existence, label them generically, grant (or deny) them *quality,* and they challenge our power to step outside the narrower parameters of our practice and expand our experiences of reading.

# 4
# Eroticism and Canonicity at the Spanish *Fines de Siglo*

IT IS A SUGGESTIVE FACT THAT IN MODERN SPAIN EROTIC LITERATURE HAS flourished especially at two analogous moments, the turn from the nineteenth to the twentieth century and our own *fin de siglo*. Between the 1890s and the first years of the new century there emerged a group of writers, led by Felipe Trigo, whose project was to create a novel of sexual experience that would reflect, and above all produce, changes in social mores. Spain's political history prevented this current of writing from following an uninterrupted chronological line of continuation, but it is widely agreed that since the reestablishment of democracy after 1975 the general environment of freedom has generated an explosion in the expression of sexuality in all the media, and that one of the forms this explosion has taken is the appearance of a clearly discernible current of erotic narrative.

The historical coincidence in the timing of these two "booms" of eroticism may be more than merely accidental. Elaine Showalter has analyzed the ends of centuries as semantically charged times in which human anxieties about past provenance and future direction are felt acutely. In her own words, "the crises of the *fin-de-siècle* . . . are more intensely experienced, more emotionally fraught, more weighted with symbolic and historical meaning, because we invest them with the metaphors of death and rebirth that we project onto the final decades and years of a century" (*Sexual Anarchy*, 2). Given that sex and gender are two of the preferred loci of anxiety of Western societies, it follows that at the turn of the century these societies look to such fields as the site of troublesome instability, and that fictional and nonfictional discourses about sexuality proliferate (although this is certainly not an implication that they do not appear at other times). The theory has seemed substantiated by the profusion of worries about sexual identity and behavior implicit in the controversies surrounding the late nineteenth-century appearance of the feminist and the homosexual as conceptions of identity, as well as in our own time the discourses of attack and defense originated in the aftermath of Women's Lib and the sexual revolution. From syphilis to AIDS, the dangers of sex polarize societies around the issues of knowledge, access, and pleasure.

As writings of their times, the erotic novel of the past turn of the century and its more recent counterpart can obviously be seen as discourses engaged with the question of the inscription of desire, and the right to the inscription of desire. The parallel, however, ends here, for the two forms are far apart, indeed a century apart, in their approaches to that issue. From the 1890s and into the 1900s, male novelists like Trigo, Eduardo Zamacois, Joaquín Belda, Antonio de Hoyos y Vinent, and others constructed a novel which, through the structure of its implicit gaze, situated woman as its object and confirmed her assigned role of passivity even while purportedly granting her erotic freedom. This distribution of positions, the relationship between active looking subject and passive observed subject, structured the understanding of the erotic experience. Moreover, as I will argue further on, this very assignment of gendered roles served to legitimize the erotic novelists' work as literature in opposition to pornography, as (masculine) high culture in opposition to (feminine) mass subculture.

Conversely, since the 1980s, as one critic writing in *Cambio 16* wrote in 1989, "la mejor literatura erótica en español es cosa de mujeres" [the best erotic literature in Spanish is a women's business] (qtd. in Pérez, "Characteristics," 175). Leaving aside the value judgment explicit in the phrase, the fact remains that a good part of the erotic writing published in Spain in the last fifteen years or so (most of which is in the form of novels, although short stories and poetry are also published) has been written by women like Almudena Grandes, María Jaén, Ana Rossetti, Isabel Franc, Mercedes Abad, and others. The change in authorship itself, and most especially the deployment of narrative themes and strategies that change the agency, point of view, and implicit readership of erotica, constitute a radical challenge to the ideas about sexuality, the who and how of desire, represented by and inherited from writers like Trigo and his "school." Concomitantly, in the erotic work of these women there is also a subversion of the assumptions of evaluation that permit the identification of high culture with masculinity and thus the constitution of a canon that conceded literariness to late nineteenth-century male-authored erotica (at least at the time of its production) and would exclude these female-authored texts from its domain. Even further, there is a questioning of the supremacy of that high culture, traditionally gendered as masculine, as the site of an adversarial stance toward repressive, bourgeois society and values, as the point of origin of experimentation, advancement of knowledge, and progress. While in the late nineteenth century sexual discourse aligned itself with intellectualism as much as with desire, thus claiming a position within a firmly established literary realm, recent erotic writing by women disputes both the masculine rationalization of the sexual and the exclusionary process of the construction of literature that determines it as a stable category identified with traditionally masculine values.

Peter Brooks has said that modern writing has been essentially epistemophilic, that is, embedded in a project to make the body signify, and that the approach to that body has been mainly that of the male gaze:

> Representing the body in modern narrative . . . seems always to involve viewing the body. The dominant nineteenth-century tradition, that of realism, insistently makes the visual the master relation to the world. . . . While the bodies viewed are both male and female, vision is typically a male prerogative, and its object of fascination the woman's body, in a cultural model so pervasive that many women novelists don't reverse its vectors. (*Body Works*, 88)

The idea is substantiated by the erotic writing of the early twentieth century, which depended structurally on the gaze as the instrument of what was indeed an epistemophilic project. These writers equated sight with both sexual possession and intellectual understanding, and both areas were conflated into the same concept of eroticism.

In order to avoid diffusing my argument with an unmanageable multiplicity of examples, I will concentrate on the work of Felipe Trigo as the directive force of this narrative current. Trigo's erotic novels, derided by intellectuals such as Unamuno, were inseparable and in a sense derived their strength from another "body" of work, this time sociological. His fiction and the nonfictional treatises *Socialismo individualista* [Individualist Socialism] and *El amor en la vida y en los libros* [Love in Life and in Books] were the two halves of a comprehensive project of social reform in which cultural and economic regeneration centered around the sexual; as he wrote, "en rigor acaso la cuestión social no es más que una cuestión sexual" [strictly speaking perhaps the social question is no more than a sexual question] (*El amor,* 285). In an earlier article I analyzed the peculiar logical circularity of his envisioned socialist-erotic utopia: a system in which the measures he proposes with the explicit purpose of liberating women and making erotic freedom and participation in the public sphere accessible to them work to limit the emancipation claimed as a goal.[1] I am now returning to Trigo specifically as an *erotic* writer, and to his novels as fictional word firmly grounded on scientificist, if not scientific, discourse. In this context the choice of vision as the privileged sense in Trigo's portrayals of erotic experience is neither accidental nor insignificant, for sight is an important vehicle to both sexual excitement and knowledge—the foundational methods of modern science being observation and experimentation. Female nudity is a stimulus for both the lover and the doctor, and Trigo, who in his life was both, does not fail to reflect the association in his novels.

In Trigo's *Alma en los labios* [Soul on Her Lips] and *La Altísima* [The Most High], as in many of his other novels, the male protagonist who seeks to experience the unrepressed "sex of the future" advocated by the author is faced with the task of creating his own "new woman"—not the New Woman of late-century feminist discourse, but neither entirely unrelated to her. In both texts, the first contact with the chosen love interest takes the form of unsuspected observation of her in a sexually evocative pose, and the progress of the sexual relationship is conveyed from the beginning through visual images. As I observed in my previous article, before the characters can have intercourse the women must always show their bodies without shame, removing their literal and figurative clothes, constantly referred to as veils. As with the biblical Salomé, the removal of one veil reveals another, and the men in the novels are always left with a desire to see more.

The visual urge does not cease to escalate until the desire to look at the woman becomes a desire to look *inside* her, and the popular *fin-de-siècle* image of the dead woman on the observation table is also recurrent in the Spanish erotic novel of the time. Although examples may be found throughout the two novels (and in others, such as Zamacois's *Loca de amor*), the most striking one appears in *La Altísima*. As part of the *educación sentimental* that will re-create her according to his desire, the protagonist, Victor, takes his lover Adria on a tour of the Madrid underworld to see "la degradación de la mujer" [woman's degradation] (222). They start at the brothel, go on to the hospital wards for syphilitic women, and end at the morgue's dissection room. As they walk among dismembered bodies, they begin to hear a song—

"la serenata de *Fausto*" [Faust's serenade] (228)—and follow its melody into a room where a doctor stands singing before "un rígido y blanco cadáver femenino, del cual estaba sacando el corazón" [a rigid and white female cadaver, from which he was extracting the heart] (229). The song's lyrics—*perché chiudi il cor* [why close your heart]—create a remarkable contrast packed with layers of meaning: a doctor plays the part of a lover who pleads for his beloved's symbolic heart—her love—as he extracts her real heart for medical observation. The image posits male desire and sight as movements of power; wanting and taking her heart are one and the same thing. The woman's sexuality, her position as object of the gaze, is associated not just with passivity but with death, her *petite mort* with a *grande mort*. And the gaze of lust is fused in this doctor-lover with the gaze of scientific knowledge, as it already implicitly is in Trigo's work. This combination of male eroticism and the quest for knowledge is worth dwelling on momentarily. As a digression, I cannot fail to point to the interesting twist it places on the early-century debate between Trigo and Miguel de Unamuno. Unamuno rejected Trigo and his "school" of erotic novelists on arguments which he developed in his articles "Sobre la lujuria" [On Lust] and "Sobre la pornografía" [On Pornography], but which are perhaps most succinctly expressed by the fictional Víctor Goti in the prologue to *Niebla*. Goti writes, referring to Unamuno:

> Su repulsión a toda forma de pornografía es bien conocida de cuantos le conocen. Y no sólo por las corrientes razones morales, sino porque estima que la preocupación libidinosa es lo que más estraga la inteligencia. Los escritores pornográficos, o simplemente eróticos, le parecen los menos inteligentes, los más pobres de ingenio, los más tontos, en fin. (49)

> [His aversion to any form of pornography is well known by all acquainted with him. And not only for the current moral reasons, but because he believes that lustful concerns are what most corrupts intelligence. Pornographic, or simply erotic, writers, seem to him the least intelligent, the poorest in genius, in sum, the dumbest.]

For his part, in his doctrinal books, Trigo criticized Unamuno as a self-proclaimed sage who pretended to disdain the sexual while having fathered numerous children, and he opposed Unamuno's supposed privileging of the brain over the sexual organs in an unnatural hierarchy. The "interesting twist" is that in his own amalgamation of sex and knowledge, erotic novel and scientific treatise, Trigo is not very far from the position he derides in Unamuno.

Trigo's novels are illustrations of his essays' theses, and the essays use quotations from the novels as demonstration of the arguments expounded. Such a symbiotic relationship is a significant strategy of legitimation through which the erotic word appropriates the authority of the scientific. By juxtaposing the gaze of possession and the gaze of scientific learning Trigo makes his writing one about more that sexual excitement. While his novels, in the context of their original readership, were undoubtedly erotic through their representation of the sexually forbidden as well as through their voyeurism and fetishism (the mechanisms through which psychoanalysis has traditionally explained the pleasure of the male gaze), the association of the act of looking with the act of learning frames, neutralizes, and therefore confers respectability (and literariness) to the sexual word.

As these novels approach sex as a *fin-de-siglo* anxiety, they reveal too an inseparable link to a second anxiety: that of literary differentiation. Writing about sexual experience actualizes the need for distinction, because any particular instance of erotic writing is always bordering on one side of a duality: erotic *literature* or pornographic *non-literature*. The former is usually masculine (active), spiritual, self-affirming; the latter is usually feminine (passive), creatural, and self-effacing (in that humans become like animals). In his study on the current erotic novel in Spain, Alberto Acereda articulates the ever-present concern:

> For a *worthy* study of the present erotic novel . . . it is imperative to clearly differentiate the concepts of "eroticism," "sexuality," and "pornography." Pornography has an obscene character, in other words [it is] shameless, uncouth, and offensive to modesty. In this sense, art is never pornographic. In the particular case of the pornographic novel, there is no truly artistic preoccupation, style is poor, and vulgar physical descriptions abound. Eroticism, on the other hand, operates on a higher plane in the novel, there is artistic elaboration and there also appear certain elements of human *psychology*. ("La actual novela erotica," 158)

Sex as a literary subject is therefore a dangerous tightrope, a tenuous line in the sand—and it matters very much on which side of it an author stands.

In a 1988 essay entitled "Literary Value and Transgression" Frank Kermode compares Nabokov's *Lolita* to a little-known 1938 English novel called *Nya*. Drawing on Tony Tanner's work, Kermode uses the index of transgression "to explain why *Nya* failed the test of time, whereas *Lolita* appears to be doing well" (51), concluding that the breaking of taboos of gender, class, or morality is the ultimate impulse of aesthetically valuable narratives. This view of art as a questioning of limits and an exploration of possibilities of being has long been held true, so that whether or not works are accorded literary status often depends on whether they are perceived as subversive rather than reactionary.

In this context it is interesting to think of Michel Foucault's analysis of sexual discourse, in particular what he calls "the repressive hypothesis," which posits sex as a censored subject that requires for its and our own liberation "nothing less than a transgression of laws, a lifting of prohibitions, an irruption of speech, a reinstating of pleasure within reality, and a whole new economy in the mechanisms of power" (*History*, 5). According to Kermode's "index of transgression," and to the degree that one accepts the premise of the "repressive hypothesis," it follows that the writer who chooses sex as a subject automatically places him or herself in a position of literary legitimacy through the liberatory power of the erotic utterance (as opposed to the possible subjugation of the erotic experience). The self-conception on the part of Trigo and other turn-of-the-century erotic novelists as reformers and heralds of the new socio-sexual Spain through the regeneration of both its erotic practices and its literature (and in this they were very much part of the generation of 98) is thus reinforced by their choice of subject.

If, however, the sex being uttered got out of control, if there was a little too much of it or it was expressed too crudely or seemed entirely gratuitous, the liberatory effect would be lost and the work in question would lose its literary aura. To this day the degree of distancing of the sexual within the text from the reader, its limitation by other aesthetic intentions, is considered a sign of quality (that is, of eroticism as opposed to pornography). In the words of Marta Altisent, "a minimal dose of sex makes a more lasting effect on the reader. Whence the difference between the erotic and pornographic novels. The erotic is an integral part, but not the prevailing part, of the text" ("El erotismo," 129). And, as Concha Alborg presents the dichotomy, "pornography and eroticism are not synonymous terms. Pornography is considered obscene; in other words its explicit sexual content is offensive and its end is, primarily, sexual excitement. Eroticism, however, suggests a reciprocity between persons or characters. . . . Erotic literature has an artistic structure with a beginning and an ending, while pornography lacks it" ("Ana Rossetti," 369).

## 4: EROTICISM AND CANONICITY

As *eroticism* and as *literature*, in summary, the early twentieth-century Spanish erotic novel depends on categorization and differentiation. Its status as erotic, as a narrative of sexual experience and pleasure, depends on the visuality that Brooks labeled "master relation" to the world. A male author and a presumably male reader enact the gaze and the voice which follows it, directing them toward an other gendered as feminine and perceived as entirely separate. This other, both observed and told (that is, defined), is identified as passive recipient of desire, and her own desire is furthermore defined as that of being desired. If the boundaries that delimit self and other, subject and object, dominance and submission, blur, the edifice of this novel will crumble. The erotic novel's status as *literature* depends on an analogous assemblage of boundaries. Given the generally upheld antithesis between intelligence and libido verbalized by Unamuno, it must take care not to be engulfed by the latter and to remain part of the collective intellectual project assigned to the truly literary at the end of the nineteenth century. Thus, paradoxically, while its very topic (sex) defines it as progressive, the fundamental impulse of erotic narrative is that of artistic self-legitimation through participation in the control and restriction—or at least the acceptable channeling—of the sexual.

Consequently, Trigo and his school construct and enforce a model of the sexual that is ultimately limited by the model of the literary they submitted to as turn-of-the-century intellectuals. At least in the case of Trigo, the formula allowed him to achieve, if not unquestionable, at least considerable literary prestige. As Luis Fernández Cifuentes explains,

> In the eight or ten years preceding his suicide (1916), Felipe Trigo was surrounded by a prestige equivalent, in appearance, to that of the consecrated novelists like Pío Baroja or Blasco Ibáñez. Already in 1907 a long review of *La sed de amar* declared him "the indisputable Galdós of the generation that had just succeeded." . . . In 1908 he was part of the jury in a literary competition sponsored by *El Cuento Semanal,* together with Baroja, Valle-Inclán, and Zamacois . . . (the prize went to *Nómada,* by Gabriel Miró, who would later maintain a respectful correspondence with Felipe Trigo). From then on Trigo's novels were reviewed in all the journals of any significance. . . . In 1909 Andrés González Blanco's tome, *Historia de la novela en España desde el Romanticismo a nuestros días* is printed. . . . The pages devoted to Trigo surpass, in number and dithyrambs, those devoted to, for example, Pío Baroja. (*Teoría,* 77–78)

To the extent that Trigo was able to combine commercial success (printings of more than ten thousand copies) and distinction (the high price of his novels restricted their audience), it was due to the intellectualist project that distinguished them from the mass of imitators who did not establish the appropriate distance regarding their subject, "those imitators of his who stripped their novels of any ulterior *message*" (Fernández Cifuentes, *Teoría*, 84).[2]

Late twentieth-century women's erotic novels implicitly dismantle the inherited models both of eroticism and of literature, even as they purportedly participate in the same tradition. In my discussion of their strategies of subversion, and again in order to keep my argument focused, I will concentrate principally though not exclusively on Almudena Grandes's *Las edades de Lulú*, winner of the 1989 Editorial Tusquets's La Sonrisa Vertical Prize and perhaps the most canonically recognized of these narratives. One of the first techniques that appears is the reversal of the dominance-submission pattern of the male gaze. This first level of reformulation of the erotic takes two predominant forms: the appropriation of sight and the performance before the looker. The woman's adoption of vision first appears as a return of the male gaze, and phrases like Lulú's "El sólo me miraba [y] le sostuve la mirada" [He simply looked at me and I held his gaze] (169) will be familiar to anyone who has read other examples of women's erotica, as variations of it reappear in a great number of such texts.

If by returning the man's look of desire the woman makes that desire mutual, thereby adding her own agency where before she was only object, it is also frequent for her to be the initiatior of the gaze, staring at a man who then assumes her previous objectified position. Also in Grandes's novel we can point to the singular opening chapter, in which Lulú recounts her excitation at the sight of beautiful male bodies in the passive sexual position regarding both women and other males. She recalls her experience watching a pornographic video and comments: "Aquella era la primera vez en mi vida que veía un espectáculo semejante. Un hombre, un hombre grande y musculoso, un hombre hermoso, hincado a cuatro patas sobre una mesa, el culo erguido, los muslos separados, esperando" [It was the first time in my life I saw such a spectacle. A man, a large and muscular man, a beautiful man, kneeling on four legs on a table, his ass raised, his thighs apart, waiting] (9). Delight, sometimes in the very sight of the male body, and sometimes, as here, in its objectification, transposes the structure of the gaze by allowing women to occupy the other side of the visual hierarchy in a way that, according to Brooks, women writers rarely do.

In addition to usurping the gaze the female characters depicted in recent women's erotic novels seize agency by showing off for the observer. Before the inevitability of the male gaze they put on their act, select the details to which attention should be paid, and ultimately *enact* seduction. Lulú, for example, makes her sexual self-display as Pablo's "little girl" work for her. She has decided while very young that she loves and will marry Pablo and, upon his return to Spain from years as a lecturer in Philadelphia, she goes to find him. She sits in the center front row of the university auditorium where he is scheduled to speak about San Juan de la Cruz, and after drawing his attention opens her coat to reveal the old school uniform she was wearing when they first had sex, back when she was twelve. Though nervous, she conceives of her actions as those of a performer: "Trataba de parecer segura, pero por dentro me sentía como un malabarista viejo y malo, que mantiene a duras penas las apariencias mientras espera a que las ocho botellas de madera que mantiene bailando en el aire se le desplomen" [I tried to look self-assured, but inside I felt like an old, second-rate juggler, barely keeping up appearances while waiting for the eight wooden bottles he holds up, dancing in the air, to plummet] (145). When Pablo walks out on his question-and-answer session and takes her home she continues her act, now feeling "muy segura" [very secure] and worried only about the *effect* of her playacting: "lo único que me preocupaba era que mi actuación resultara excesivamente teatral" [the only thing that worried me was that my act might appear excessively theatrical] (149). Through this escalating performance—"volví a acariciarme para que él me viera" [I caressed myself again for him to see me] (154), etc.—she propitiates a sexual encounter that will culminate with the desired marriage proposal.

Lulú, therefore, arrogates the power of the gaze by using it to her advantage. And while it may be argued that this only leads her into Pablo's field of control—the rest of the novel is largely about her questionable attempts to grow up and away from him—the fact remains that she is never merely his conquest. The woman's sexual show wins a prize, and this evokes of course the paradigm of Salomé (though its character here is essentially opposite to that of its appearance in the early twentieth-century novel). Through the dance of the seven veils Salomé exploits her position as an object of beauty and pleasure, tantalizing and confusing the gaze for her own gratification. The dancer's pleasure is furthermore castrating—she beheads him who beholds her—and hence the fear she inspired from the point of view of the *fin-de-siglo* male writings.

Other erotic texts by women overtly parody the idea of this Salomé-Medusa, incarnated, for example, in the Marta of Ana Rossetti's short story "Siempre malquerida" [Always Unloved]. This perpetually unsatisfied heroine entices her new lover, Marcos, toward the satisfaction of her own sexual desire in a scene reminiscent of Herod's banquets. She feeds him cherries she moves through her own body, bringing them and him closer and closer to her sex; but "cuando Marta quiso que el reclamo atrajese al perseguidor a su destino no consiguió inducirlo a morder el anzuelo" [when Marta wished the lure to attract the pursuer to his destination she was not able to induce him to swallow the bait] (81). Finding a sight he didn't expect, Marcos surreptitiously flees the scene, so that "las nueve semanas y media apenas sobrepasaron nueve horas y tres cuartos" [the nine and a half weeks barely exceeded nine hours and three quarters] (82). This modern-day Medusa who inadvertently brought Marcos face to face with horror is left disappointed and especially perplexed at the mysteries of male conceptions of sexuality that exclude the naturalness of her body. She wonders "a qué se referiría él cuando proponía tocar el fondo, sumergirse en la depravación y ensayar las obsesiones de las fantasías secretas si era incapaz de asumir que ella amaneciese con la regla" [what he could have meant when he proposed to touch bottom, dive into depravity, and try out the obsessions of secret fantasies, if he was incapable of accepting that she might wake up with her period] (82). Beyond its perverse humor, this phrase speaks directly to the instinctive disgust with women's bodies that often appeared in early-century male-authored erotic narrative, whose new sexual goddess was still the idealized woman of Victorian fantasy.[3]

The previous examples show a specifically female use of the structure of the gaze that nevertheless remains within the parameters of eroticism laid out in the male-authored novels. In her essay "Is the Gaze Male?" E. Ann Kaplan answers the title question by stating that "the gaze is not necessarily male, but to own and activate the gaze, given our language and the structure of the unconscious, is to be in the masculine position" (319). The above-mentioned solutions to the problem of representing women's sexuality maintain a binary and unequal structure of desire in which each position is statically gendered. Consequently, for a woman to reverse the gaze does not necessarily imply a reformulation of the position of female as object and not subject. There are, however, in these women's works more radical experiments with the subjectivity of desire.

Before returning to *Las edades de Lulú,* one of the strongest challenges to configurations of gender and sexuality, I would like to mention one other text which posits a possible alternative to the dominance-submission pattern. The book jacket of Isabel Franc's novel *Entre todas las mujeres* [Amongst All Women], a finalist for the 1992 La Sonrisa Vertical Prize, summarizes thus its plot about a middle-aged Spanish woman anxious about her lesbianism:

> En su desesperación por "regenerarse"—y, en realidad, siguiendo las indicaciones de un psiquiatra del Opus, quien le aconseja, para aplacar sus ánimos, enamorarse de la Virgen—, se deja arrastrar en la gratificante fantasía [presented as reality by the narrator] de reencarnar a Bernadette Soubirous, la niña que recibió los favores de la Virgen de Lourdes a mediados del siglo pasado. Nadie, entonces, supo imaginar de qué naturaleza fueron estos favores

> [In her desperate attempt to "regenerate herself"—and, in reality, following the recommendations of an Opus psychiatrist who advises her to fall in love with the Virgin, to appease her spirits—she allows herself to be swept away by the gratifying fantasy of reincarnating Bernadette Soubirous, the girl who received the favors of the Virgin of Lourdes in the mid-nineteenth century. No one, then, could imagine the nature of these favors.]

The first-person narrator, through the persona of Bernadette, who occupies most of the novel, tells of a new kind of gaze that posits an alternative to the binary, gendered structure of the male sexual gaze.

In the above-mentioned article, E. Ann Kaplan suggests a solution to the problem of women's ability to appropriate pleasure. She argues that there are untheorized fissures in the Lacanian psychoanalytical construction of the development of subjectivity through which women can begin to alter the discourse of desire. One such gap would be the "pre-Oedipal plenitude with the mother," a time when another gaze configuration is experienced:

> Things have been structured to make us forget the mutual, pleasurable bonding that we all, male and female, enjoyed with our mothers. Some recent experimental (as against psychoanalytic) studies have shown that the gaze is first set in motion in the mother-child relationship. But this is a *mutual* gazing, rather than the subject-object kind that reduces one of the parties to the place of submission. ("Is the Gaze Male?," 324)

What Kaplan points to is a matriarchal order of subjectivity in which the boundaries between self and other that support the male gaze's (and the male erotic novel's) process of objectification are erased in favor of a relationship of commonality. Since the prelinguistic union with the mother also precedes the imposition of the incest taboo, an evocation of that union would seem to suggest a sexuality without sin or shadow of perversion.

As if in accordance with Kaplan, Isabel Franc endeavors to portray just such a bond of pleasure with the archetypal mother. In this novel the look at another's body literally turns into a vision. For Bernadette to behold the apparition of the Lady is the apotheosis of passion, a look in which the subject possesses entirely that which no one but her can see. Furthermore, not only does Bernadette see a reflection of herself—of her femininity, her beauty, and her virginity—in the other, but the vision of the Virgin also transcends her otherness through their veritable communion: "Manos y brazos se perciben y se confunden con espaldas y caderas y todo es uno y no hay cuerpos sino un cuerpo y no hay pieles sino una sola piel" [Hands and arms are sensed and confused with backs and hips and everything is one and there are no bodies but one body and there are no skins but only one skin] (*Entre todas*, 123). Bernadette increasingly feels the Virgin's otherness as selfhood even outside the moments of sexual connection. She is able, for example, to make the Virgin materialize in her own bed at night through her imagination, and during the day her conscience unfolds into a double one: "Una voz *interior* me ordenaba ir a la gruta, una voz *que no era mía*" [An *inner* voice commanded me to go to the cave, a voice *that wasn't mine*] (99, my emphasis). This voice, at once *internal* and *alien*, signals the overcoming of self and other through Bernadette's desire, so that in giving herself she absorbs the other.

Despite the book jacket's warning that "algunos clamarán al escándalo, otros a la herejía" [some will decry scandal, others heresy] there is not much sense of heresy. Narrated in the first person through the persona of Bernadette, the text captures her qualitative innocence. It goes *beyond* innocence—neither Bernadette nor the primary middle-aged narrator who fuses with her ever assume their practice as sinful or unnatural, and in both of them there is a consciousness of martyrdom. Intradiegetically, lesbianism is granted divine status; it is a doctrine to be transmitted through a matriarchal line, from woman to woman, according to the Virgin's own instructions to Bernadette: "'No reveléis a hombre alguno lo que hacéis aquí conmigo, ni vuestro mismo confesor debe saberlo; amad a las mujeres y enseñadles lo que yo os he transmitido'" [Don't reveal to any man what you do here with me, not even your own confessor must know; love women and teach them what I have transmitted to you] (103). Extradiegetically, it is granted messianic status as the "third gender" that will transcend subject/object divisions and thus proclaim a superior kind of love.

Franc's novel already suggests certain movements—the replication of the self and the blurring of the self-other boundary—that have important implications for the configuration of the gaze assumed by Trigo and the other early-century novelists. Such structural breaks have also been theorized by recent women theorists, perhaps most notably Judith Butler. In her book *Gender Trouble,* Butler describes gender identity as neither natural nor cohesive, as the institutions of power—referred to as the heterosexual matrix—make them seem. Rather, gender and its manifestations, one of which is desire, are *performative* practices: in other words, the actions of desire usually assumed to express gender are in fact constitutive of gender. The development of identity and sexuality theorized by, for example, psychoanalysis, "can be read only as normalization within the heterosexual matrix" (27).

Such normalization occurs through the establishment of boundaries between "inner" and "outer" (two words for "self" and "other") as positions relative to the body's surface. Building on Mary Douglas's anthropological study *Purity and Danger,* Butler posits that the skin signifies the limits of the social: "[one] might well understand the boundaries of the body as the limits of the socially *hegemonic*" (131). Since boundaries, margins, borders are always the site of self-definition and regulation, the inner/outer binary is the fundamental distinction that stabilizes the coherent subject, and "for inner and outer worlds to remain utterly distinct, the entire surface of the body would have to achieve an impossible impermeability" (134). The body's permeability thus appears problematic, and consequently must be regulated: only forms of penetration or pollution that will further the needs of the self-perpetuating social apparatus are sanctioned. Within this sexual economy, "the rites of passage that govern various bodily orifices presuppose a heterosexual construction of gendered exchange, positions, and erotic possibilities" (133).

Against this pre-established grammar of gender and desire, the potentially subversive subject has to acknowledge his or her powerlessness. One cannot be outside the sexual economy, and from this arises the concern expressed by critics like Kaplan to find "untheorized fissures" from which to propel change. Butler re-addresses the same dilemma: "If there is no radical repudiation of a culturally constructed sexuality, what is left is the question of how to acknowledge and 'do' the construction one is invariably in. Are there forms of repetition that do not constitute a simple imitation, reproduction and, hence, consolidation of the law . . . ?" (31). Her answer is predictable: the parodic distancing from naturalized identities of desire in order to reveal them as learned, political, and local is the most powerful mode of sedition available in our cultural framework.

Butler's envisioning of how these parodic operations might occur in life or in literature is the most disappointing part of her work—she concentrates only on drag as a denaturalization of gender identity. The erotic women's texts I am writing about nevertheless seem a practical test of a theory such as Butler's. Read against Trigo's anxiety to seal off his protagonists' bodies from the female "other" and behold them only as prepackaged fetishes of their own phallus, aseptically beautiful, Marta's display of her menstruation for Marcos to feast on is a destabilizing strategy. Read against the binary structure of the male gaze, Bernadette's fusion with the Virgin, and the secondary narrator's fusion with Bernadette in a long line of women who have perpetuated the "doctrine" of lesbianism, introduce uncertainty between "inner" and "outer" as well as infiltrating other numbers into the fundamental duality of desire—a desire that neither depends on nor challenges the matrix of the heterosexual couple.

This type of dissipating, denaturalizing maneuver is probably best codified in Grandes's novel. *Las edades de Lulú* is, especially from a traditional feminist point of view, a disturbing text, and it is even hard to recount it without leaving out some contradictory loose ends. The storyline follows Lulú from age twelve, when she loses her virginity with Pablo, through age thirty, when she leaves him, and on to a couple of years later, when she goes back to him. The ending seems a problem in relation to her trajectory. After building their whole life together upon the role-playing of daddy and his little girl, playing increasingly dangerous sex games in which her trust for him ultimately safeguards her, he crosses the line one night during a party when he blindfolds her and both he and another man simultaneously penetrate her. Her pleasure and thrill become horror when at the moment of collective orgasm he takes off the blindfold and she identifies the other man as her brother (and his best friend) Marcelo.

## 4: EROTICISM AND CANONICITY

Lulú ends the marriage and begins a quest for her own identity, but this quest mirrors her past through new, increasingly dangerous, sex games. She begins hiring numerous pairs of hustlers with whom she engages in sexual acts in which her position varies: she may be in the middle or at either end. As she approaches moral rock-bottom, she finally crosses another line—and the problem of where the line is has been on her mind throughout the novel—and gets paid to participate in a sadomasochistic nine-person orgy to be performed for a male "customer." Things get entirely out of hand and she is nearly beaten to death before Pablo, with whom she has unsuccessfully tried to reconcile earlier, comes in and rescues her. We then find out that he had been aware of her actions all throughout and in fact manipulated the whole sequence of events:

> Me esforzaba por buscarle un sentido al verdadero origen de las marcas impresas en mi piel. . . . Luchaba contra aquella certeza disfrazada de sospecha y no encontraba alternativa alguna, no existían alternativas, él había estado allí, moviendo los hilos a distancia, pero aquello era demasiado duro, insoportablemente duro para las escasas fuerzas de una niña pequeña, soy una niña pequeña, concluí, y mañana pensaré en todo esto, mañana. (257)

> [I tried hard to make some sense of the true origin of the marks branded on my skin. . . . I struggled against that certainty disguised as suspicion and could not find any alternative, there were no alternatives, he had been there, pulling the strings from a distance, but that was too hard, unbearably hard for the meager strength of a little girl, I am a little girl, I concluded, and tomorrow I will think about all of this, tomorrow.]

The end of the novel follows, with Lulú recuperating in her own bed, dressed with a baby's blouse she had often worn during her sexual make-believe with Pablo, and smiling as he spoils her, bringing her favorite pastries.

Does Lulú's final smile indicate a fairy-tale happy ending or her ultimate annihilation as a subject? This problem, relevant from an approach to the novel as a sexual bildungsroman and a desire to find it assertive of women's sexuality, becomes irrelevant if we look at Lulú as a reflection of the "parodic proliferation" that according to Judith Butler "deprives hegemonic culture and its critics of the claim to naturalized or essentialist gender identities" (*Gender Trouble*, 138). Lulú's itinerary cannot be understood merely in terms of objectification and victimization, as has been the case from certain feminist perspectives.[4] At the structural level, the character of Lulú is the incarnation of the performativeness of gender and desire. She performs all possible roles: the little girl, the femme fatale, the lesbian (fantasized or real), the wife, the middle-aged patron of gigolos, the incestuous sister. When she views the initial video with the beautiful men "intercambiándose los papeles entre sí" [exchanging roles] (*Las edades,* 88), she says that "me inspiraban una especie de furor maternal" [they inspired in me a sort of maternal furor], acting out sexually the mother which she also is in her own life, as well as conflating motherly instict with traditional concepts of women's unbridled sexuality (as in the nineteenth-century *furor uterino*). Lulú becomes the plethora of erotic and identity positions available to women, and her character as a repertoire rather than a static personality is reinforced by two textual elements: her complete opening up of the sealed boundaries of the body so important to the Trigo school, and the both metaphorical and metonymic use of the figure of the homosexual.

Her first three sexual encounters with Pablo—not her only ones during an adolescence of experimentation—are singled out not only because she loves him but because each is a rite of initiation, opening up one more orifice of her body: first the mouth, then the vagina, then the anus. This progressive aperture, first of the socially sanctioned channels, and subsequently an act of transgression, culminates in the final orgy in which she is hung by her neck, scratched by another woman's nails "abriendo heridas largas y toscas" [opening long and rough wounds] (247), pierced by pincers, bitten and beaten, her body finally broken down and opened up in a state of absolute permeability. This victimization, which certainly horrified me at first reading, is, however, relative, and does not represent her destruction. One must keep in mind that the novel ends with Lulú assuming yet another of her identities, smiling and getting ready to *eat*—that other pleasurable reversal of sealed identity in which we bring the outside into our bodies. Ultimately, she is always able to reinvent herself in the cycle of dissipation and reconstruction that is her pleasure. Much like Isabel Franc, Grandes conceives of a sexuality that defies the ideas of a sealed body and a clear demarcation between self and other; unlike Franc, however, she does so without turning away from the experience of violence that is sometimes essential to acts of transgression.

Grandes's use of the homosexual figure also contributes to the parodic denaturalization of sexual identities. Early in the novel, one of Lulú and Pablo's games is to have threesomes with the transvestite Ely. Ely, who with her shrunken penis is already a copy of Pablo (a parody or diminutive of *él*, "him"), is also a physical copy of Lulú (with her breasts), and replicates her actions as they take turns in pleasing Pablo. But if Ely is the copy, the originals she copies are also copies: Lulú has come up with her sexual persona after shopping with Ely for costumes and props, and Pablo imitates Lulu's brother Marcos, ultimately exchanging roles with him. All the characters exist as performances of their (and others') sexual roles. In the novel there is no fixed identity, and consequently all identities—subject and object, male and female, heterosexual and homosexual, victimizer and victim—can be put on *and taken off*. Victimization as such is thus deactivated, because Lulú exploits, and enjoys, all possibilities of gender and desire performance.

Through a different theoretical framework from the one used here, Juan Duchesne has come to a comparable conclusion. Based on the analysis of Lulú's attitude toward the homosexuals of the video episode, whom she wants to sodomize, not by turning into a man or even by impersonating a man (with a dildo), but from within her own sexual consciousness, he posits that the novel "does not seek a univocal correspondence between self and desire," and that Lulú "will possess the phallus expressly extricated from the penis, setting in motion a complex series of symbolic and bodily configurations" ("Sorpenderla mirando," 64). For this critic, identity in *Las edades de Lulú* is "diasporized," a concept he borrows from the following passage by theologists Boyarin and Boyarin:

> A diasporized gender identity is possible and positive. Being a woman is some kind of special being, and there are aspects of life and practice that insist on and celebrate that specialty. But this does not imply a fixing or freezing of all practice and performance of gender into one set of parameters. . . . Rather than the dualism of gendered bodies and universal souls . . . we can substitute partially Jewish, partially Greek bodies, bodies that are sometimes gendered and sometimes not. It is this idea that we are calling diasporized identity. (qtd. in Duchesne, "Sorprenderla mirando," 64)

The same could be inferred from many other passages in the novel, including the one that is literally and figuratively its climactic moment—the unwitting act of incest in the threesome between Pablo, Lulú, and Marcelo. At this moment, Marcelo and Pablo are simultaneously heterosexual and homosexual; Lulú is simultaneously legitimate wife and incestuous sister, concrete lover desired by (and desiring of) the two men, and evanescent membrane separating them. Her many experiences with hustlers after she leaves Pablo repeat this performance (which already repeated the initial video scene) despite the variety of positions she assumes in the encounters, which do not always replicate the original sexual arrangement. Instead they introduce self-consciousness and perhaps confusion: shall I watch or participate? which role shall I assume? which one of them shall I become, and which will become me? The repetition in the text focuses on what is essential to its idea of sexuality—the plurality of identity—as well as embodying Butler's ideal of a repetition that does not constitute imitation or consolidation of the law. In this manner the novel destabilizes the duality inherent to the structural gaze of the early-century male-authored novels, indulging in an iconoclastic concept of desire and gender: "This is not . . . the harmonious, eudaemonist, ideal eroticism invoked by certain feminisms, but a pornographic acting-out permeated by the obscure play of violence and pleasure, without ceasing, because of this, to be a feminist product, though [now it is so] in a much more disturbing and enigmatic way" (Duchesne, "Sorprenderla mirando," 64).

To varying degrees, from heterosexual or lesbian positions, *Las edades de Lulú* and the other texts mentioned undermine the binary and hierarchical categories on which desire hinged for early-century erotic writers. They construct sexual images that disregard or disable the limits imposed by religion, by conventional morality, by aesthetic standards, by "natural" gender, and sometimes even by feminist or political commitment, thereby rupturing the ascendancy of any of those discourses over the raw fact of uncensored desire. This movement is completely opposite to the attempt at the legitimation of the sexual by other, "superior" impulses found in the work of Trigo and his contemporaries. That a novel like *Las edades de Lulú* is at odds with some feminist conceptions of female sexuality only confirms the radicalness of its use of sexually explicit representation, for it concentrates on a pleasure that cannot be in any way subdued, subordinated to a cause, rationalized or intellectualized. Since the languages of reason and intellectualism have been traditionally associated with the masculine, such a novel represents a credible attempt at bringing a certain kind of "feminine" expression into the literary field.

## 4: EROTICISM AND CANONICITY

The assault perpetrated by these novels both on early-century masculine notions of desire and on any prescriptive concept of sexuality is inseparable from their assault on the configuration of the canon of Spanish literary narrative. As Andrew Ross has shown, the criticism against pornography's portrayal of erotic practices and against its lack of literary quality have historically had much in common:

> While [the feminist antiporn critique] proposes to redefine cultural conflict along gender rather than class lines, it reproduces the same languages of mass manipulation, systematic domination, and victimization which had been the trademark of the Cold War liberal critique *of mass culture*. Both share a picture of a monolithic culture of standardized production and standardized effects, and of normalized brutality, whether within the mind or against the body. While lack of mutual affection has replaced lack of aesthetic complexity as the standard grounds of disapproval in antiporn analysis, the charge of propagandism is repeated, and the renewed use of the rhetoric of protection and reform has sustained the privilege of intellectuals to "know what's good" for others. (*No Respect*, 226, my emphasis)

Like their turn-of-the-century counterparts, the new women writers of erotica have had to face the fact that how sex is presented in a text, and whether it is an integral and "justified," or a prevailing and "unjustified" element says something not only about the treatment of the theme but about the literariness of the text. Unlike the earlier male writers, they have chosen not to conform to this standard, but to cross the line in the sand.

In this context, it is interesting to observe how resistance to the models of sexuality these writers present is often accompanied by a denial of their literary status. James Mandrell, for example, translates their supposed failure to transform "the inherently masculine interest of erotica" ("Mercedes Abad," 282) into a failure to retain the status of erotic literature over that of pornography. Underlying his argument is the concern over these texts' ambiguous value position, "'popular'—yet 'high-brow'" (279), inseparably linked to their position on sexuality. Lou Charnon-Deutsch focuses on *Las edades de Lulú*'s model of female subjectivity and desire *because of* the text's importance in the literary field:

> Tusquets' appraisal of *Las edades de Lulú* as significant literary erotica and the rapidly escalating cult and commercial status of the novel give it the institutional and intellectual authority of high literary value. This inter-

pretation would place *Lulú* beyond the bounds of pornography because, it is argued, a literary framework makes art of the pornographic, pushing it into a non-politicized realm of inquiry. . . . [But] simply to classify the novel as erotica . . . is to eschew the sexual issues that reduce the reader's possible responses to the text's construction of subjectivity. It is our contention that *Lulú* as literary pornography offers limited critical plurality, for it restricts rather than opens up potential readings and interpretations. ("Regarding," 303)

With this line of argumentation, Charnon-Deutsch places herself within the tradition of antipornography critique that sees it as discourse that denies readers' freedom of interpretation, demanding a fixed (objectionable) reading.[5] The boundary between the aesthetic and the sexual appears as a porous one, and the disapproved use of the sexual is likened to propaganda as a form of writing dangerous in its power to rob the reader of agency. Just as it happened with the propagandistic novels of the Civil War discussed in the previous chapter, this view of the texts' use of their subject matter entails a negative judgment about their literariness.

Without a doubt, Almudena Grandes and the other women erotic writers—as well as their publishers—are acutely aware of the need for distinction from pornography that has always informed erotic literature. They are also aware of the paradoxical fact that while the canon is an instution of power—imposed by those who are in power as well as granting power to those it recognizes—it also limits the possibilities of canonical authors for "making trouble," for stepping outside certain norms of decorum. Perhaps because of this, they often situate their work from the outset in the space of the extraliterary: thus, for example, the text of the book jacket of María Jaén's 1986 *El escote:* "Después de oir el lamento de aquellos que se quejaban por la ausencia de una '*subliteratura*'—signo evidente de normalidad—autóctona, por fin nos llega esta maravillosa novela" [After hearing the lament of those who complained about the absence of a native "*subliterature*"—an evident sign of normalcy—at last we get this wonderful novel] (qtd. in Vilarós, "Confesión," 147, my emphasis). In the same way, the inside cover of Franc's *Entre todas las mujeres* addresses the "amantes de la buena literatura *de género*" [devotees of good *genre* literature] (my emphasis).

By placing themselves on the "wrong" side of our line in the sand these women authors address the association of mass culture with woman that Andreas Huyssen has discussed in his book *After the Great*

*Divide.* There he reflects on how "the political, psychological, and aesthetic discourse around the turn of the century consistently and obsessively genders mass culture and the masses as feminine, while high culture . . . clearly remains the privileged realm of male activities" (47) and, on another page, how "the fear of the masses in this age of declining liberalism is always also a fear of woman, a fear of nature out of control, a fear of the unconscious, of sexuality, of the loss of identity and stable ego boundaries" (52). Huyssen captures perfectly the way in which ego boundaries, sexual boundaries, and literary boundaries are metonymically linked, and in which consequently threats to any one of these divisions are threats to all of them.

In contrast to feminized mass literature, the masculinized "high" culture product fashions for itself an image as polivalent, self-conscious, ironic, experimental, and *scientific*. In Huyssen's words, "its experimental nature makes it analogous to science, and like science it produces and carries knowledge" (53). It is also revolutionary: "Only by fortifying its boundaries, by maintaining its purity and autonomy, and by avoiding any contamination with mass culture . . . can the art work maintain its adversary stance: adversary to the bourgeois culture of everyday life as well as adversary to mass culture and entertainment which are seen as the primary forms of bourgeois cultural articulation" (54). Against this background, the women writers mentioned place themselves in the space of "popular" literature, which does not presume to further knowledge, advance art, or challenge the hegemony of industrial consumer society.

The trick, of course, is that the nonthreatening "popularity" of this production is only apparent, for these texts have entered the canon and the curriculum even as they retain maximum commercial appeal. Through the primary venue of La sonrisa vertical and similar collections they are produced by the same publishing houses and sold to the same audience that consumes "legitimate" literature—almost forcing the same group of readers to divide themselves into two entities, the connoisseurs and the consumers, in a schizophrenic code of reception. The most successful works, however, get to cross over openly: when *Las edades de Lulú* was translated to other languages it was often for "regular" non-erotic collections, and it is now edited in Tusquets's mainstream Fábula series (often purchased as textbooks in academic contexts). Grandes herself does the literary talk circuit just like and often with her significant other, poet Luis García Montero, and there were great literary expectations for her following novels and short stories.

By wielding the weapon of the territory proverbially attributed to women—sex and the body, "debased" language, the intimate and the domestic—these women writers have also invaded the halls of academia. As I alluded to above, their works are often included in university syllabi (perhaps the most concrete manifestation of the canon, or of canonical operations), and critics approach them through the same techniques of reading and analysis as they approach texts traditionally considered literary according to high-modernist criteria. Looking leads to seeing, and these readings have revealed the works as both rich in possibilities of interpretation, and symbols of an adversarial stance through their oppositional status with regard to patriarchal or otherwise establishment culture. Through these two movements, they are once again associated with two of the most widely shared indexes of literary standing.

Ultimately, as Mandrell had observed, the works alluded to are "popular yet highbrow," as erotic/literary as they are pornographic. These women writers take it as a given that they cannot be outside either the sexual or the literary economy, and instead participate in both through denaturalizing strategies. They place one foot in the center of the field of power of canonical literature and the other squarely in the realm of the senses, showing that, as Carolyn Dean has observed, "the divide between aesthetics and pornography [is] always already decided and yet undecidable, always already constructed and yet under construction, an expression of cultural hegemony so totalizing that pleasure becomes merely an extension of power and yet a site where presumably subversive pleasures can be imagined" ("Pornography," 64). Their insistent hovering around that divide—as Lulú herself muses in *Las edades,* "la raya me tentaba" [the line attracted me] (225)—threatens the purity of the literary and its autonomy from mass culture. This attitude is evidence of a change in paradigm that clearly separates them from the *fin-de-siècle* erotic writers, and which is perhaps more fundamental than the change in the understanding of sexuality. In the end, they assume in the literary field the same plurality and permeability that they assume in the field of pleasure. Unsatisfied with the categories that limit them, these writers challenge the reliance on categorization and differentiation that supported modern thought, replacing them with a brand of having their cake and eating it too that we may, or may not, call postmodern.

# 5
# Manuel Vázquez Montalbán and the Spanish Literary Institution

As A WRITER IN THE CONTEMPORARY SPANISH LITERARY FIELD, MANUEL Vázquez Montalbán holds a very particular position: he seems firmly entrenched in the border between what Pierre Bourdieu calls the field of large-scale production—which submits to the laws of the market—and the field of restricted production, which develops "its own criteria for the evaluation of its products, thus achieving the truly cultural recognition accorded by the peer group whose members are both privileged clients and competitors" (Bourdieu, *Field*, 115). In the qualitative spectrum of contemporary authors, Vázquez Montalbán clearly stands apart from figures like those of Alberto Vázquez Figueroa or Antonio Gala—widely acknowledged as symbols of commercial or mass fiction—for the way in which he has engaged the audience of professional literary critics. But for that audience, he does not achieve the stature of a novelist like, for example, Juan Benet. He is both too literary and too commercial, and a look at the uneasy critical reception of his work makes evident the many and to a great extent unexamined presuppositions academics have about the relationship between the literary market and artistic quality.

Vázquez Montalbán, who is a hot ticket for publishing houses, is more unequally received by those specifically concerned with symbolic or cultural value. A personal anecdote serves to illustrate the point. As I wrote the earliest versions of this chapter, I was also coordinating a symposium entitled Creation and Tradition, The Creation of Tradition, held at Brown University in November of 1997, with Vázquez Montalbán as one of four guest speakers engaged with the subject of contemporary writing and the canon. As different people from literary and academic environments heard of the Brown symposium, I was exposed to a range of quite strong reactions. First there was the Spanish editor, who must unfortunately remain unnamed, who declined our invitation because he would have felt uncomfortable speaking his mind about literature, writers, and the market in the same room with Vázquez Montalbán. Then there were those scholars who made snide remarks about the apparently infinite supply of new material for the presses Vázquez Montalbán can churn up. On the other hand, the many favorable comments on the part of the same audience were often somehow qualified, as in "I don't think his novels are very good, but I just can't put them down." Such a love-hate relationship with a writer may be quick to surface in academics' nonacademic talk, but it is also rooted in deep beliefs about the nature of the work of literature, and is the product of nothing less than the most widely shared assumptions about the concept of literariness.

Writing in 1981, René Wellek dismisses what he considers the two basic definitions of literature, "literature is fiction or literature uses language in a special way" ("Literature," 21), and describes it instead as writing "characterized by the dominance of the aesthetic function" (24), the latter defined as that within a text which "yields a state of contemplation, of intransitive attention which cannot be mistaken for anything else . . . [an experience] as self-evident as the color of snow or the sensation of pain." However imprecisely defined, this literature exists in clear opposition to another body of imaginative writing, "colportage, *Kitsch,* pulp-fiction, *Trivialliteratur,* or whatever we choose to call it" (21). While literary forms are in constant interchange with subliterary forms, and although "detective stories, science fiction, Gothic romances, Westerns, and even pornography" can be differently valued, the ultimate limit is, in Wellek's words, that "we cannot get around the question of quality."

In a 1986 article entitled "On the Category of the Literary," Thomas Greene also attempts to answer the question of "what if anything characterizes those works that we have traditionally claimed for our particular disciplinary province" (217). Greene's response is that there is a type of text that provides a "unique and recognizable" experience through its availability for "dynamic collaboration" (218) with the reader, and that this criterion "does delimit a category and a canon, even if [that] canon is not perfectly identical to the traditional literary canon." While a "minor" (219) or nonliterary work "reveals its participation in a conventional coded practice," a "major" or literary work "challenges its semiotic universe with its own revisionary practice." In 1990, Antony Easthope provides a similar definition when he makes the "effect of presence" and functional polysemy ("The Question," 386) the identifying marks of the literary text. And while, unlike Wellek or Greene, Easthope—who is already moving toward a position within cultural studies—would not consider the truly literary a separate category from popular literature, his position does maintain a gradation within an ample spectrum of writing: "If literature consists merely of texts that are more functionally polysemous than others, I can foresee no good reason why they should not be studied together as examples of signifying practice" (387).

There is no doubt that the positions of these three critics can be (and have been) vehemently debated from the theoretical point of view, since their arguments sound highly essentialist even when they claim not to be writing about intrinsic essences. My interest here is not, however, in the validity of such reasoning, but rather in its prevalence, because to the very beginning of the twenty-first century, we all to one degree or another share the main conceptions of the literary that they put forward: a text or form that is extraordinary rather than ordinary, that goes beyond the participation in a set of conventions such as those imposed by seriality, that is complex rather than simple or open, and that can be read at various levels, providing the ground for richness of interpretation. In other words, the terms in which literary quality is most often defined exclude the properties of formulas like science fiction, *novelas rosa,* or detective stories. The academic prejudice against the bestseller as commercial phenomenon is thus an extension of the belief in literature as a specialized product whose uniqueness is apprehensible through an uncommon kind of gaze, what Bourdieu terms "the pure gaze" (264).

The incursion of a previously recognized writer into a "popular," "subliterary," or "commercial" genre consequently provokes a strong critical reaction, not limited to the cavalier comments made via email about an upcoming symposium. There is thus no scarcity of published criticism about Vázquez Montalbán, and I find that it overwhelmingly concentrates on his detective fiction, to the detriment of attention to his poetry or other prose like *Galíndez* (1990) or the *Autobiografía del General Franco* (1992). As for criticism of the Carvalho series, the minority of it is descriptive or exegetic of matters not related to the choice of form, whereas the majority concentrates on the question of genre in itself. Some of this criticism is openly imbued with a degree of perplexity at this pairing of author and form; Luis Costa expresses it most candidly when he writes:

> Will we continue to read these works seriously because they have an intrinsic value, or, on the contrary, do we read them with interest and un-

dertake their study because they are works by Vázquez Montalbán? If this is the case, we encounter the need to justify their study on the basis of a faith on the value of the author, and, consequently, [on] the certainty that within their deepest folds, in those places we wouldn't dare scrutinize in a less skilled writer, we will find a key or series of keys, not as much to the function of the detective novel [novela negra] in Spain, but to the literary persona of Vázquez Montalbán. But we run the risk of having our leg pulled. Perhaps after the series concludes the plan of the *oeuvre* will be evident. So far, aside from [granting] its value as entertainment novel, or as a gastronomical guide to the Spanish provinces, we have to suspend judgment. ("La nueva novela," 305)

Most critics, of course, do not postpone judgment, and some judgments of Vázquez Montalbán and his writing of detective fiction are quite sharp. Joan Ramon Resina, for example, departs from an account of the semiotics of the detective novel to debate other critics who find in Vázquez Montalbán a postmodern or poststructuralist transcendence of the form. Resina considers Vázquez Montalbán's handling of established conventions like the inclusion of culturally specific information, the device of iterability, and the traditional functions of the detective and the criminal, a return to one of the *traditional* uses of the detective novel, that of the reactionary legitimation of official order. For him, the Galician "h" in Carvalho's name functions as the mark of the positive in the melodramatic detective form, whereas "Catalanness [la catalanidad] takes on the function of a negative mark" (*El cadáver*, 107). In this way, Vázquez Montalbán's detective fiction contributes to "the historical violence institutionalized in the ideology of centralism, [which] receives here its justification as legitimate defense against the speculation and sophistry of an irresponsible or frankly criminal collective."

At the opposite end of the evaluative spectrum are those critics who understand Vázquez Montalbán's use of the detective formula as a structure around which to organize aesthetic or cultural constructions that go beyond the original limits of the form. The term "postmodern" used by José Colmeiro, or that of "postclassical" preferred by Gonzalo Navajas ("Género," 247) have been used to allude to the Carvalho novels as works which leave behind traditional hierarchical divisions between "high" and "low," combining both and reducible to neither. For Malcolm Allan Compitello, Spain's "new detective novel" is an example of the postmodernist, metaphysical detective novel which, "by redefining the possibilities of detective fiction . . . demonstrate[s] the capacity of ART to overcome kitsch" ("Spain's," 184). He applies this description specifically to Vázquez Montalbán, of whom he writes: "The tinkering with the formal properties of a genre to create specific ideological and literary effects is as fundamental to an understanding of this writer's fiction as it is to . . . postmodernist writers [like Borges and Robbe-Grillet]. . . . We are faced with a writer who turns to the detective mode to make a break with earlier narrative praxis" (185). Vázquez Montalbán "takes a highly formulaic form and transfoms it into one that is not so" (189), and by so doing rewrites "the canon of the avant-garde" (185).

The approaches mentioned have produced a number of incisive and valuable readings, in which critics have found the literary—that is, the complex, the original, and the polysemous—transforming and transformed by the traditionally nonliterary. The significant consequence of such readings is of course to bring these texts to our school, and to modify the canon of contemporary Spanish narrative by using the critical gaze to find the aesthetic in places where it may not have been obvious. What has not appeared alongside these readings, in my opinion, is criticism that considers Vázquez Montalbán's novels *as* detective narratives and bestsellers, without concentrating on the ways in which they surpass this status or dismissing them because of it. As serial products always, in a structural sense, identical to each other, as fictions read by a nonintellectual class which seeks the pleasure of recognition rather than that of innovation, as *cuentos* (or stories) that generate *cuentas* (or money), the Carvalho novels have little place in our canon. Despite the popularity of cultural approaches to literature and despite increasing awareness of sociological arguments like Bourdieu's, academic critical vocabulary within the field of literary studies is still timid when it comes to accounting for certain reading experiences of the sort provided to a large audience by the detective novels of Vázquez Montalbán.

Criticism has been quicker to apply "aesthetic" readings to mass and popular culture than to explore, *as a corollary to those readings*, other possibilities which do not correspond to our academic, analytical training but are nevertheless dominant in the field of literary production. The bias of the close reading and the accompanying "aristocracy of critical activity" (Fromm, *Academic Capitalism*, 6) have been sharply criticized by Harold Fromm in his often unfair, sometimes objectionable *Academic Capitalism and Literary Value*, a book that nevertheless touches on some of the most sensitive sore spots of academic criticism. For Fromm, professional critics are increasingly appropriating the power to define art—hence also the canon—as well as the power to impose their definition on the general educated public. This "professionalism" has the result of undermining "the confidence of nonspecialist readers, who fear they can no longer trust their own feelings" (4), and obscures the very important question of who constitutes the authentic audience for any given art. Fromm comments on a case in which the rejection of "ugly" postmodern public sculpture on the part of two university professors of philosophy and history of science was dismissed by art critics as philistine "Knownothingism" (60), and concludes that

> if . . . we keep disqualifying more and more constituencies as inauthentic, until we finally dismiss the audience consisting of . . . [extremely well-educated laymen], there will be almost nobody left besides the experts. What this suggests is that once we believe an audience to have some sort of literary or musical competence, they must be part of the bona fide arbiters of taste who establish value. (62)

In an insight that he does not himself proceed to follow, Fromm clarifies that for critics, this should not be "an either/or question: cultural theory or else maundering impressionism, but a matter of multivalent inclusiveness" (7).[1]

The attitude that Fromm criticizes has to do with one of the chief functions, if not the chief one, that criticism has historically assigned itself, especially in its develoment within academia. This function, that of the expert definition and protection of the domain of art, is clearly stated at many points in the history of criticism. To remain within the Spanish tradition, I will quote Urbano González Serrano, one of the most important critics of the late nineteenth century, who writes in 1892 that the "primera condición de la crítica" [first quality of criticism] is an "amplio *saber mirar y ver*" [broad know-how to look and see] ("La crítica," 124). The knowledge of how to look enables the critic to see what others cannot, and engenders the obligation to preserve and transmit that vision, but paradoxically through the regulation of access to it. In 1871, writing against the popular slapstick comedy, Antonio Alcalá Galiano stated that mission as that of a "cruzada literaria" [literary crusade] responsible for "restaurar la ortodoxia del arte" [restoring the orthodoxy of art] as the taste of a few against the taste of the masses: "Solía decir Epicuro: 'esto es justo, porque el pueblo lo encuentra malo.' Aplicando, invertido, . . . el malicioso juicio de aquel discreto filósofo, podemos decir: 'esto es malo, porque el vulgo lo encuentra bueno'" [Epicuro used to say: "this is fair, because the mob finds it bad." Applying, in reverse, the malicious judgment of that shrewd philosopher, we can say "this is bad, because the mob finds it good" ("El género," 207).[2]

Much more recently, in the United States, John Guillory has elaborated a theory of the relationship between criticism and the canon that scrutinizes the former's role as regulator of culture. For Guillory, criticism is a discourse subordinate to the institution of the school, or more specifically the university, which itself functions as the administrator of cultural capital. Literary works are "the cultural capital of educational institutions," and the school acts as "a system of credentialization by which it produces a specific *relation* to culture" (*Cultural Capital*, 56). In other words, criticism and the school establish quality as a set of qualities or value as a set of values that define certain works as canonical, that is, an inheritable treasure. And they negotiate both that configuration of literature as a tradition and the connection that different reading populations—particularly those who go through the school—will have with it. Mary Louise Pratt, cited by Guillory, establishes this connection as "a narrowly specific cultural capital that will be the normative *referent* for everyone, but will remain the *property* of a small and powerful caste that is linguistically and ethnically unified" (Guillory, *Cultural Capital*, 46).

While the liberal critique of the canon (feminism, ethnic studies, Queer studies, cultural studies) rejects this attitude, according to Guillory it has failed to acknowledge the extremely important fact that both canonical and noncanonical works constitute "the same *kind* of cultural capital" for the same communities (45). Thus, for him, attention must be shifted away from the "ideology of tradition" (63), that is, the defense of *either* a central tradition or alternative "countertraditions of noncanonical writers" (63). The central concern, then, is not the preservation of the canon or even the expansion of its possibilities of inclusiveness, but the larger problem of the educational system as an apparatus of access and credentialization. This shift is not only desirable, but also unavoidable, given the crisis of the humanities in the university, which does not stem from the endangerment of the Western canon, but rather from the emergence of a "professional-managerial class" (45) for whom the knowledge of the great works of literature is much less relevant than the acquisition of technical skill.

The conclusion is that, as a matter of both survival and responsibility, criticism must refashion itself. In Bourdieu's words, "we must ... work to *universalize in reality the conditions of access* to what the present offers us that is most universal" (qtd. in Guillory, *Cultural Capital,* 340). In Guillory's terms, "the point is not to make judgment disappear but to reform the conditions of its practice" (340). Doing this is, of course, a gargantuan task, and one that even Bourdieu and Guillory present in the most abstract of terms. But, even if we take the university and its function of credentialization as social givens, one possible, if circumscribed, avenue within literary studies is to turn away from the unsustainable duties not only of determining a limited canon of ostensibly valuable (complex, polysemous) texts but additionally *of acknowledging only a limited range of modes of engaging with those texts:* namely, the operations of (close) reading, from a spectrum of theoretical or even political positions, that we now group under the rubric of "critical." A true "science of the literary field," to use Pierre Bourdieu's term (*Field,* 30), must not limit itself to creating texts in its own image, that is, to effecting the readings that most stimulate its practitioners and that set them apart from the common public. Instead, criticism should pierce the very boundaries that brought it to and maintain it in existence, both including and analyzing the reading practices of the "uncredentialed" and the texts that reach them *as* they reach them and not only as we can reach those texts.

According to Bourdieu, the cultural field is structured by the distribution of available positions and the consequent struggle between the "position-takings" (35) of its members. Clearly he writes as a sociologist, as Guillory writes as a theorist and I write as a critic and professor of Spanish literature in American academia. From his position as a writer in Spain, Manuel Vázquez Montalbán adopts a surprisingly similar approach. In his critical work *La literatura en la construcción de la ciudad democrática* [Literature in the Construction of the Democratic City] (1998) he traces the historical development of literature from its origins as foundational myth administered by the small caste of those who could read, through the industrial revolution and the appearance of the mass of readers, and through the present end not only of the century but of the millennium. He describes as follows his view of the literary phenomenon as it now exists:

> En la parte del mundo donde funciona un mercado libre de lectura, con todas las correcciones en profundidad que se puedan hacer a la economía de mercado, ha desaparecido progresivamente la función de los tutores culturales, desde el mecenas al crítico, y se tiende a la relación directa entre autor y lector y a una tal pluralidad de cánones que resulta difícil insistir en su inventario ante los distintos niveles de propuesta es-

tética, muy diferenciadas las audiencias cualitativa y cuantitativamente consideradas. El santuario de la Literatura y el Arte como recintos sagrados legitimados por el idealismo o el materialismo histórico . . . no resistió la lógica de la evolución interactiva de la escritura y la lectura, pautada directamente entre la operación de escribir y la de leer. (167–68)

[In that part of the world in which a free reading market functions, (even) with all the in-depth amends that could be made to the market economy, there has been a progressive disappearance of the function of cultural tutors, from the patron to the critic, and a (growing) tendency toward the direct relationship between author and reader, and toward such a plurality of canons that it becomes difficult to insist in keeping track of them, given the different levels of aesthetic proposal, and the clear difference between audiences, qualitatively and quantitatively considered. The sanctuary of Literature and Art as sacred enclosures legitimated by idealism or historical materialism . . . did not withstand the logic of the interactive evolution of writing and reading, established directly between the operation of writing and that of reading.]

From the observation of this state of affairs he infers a number of consequences, some of which bear quotation here:

1) que la Literatura no parte del mandato exclusivo de la Tradición y mucho menos de la tradición nacional; 2) que se han convertido en referentes canónicos tradiciones muy diversas y a veces legitimadas por códigos no estrictamente literarios . . . 3) el no lugar del comisariado político, cultural o político cultural en el pasado ejercido por el Estado o *la crítica* en la fijación de cánones . . . 7) que el ensimismamiento literario puede conducir a una literatura arqueológica, gozada con el valor añadido y legítimo de obsolescencia y anacronismo . . . 10) que ante la relativización de los cánones, la crítica está obligada a aprender a leer en cada obra [su] propuesta y a renunciar a una residual, obsoleta, morbosa tendencia a la pretextualidad. (172–73)

[1) that Literature does not follow the exclusive mandate of Tradition, and much less of national tradition; 2) that very diverse traditions, sometimes legitimated by codes that are not stricty literary, have become canonical referents . . . 3) that the political, cultural, or political-cultural policing exercised in the past by the State or by criticism in the establishment of canons has been overruled . . . 7) that literary conceit can lead to an archaeological literature, enjoyed with the added and legitimate value of obsolescence and anachronism . . . 10) that, faced with the relativization of canons, criticism must learn to read in each work its own proposal, as well as renounce a residual, obsolete, morbid tendency to pretextuality.]

For Vázquez Montalbán, the necessary opening up and relativization of the category of literature does not, as we will see below, imply the total surrender to the laws of the market or the fall into the mechanical reproduction of formulas. There is, for him, a collective reading subject who can insure both the pluralization and the continuity of artistic preoccupations. It is the literary critic in his or her role as *director* of readings who fails to step beyond academicism and to assume "la sospecha o sanción más válida de la postmodernidad: la inutilidad del vanguardismo como una demostración del crecimiento continuo del espíritu" [the most valid suspicion or sanction of postmodernity: the uselessness of vanguardism as proof of the continuous growth of the spirit] (179).

How, then, can academic criticism read Vázquez Montalbán, a writer whose often-chosen genre, majoritary readership, and reflection on his work seem to beg for the use of alternative interpretive techniques? One answer is, nevertheless: the way it has already been reading him. Resina, despite his disagreement with the political underpinnings of the texts as he understands them, effectively draws on deconstruction and semiotics to trace Vázquez Montalbán's relationship to and interpretation of a literary tradition and its ideological ties to the middle class. Like Navajas, Colmeiro, and other critics, he too perceptively emphasizes the fundamental structure of duality that supports this writer's novels: the thematic tension between conventional detection and social criticism, the contextual tension between high and low culture. Most of these critics inscribe the language of such dualities within the fragmentary imaginary of postmodern (or postclassical) culture, thus keenly linking Vázquez Montalbán to another contemporary tradition of thought and writing.

In *La literatura en la construcción de la ciudad democrática* the author himself follows the analytical line of such readings. This work is a rare retrospective reflection in which Vázquez Montalbán sketches his view of the historical progression of the role of "literature" in modern European social contexts and situates himself within that heritage, with reference to and in dialogue with criticism about his work. He states the indexes that have constituted him as a writer, and that constitute the interpretive references for his work: "Socialismo, franquismo, postmodernidad y literatura, he aquí una reflexión teórica complementaria de todo cuanto he escrito" [Socialism, Francoism, postmodernity, and literature, here is a theoretical reflection that complements everything I have written] (14). He elaborates on the circumstances of his disenchantment with the failed utopian projects of the socialist city and of the post-Franco democratic city, and goes on to define the terms of his own proposal and the significance of his own generic and thematic choices.

Perhaps because of the dialogue with criticism, in this text Vázquez Montalbán assumes a voice that sounds more critical (analytical) than testimonial or autobiographical. His consideration of his own work is thus thoroughly contextualized by a sophisticated analysis of the role of "subgenres" in postmodern culture: adventure literature, understood as the matrix of detective fiction, "fue la expresión de la cosmogonía imperial burguesa y ahora es la expresión de la ruptura y resituación de esa cosmogonía, en el marco de una ciudad llena de deconstrucciones" [was the expression of the imperial bourgeois world view, and it is now the expression of the rupture with and replacement of that world view, within the frame of a city full of deconstructions] (114). Against this scenario, Vázquez Montalbán's own detective fiction is born, not just as a new instance of the genre, but as its citation or its repetition, in the sense that Peter Brooks gives to the latter term (although he is referring specifically to repetition of motifs within a text): "To repeat evidently implies resemblance, yet can we speak of resemblance unless there is difference? Without difference, repetition would be identity. . . . Repetition always includes the idea of a variation in time, and may ever be potentially a progressive act" (*Reading*, 124). Such repetition confers on Vázquez Montalbán's novels the character of critical commentary both on the genre and on the reality of the capitalist city: "una sociedad, como la española de los años setenta, abocada ya al delirio neocapitalista y parademocrático, dependiente de la doble verdad, la doble moral y la doble contabilidad del capitalismo avanzado" [a society, like that of the seventies in Spain, already headed toward neocapitalist and parademocratic delirium, dependent on the dual truth, the dual morality, and the dual bookkeeping of advanced capitalism] (*La literatura*, 145).

With social commentary as his ultimate aim—"el desafío de . . . escribir un ciclo de novela-crónica de la realidad" [the challenge of writing a cycle of novel-chronicle of reality] (145)—Vázquez Montalbán appropriates the conventions of detective fiction, avowedly without entirely subscribing to them:

> Yo deconstruía la convención de la novela policiaca quitando importancia a sus mandatos originales basados en el respeto al misterio como condición *sine qua non*, utilizando la trama intriga como un mero pretexto para forzar a un viaje literario por el espacio-tiempo delimitado en

cada novela, siempre adscrito al espacio-tiempo de la sociedad historificable. Es tan fácil y aleatorio descubrir en mis novelas quién ha matado a quién, son tan leves los rituales de la novela policiaca que sin duda podrían defraudar a los auténticos puristas del género y eso pretendía.... Mis novelas llamadas policiacas podían leerse desde distintos niveles porque implicaban diversos patrimonios narrativos escapando a la unidimensionalidad de la novela de género. (145–46)

[I deconstructed the convention of the police novel, turning away from its original mandates, based on respect for the mystery as *sine qua non* condition, using the intrigue plot as a mere pretext to force a literary voyage through the space-time delimited in each novel, always attached to the space-time of historical society. It is so easy and fortuitous in my novels to find out who has killed whom, the rituals of the detective novel are so light, that they could without a doubt disappoint the true purists of the genre, and that was my intention.... My so-called police novels could be read from different levels, because they implied diverse narrative traditions, escaping the one-dimensionality of the genre novel.]

This operation is clearly identifiable with the "repetition with difference" (Hutcheon, *Theory*, 44) that has been hailed as the definining mark of postmodernism, a label that Vázquez Montalbán accepts in the knowledge of its "indagación teórica ... en las universidades norteamericanas" [theoretical questioning ... in North American universities] (113). He nevertheless insists on one important reservation: insofar as the term "postmodernism" might signal a turn away from historical thought or political commitment, it does not, for him, accurately reflect his literary vision.

An interesting parallel emerges between Vázquez Montalbán's account of his literary project and the attempt at the transcendence of commodity fetishism Kevin McLaughlin finds in the rhetoric of Marx's *Capital*. According to this critic, "Marx resists the language of the commodity by miming it" (*Writing*, 15). By simultaneously adopting and denaturalizing the vocabulary of political economy, Marx seeks to reveal its arbitrariness as a sign, and to make evident the hidden social character of economic relations. In this way, "imitation, ... and citation in particular, is a leading strategy by which Marx aims to set his own work apart from the monstrous amount of research, by 'political economists' and others, that is behind it." Consciousness is generated through the decontextualization of languages previously received automatically: "The difference to which Marx calls attention here is that between an unconscious way of behaving and a critical awareness, between 'blindly going through the motions' prescribed by the language of commodities and stopping to reflect on that language" (16). The work places itself in metonymical relation to the discursive context of which it forms part, using repetition as a critical device whereby it both attempts the context's transformation and asserts its own individuality.

Vázquez Montalbán's quoting of the language of detective fiction in order to chronicle and critique post-Franco Spain finds yet another parallel in McLaughlin's description of Honoré de Balzac's approach to his own participation in "industrial literature." As the first French writer to publish a serialized *feuilleton* novel (in 1836) and a successful participant in the world of journalism, Balzac was forced to confront his double position in the French literary institution and to ponder the question of "what is the essential difference between 'literature' and this contaminated writing of the market" (McLaughlin, *Writing*, 29).[3] He found the answer in the one feature alien to the "incomplete" character of all serialized fiction, that is, unity: "from early in his career Balzac considered the establishment of his fame to rest on the unity of his work" (42). The project of *The Human Comedy* is to record and interpret French history, so that the writer becomes both its secretary and its *author*—the one who attempts to give it wholeness and shape, who authorizes it through his endless search for meaning. This process shifts attention "from individual works as centers of authority" (48) to the *plan* as that which legitimates each individual narrative, separating it from the waste of other mass-produced, but purposeless, fictions.

Read in this context, *La literatura en la construcción de la ciudad democrática* is a text of utmost importance. It summarizes—unites— many of Vázquez Montalbán's previous incursions into self-criticism, scattered in interviews and journalistic pieces, and thus supplements and completes his novels. For the nonpurists who may have been reading the Carvalho narratives simply as detective fictions—filling in the gaps of perceived lacks in suspense or in faithfulness to the platonic model of the genre—*La literatura* provides a guide to informed reception. The enigma in each novel—in fact, each novel in itself— is to be read as a vehicle for the communication of something that exceeds it. The customary move toward clarification in detective fiction must thus lead the reader to a clarification of another sort, in a process that makes each novel of the Carvalho cycle the very incarnation of metaphor. Moreover, the stated aim of the cycle—the critical political chronicle of the capitalist city—removes the Carvalho novels from an isolated "paraliterary" status, linking them to the rest of Vázquez Montalbán's production, from the early, and almost accidental, *Crónica sentimental de España* (1969) to *Galíndez*, the *Autobiografía del General Franco*, and, more recently, *O César o nada* (1998).[4]

Vázquez Montalbán's work, which might, like Balzac's, be grouped under one title (one might follow his lead and choose *Memoria y deseo*), is united by a thoughtful, extended reflection on power (146).[5] And the paradigmatic writer who can carry out such a reflection is imagined in terms that are also reminiscent of Balzac. In the epigraph to his previous volume of criticism, *El escriba sentado* [The Sitting Scribe] (1997),[6] Vázquez Montalbán finds an apt analogy for the writer in the Egyptian scribe, recorder and decoder of history, both humble and wise, and protected by the gods and the pharaohs:

> Las manos sabiamente posadas sobre las rodillas, un mono babuino encaramado sobre un pequeño pedestal. Sería sacrilegio confundirlo con un animal doméstico. Este mono es una de las formas del dios Thot, patrón de los escribas. Así nos lo recuerdan la inscripción situada en la base del pedestal y la actitud del escriba, humildemente sentado a sus pies. El escriba despliega sobre las rodillas un papiro inscrito e inclina la cabeza en señal de devoción; la inscripción que enmarca este pequeño grupo escultórico consiste en invocaciones a Thot, "Señor de las palabras divinas" en beneficio del escriba, del que se enumeran sus títulos. Se trata de un altísimo personaje llamado Nebmertuf, *sacerdote, archivero y escriba real con rango de ministro*. Amenofis III, su soberano, le concedió el insigne favor de quedar representado a su lado sobre los muros del templo de Soleb. (11, my emphasis)

> [His hands wisely resting on his knees, a baboon perched on a small pedestal. It would be a sacrilege to mistake it for a domestic animal. This monkey is one of the forms of the god Thot, patron of scribes. We are reminded of this by the inscription on the base of the pedestal and the attitude of the scribe, humbly sitting at its feet. The scribe displays on his knees an inscribed papyrus, and bows his head as a sign of devotion; the inscription that frames this small sculpture consists of invocations to Thot, "Lord of the Divine Words," on behalf of the scribe, whose titles are enumerated. He is an important personage named Nebmertuf, *priest, archivist, and royal scribe with the rank of minister*. Amenofis III, his king, granted him the notable favor of being depicted next to him on the walls of the temple of Soleb.]

In these lines quoted from a description of the sculpture *El dios Thot protege al escriba Nebmertuf*, the baboon—easily mistaken for a pet, but actually the figure of the god—has a significant role. It joins the world of the ordinary to a higher, divine order, symbolizing the writer's pivotal position between the two. Accordingly, in his own quest as a writer, Vázquez Montalbán (like Balzac) attempts to represent history through the weaving of discrete stories, the political and the social through the private and the commonplace.

Vázquez Montalbán's self-definitory account might of course be read as a strategy of canonization. As I suggested at the beginning of this chapter, few writers of today have had to endure the constant questioning to which he has been subjected, and I know of none other about whom an academic critic might have wondered, in print, if his work were some kind of hoax. This critical attitude has engendered a certain defensive answer, implicit in statements such as the one made to an *El País* interviewer, that it is more difficult to write the Carvalho novels than the ones considered "serious": "Puede que parezca fácil, pero es mucho más difícil que escribir novelas en las que te lo puedes permitir todo.... Es curioso que a mí me cuesta más esfuerzo escribir los *carvalho* que los libros por los que me han dado premios, los considerados serios, literatura con mayúsculas" [It may look easy, but it is much harder than writing novels in which you can allow yourself anything.... It is odd that it takes a much greater effort on my part to write the *Carvalhos* than the books for which I have received awards, those considered serious, literature with capital letters] (Moret, "Manuel Vázquez Montalbán," 41). However, beyond its interpretation as a defense mechanism, Vázquez Montalbán's particular reading of himself, written in the language of the critics, represents a serious attempt to come to terms with his own position between high and low culture, and within the literary market of which he forms an important part. As in the case of Balzac, the writer's critical theory about his work, and the figuration of that work as a theory in itself, respond to a need to define his relationship to the literary commerce that both serves him and threatens to absorb him.

Vázquez Montalbán brings mass culture to literature as an "ajuste de cuentas con la pedantería intelectual" [settling of accounts with intellectual pedantry] (143), and as a compromise with his personal experience. In his youth the writer looks at available models and verifies that "ni el mundo ni la tía de [T. S.] Eliot son como mi mundo ni mi tía Daniela" [neither T. S. Eliot's world nor his aunt are like my world or my aunt Daniela] (*La literatura,* 130). As a communications professional, he also acknowledges the cultural power of mass media as ideological and educational devices, in contrast with the "papel relativizado que la literatura tenía como elemento de creación de conciencia" [relativized role that literature had as an element for the creation of consciousness] (129). He recognizes himself as a hybrid character: "Yo era y soy un mestizo cultural y social, me he alimentado de la cultura popular y de la universitaria, vengo del proletariado más destruido y soy un burgués muy reconstruido por una elemental colección de máscaras" [I was, and am, a social and cultural crossbreed, I have fed on popular and university culture, I come from the most demolished proletariat, and I am a bourgeois, very reconstructed by an elementary collection of masks] (130). His particular perspective will become his weapon in an operation in which literature, though theoretically relieved of historical responsibility as an instrument of change (129), is nevertheless recovered in just such a character: as the critical conscience of the failure of the democratic project, of its takeover by the logic of savage capitalism until the dreamt-of utopia becomes a "ciudad de mercados" [city of markets] (14).

But this weapon has a double edge. For this literature, and, most specifically, the Carvalho novels, to have an opportunity of success as an agent of cultural revolution (104) in the way described by the author, it must exceed what it has of mass culture—it must establish with it a relationship of repetition rather than identity. It must also find a reader prepared to identify that repetition, to crack its code and decipher its values. This reader is not identical to any one of the more than two million individuals who have already bought the Carvalho novels (according to figures given in 2000 by Editorial Planeta): "No hay que confundir el público con el mercado, sino considerarlo como una vanguardia de ese mercado" [One must not confuse the audience with the market, but consider it an avant-garde of that market] (*La literatura,* 82). Among the hundreds of thousands of actual readers with whom the text will engage in a productive struggle—"una cosa es reconocer [al] . . . lector realmente existente y otra satisfacerle en todos sus gustos, sin ningún forcejeo" [it is one thing to recognize the . . . reader existing in reality, and another to satisfy all his tastes, without a struggle] (178). The work must find, or create, its ideal receivers: "el sujeto que está en condiciones de enfrentarse a la dictadura del mercado, y a lo peor de la globalización, . . . el sujeto colectivo del lector ilustrado capaz de orientar y pluralizar el gusto, más allá de la tradición, concibiendo la tradición como un patrimonio en movimiento" [the collective subject capable of standing up to the dictatorship of the market, and to the worst of globalization, . . . the collective subject of the learned reader capable of guiding and pluralizing taste, beyond tradition, conceiving of tradition as a fluid endowment] (179).

For the author, the audience who can understand his offer is thus composed of *readers* as opposed to *consumers*. Though they exist within the city of markets, they can master their own condition and share in the writer's conscience, his sentimental chronicle of they way things have been, why they have been so, and how else they could be. The difference between reader and consumer lies precisely in this liberatory conscience, as opposed to the controlling tyranny of the market:

> Conciencia controlada, pero no por un poder represivo directo, evidente, que aparece de pronto en unas pantallas televisivas por las calles, como en las utopías negativas, sino en nombre de un sujeto que nadie ha comprobado si existe o no existe, pero que sería algo así como el consumidor mayoritario... de verdades políticas, de leche en polvo, de pautas de conducta, de fines de semana, de itinerarios ideales de verano, ese consumidor mayoritario en nombre del cual prácticamente se hace todo, se crea todo y se planifica todo, desde una campaña electoral hasta una programación de televisión e incluso cualquier liviana propuesta de cambio correcto. (95)

> [A conscience controlled, not by a direct, evident, repressive power, that suddenly appears in television screens on the streets, as in the negative utopias, but in the name of a subject whose existence no one has verified, but who would be something like the majoritary consumer... of political truths, of powdered milk, of rules of conduct, of weekends, of ideal summer itineraries, that majoritary consumer in whose name practically everything is done, created, and planned, from an electoral campaign to television programming, or even the slightest proposal for correct change.]

The generative interactivity of the literary project requires, then, the private act of communication between the writer and a lucid reader that takes place in a "novela de calidad éxito de ventas" [quality bestselling novel] (178), different from the mere bestseller precisely because of its project.

Vázquez Montalbán's account of his position taking within the field of literary production in post-Franco Spain comes surprisingly close to the reading of his *propuesta* a critic might reach by following Bourdieu's advice of reconstructing the relationship between the field as it exists at a given moment in a writer's career and that writer's habitus, the space of dispositions that leads him or her (but not mechanically) to a particular type of creation.[7] But if it is the task of writers to concentrate on the coherence of their projects, the task of critics should not be limited to understanding the different aspects of those projects (in the cases where authors' accounts exist and are accepted) or even to constructing themselves alternative accounts of textual or ideological functioning—and here we turn to another answer to the question of how to read Vázquez Montalbán. The significance of this author in contemporary Spanish literature—his character and his consequence—is not exhausted by the way in which he juxtaposes mass and high culture in order to effect, through the edifice of a complex text, a sharp social critique. The critic concerned with literature as a system not composed only of texts, or even of writers—as a field of cultural production—will also look at any literary event, *el hecho literario,* as the site of confluence of many different types of relations.

As Itamar Even-Zohar describes it, literature, understood as "the literary system" consists of a series of factors, all equally endogenous. At one end is the *producer* (the writer) who creates a *product* (the text) that will be received by a subject now understood as *consumer* (a term which does not obey a desire to recuperate literature for capitalism, but rather, as we shall see, to denote a subject engaged in a larger set of activities than that implied by the word "reader"). Any given text is produced or received in reference to a repertoire, that is, to a figurative grammar of usable and recognizable materials that includes language itself, as well as genres or formulas, but also models of behavior (for all persons and objects involved in the system) and ideas about the possibilities available to writers, readers, or any other participant in the literary world (in this sense, the concept of repertoire is related to Bourdieu's notion of habitus). Additionally, literary activities take place within the constraints of the *institution,* more or less analogous to Bourdieu's field:

> The "institution" consists of the aggregate of factors involved with the maintenance of literature as a socio-cultural activity. . . . [It] includes at least part of the producers, "critics" (in whatever form), publishing houses, periodicals, clubs, groups of writers, government bodies (like ministerial offices and academies), educational institutions . . . the mass media in all its facets, and more. (*Polysystem,* 37)

The institution, in turn, intersects partially with the *market* in which all literary products and agents circulate and which comprises "not only overt merchandise-exchange institutions like bookshops, book clubs, or libraries, but also all factors participating in the semiotic ('symbolic') exchange involving these" (38).

What critical readings of Vázquez Montalbán—his own included—do is elaborate theses about the texts according to the repertoire of criticism. Some readings (like his) also attempt to reconstruct the repertoire of the author; others, insofar as they tackle, for example, the role of popular culture, refer to the institutional repertoire that governs the production and reception of this work. What has not been attempted—as it generally isn't in the field of criticism—is an assessment of the importance of the consumer (and the market behind him or her) as constitutive element of the literary event designated by the name of its producer, beyond the simple facts a) that the ample sale of his books enables him to exist as a (successful) writer, and b) that the commerce generated by these sales supports a capitalist cultural system, with all the ideological objections any liberal critic might raise to that system. Such an approach would not invalidate interpretive critical approaches, but rather supplement them and enable literary studies to look upon a rarely considered domain.[8]

It might rightfully be argued that the critic cannot step outside himself to reconstruct the reception of the consumer ("layperson"), or, in other terms, that it is impossible to step outside one's own interpretive community to read as others do. The lack of homogeneity among the individuals who might be considered to belong to the community of nonspecialist readers or consumers of any literary text is one more obstacle to be overcome in the effort to bridge the gap between the ivory tower and nonacademic experiences of literature. The difficulty of this enterprise should not, however, preclude its undertaking. Though it is impossible for the critic to inventory all actual models of nonspecialist reading practice, she can point to plausible models manageable from the sphere of the classroom or the article. As Pierre Bourdieu advises,

> scientific progress may consist, in some cases, in identifying all the presuppositions and begged questions implicitly mobilized by the seemingly most impeccable research, and in proposing programmes for fundamental research which would really raise all the questions which ordinary research treats as resolved, simply because it has failed to raise them. (*Field*, 65)

Since no critical account can ascertain once and for all the meaning or the value of any given text or author, what is important is to address, if only partially, the many facets that come into play in their creation. This does not disqualify textual analysis as it has been practiced and continues to be practiced, but it begs for attention to the elements of literature that criticism has traditionally ignored. If we all construct the texts we read through the selection of relevant textual (and cultural) facts, it is certainly possible to expand our perception to consider new facts and thus create new texts.

The reason why Even-Zohar names the receiver of the literary product *consumer* is that the functions of this receiver are not limited to reading alone. One of the chief ways of coming into contact with texts is what he calls *indirect consumption:*

> All members of any community are at least "indirect" consumers of literary texts. In this capacity we, as such members, simply consume a certain quantity of literary fragments, digested and transmitted by various agents of culture and made an integral part of daily discourse. Fragments of old narratives, idioms and allusions, parables and stock language, all, and many more, constitute the living repertoire stored in the warehouse of our culture. (*Polysystem*, 36)

Indirect consumption—the infiltration into private and collective imaginaries through ways other than literary reading—is certainly not limited to texts of popular culture. On the contrary, it is also a feature of the classic, as the most minimal inventory of the uses to which the figure of Don Quijote or Federico García Lorca's poetry have been put will confirm. The many ways in which Carvalho circulates in the Spanish cultural market—including films, TV, and "happenings"—are therefore an integral part of the novels' participation in the literary system.[9] In this context, the study of an author must take into account as an essential fact the degree to which that author becomes a "brand" and the effect that his recognition as such has not only on the subsequent purchase of his or her works, but on their reception at all levels. Is it extrinsic to the literary fact of Vázquez Montalbán's work that a number of Carvalho's recipes have been collected in a cookbook? There is a way in which such an alternative form of "delivery" brings this imaginary world closer to readers, and even to non-readers: people who have only heard of the character, or who find out about the character through their contact with the cookbook.

Even "'direct' consumers" (Even-Zohar, *Polysystem*, 36) of literary texts engage with these in ways not limited to their private reading.

The fact that there are readers who may want to share in Carvalho's "reality" by replicating his culinary experience, or at least by imagining doing so, indicates that there is something beyond the fantasy of reading that can be sought in a text. From this point of view, it is also significant to assess what the reading (or the general knowledge) of a character, a work, an author provides to the persons who have it. Not the least, this knowledge confers onto someone the status of a reader, with whatever social advantages stepping into this image may bring. But this is not just a matter of the cynical appropriation of a socially privileged role, and there is a sense in which Vázquez Montalbán's joining of "high" and "popular" or "mass" culture can be considered a true settling of accounts with intellectual pedantry. He himself points to this move in referring to the position of Somerset Maugham in the English literary world of the fifties and sixties: "el prototipo de autor de bestsellers de una cierta dignidad literaria, conectado con los subgéneros de tradición popular, pero regalando a sus lectores la condición de partícipes de una relación literaria" [the prototype of the author of bestsellers of a certain literary dignity, connected with the subgenres of popular lineage, but granting his readers the status of participants in a literary relationship] (*La literatura*, 175).[10]

Vázquez Montalbán emphasizes communicability as a way of incorporating readers into the literary experience:

> Puede decirse que hoy, sobre un mercado medianamente culturalizado, casi toda la literatura que está en los libros de historia de la literatura sería suficientemente recibida por el lector. . . . Lo que ha contribuido poderosamente a perpetuar la división de un público predispuesto a leer, ha sido la actitud anticomunicacional de algunos escritores y el nefasto papel desempeñado por un brujo de nuevo tipo, incorporado a la fiesta de la cultura, casi siempre a manera de parásito, desde finales del siglo XIX: estoy hablando del crítico, cuando no asume la relativización de su propio papel. (173–74)

> [It may be said that today, with a fairly cultured market, almost all the literature in the literary history books would be sufficiently well understood by the reader. . . . What has powerfully contributed to perpetuating division within an audience predisposed to reading has been the anticommunicative attitude of some writers, and the ill-fated role played by a wizard of a new type, included in the feast of culture, almost always as a parasite, from the late XIXth century on: I am referring to the critic, when he does not assume the relative nature of his own role.]

To the extent that Vázquez Montalbán's narratives, and especially the Carvalho novels, are accesible to a wide audience of nonspecialist readers, yet culturally distinguishable (through the author's reception of critical attention, literary prizes, etc.) from a large set of bestsellers accorded no degree of literariness, they bring the mass of readers to the sphere of high culture, even to a higher degree than other widely read narratives that do not adopt the familiar form of detective fiction (say, Lucía Etxebarría's *Beatriz y los cuerpos celestes* [1998]). As Vázquez Montalbán himself points out in referring to Virginia Woolf, an author passes on—"contagia" (175)—his or her aura to readers.

I have referred to the *familiar* form of the detective novel, suggesting that this particular type of narrative communicability is different, at least in degree, to the one readers might find in a novel about a young woman's sexual awakening. In attempting to include "the reading practices of the uncredentialed" as a subject for literary study, it is also appropriate, then, to consider, in the context of their *direct consumption* of literary texts, how such practices may differ from the analytical interpretive readings characteristic of criticism. While it would be ingenuous to think that individuals who are culturally sophisticated enough to buy and read novels do not pay attention to their structure, it is plausible to postulate that they do not apprehend it in the same way as professional readers. Indeed, one might posit a reading based on familiarity as opposed to the defamiliarization that has structured critical reading—not only formalist—throughout the twentieth century.

In chapter 1 I mentioned, with regard to the reception of the nineteenth-century serial novel, Thomas Pavel's narratological thesis of reading strategies based on precedent, as opposed to novelty. While the critic is likely to look for the (perceived) rupture or gap that will allow him or her to theorize the work's model of textual or ideological subversion, the nonspecialist "sophisticated" (Pavel, "Literary Conventions," 58) reader—already past the stage of the "naive" (57) reader who discovers every textual element for the first time—can recognize a text's system of constitutive conventions and preconventions. Constitutive conventions are a repertoire of rules that function as basic grammars giving access to the work: "narrative patterns that require from the reader knowledge of the established conventions: first person narrations, epistolary novels, and detective stories are recognized and enjoyed by virtue of an entrenched agreement" (56). Preconventions, for their part, "include those literary regularities that do not reach the high uniformity of conventions and can therefore be understood as local rules or hints in a particular group of literary games" (57).

Pavel suggests the model of the game to describe the experience of a hypothetical reader deploying strategies of recognition. Skill and proficiency are keys to the "sophisticated" reader's nonspecialist reception:

> In a game-theory perspective, literary texts are assumed to be built around a few basic rules that give access to the text; while a naive reader knows these and only these rules, more advanced strategies can gradually become available through training and practice. Just as good chess players not only master the elementary rules of the game but are capable of applying such strategic laws as the principle of intermediary goals, or the principle of controlling the central squares, good readers know how to detect regularities that are invisible to less-trained readers. Advanced readers may know in advance the matrimonial outcome of *Jane Eyre* and enjoy the tortuous progress toward it. (57)

In this context, the Carvalho novels' repetition of the detective paradigm, as well as the repetition inherent to the seriality of the cycle— Vázquez Montalbán's quotation of his own model—make them archetypical of the ways in which the nonspecialist reader can engage with a text. On the one hand, this reader will exercise the skill acquired through the previous knowledge of the conventions of detective fiction; on the other hand, he or she will also be able to identify the preconventions particular to the Carvalho series. What this means is that even the reader who does not semiotically interpret the significance of Carvalho's ritual burning of books, of his passion for food, of his relationship to a prostitute, or of his disdain for the police and conventional justice—though many will, certainly according to their own cultural repertoires—is undergoing a significant and significative reading experience.

Such readers' recognition of the preconventions specific to Vázquez Montalbán's novels makes them "participants in a literary relationship," as well as capable of building on it to acquire an ever-greater proficiency "through training and practice." Against this background, one should note that the acknowledgment on the part of the reader of the minimal faithfulness to the convention of the mystery that Vázquez Montalbán confesses ("it is so easy and fortuitous in my novels to find out who has killed whom") may not function as the frustration of an expectation, as he assumes it to, but rather as a local preconvention that readers might integrate into a totalizing vision. Nevertheless, insofar as one can suppose that a certain part of the mass of readers who come to the Carvalho novels in search of a "popular" reading experience (of detective novels with no aesthetic pretensions) discover, through increasing familiarity with their preconventions, a more sophisticated model of the literary experience, his work can again be considered a settling of accounts with traditional configurations of the field. Through the incorporation into the literary system of a group of readers (or consumers) formerly excluded from it, the cultural phenomenon of the Carvalho novels fulfills the author's desire to bring his own cultural hybridity to bear on the sanctuary of literature, and to attack its institutional role in the failure of the democratic city.

This understanding—one of the many possible—of the nonspecialist reading experience of the Carvalho cycle brings it close to the origins of the modern Spanish novel in the mid-nineteenth-century serial novel, a form radically endowed with a transforming power, both in regard to social order (if from an opposite ideological perspective) and in regard to the literary field. Concerning this, it is significant to remember how the pre-realist nineteenth-century novel of contemporary manners was fundamentally interested in urban order and deviance, intrinsically conceived as a serial product (both a series of installments and a series of novels about the same characters), and essentially directed at a mass of readers as yet undifferentiated into hierarchical categories. In this sense, it is possible to take quite literally Vázquez Montalbán's assertions about the present state of literature as going back to the basics, "el retorno a los comienzos, a algo tan elemental como que la literatura es la literatura y que eso no se considere una declaración metafísica, sino la constatación de una evidencia cultural" [the return to the beginning, to something as elementary as literature being literature, without it being considered a metaphysical declaration, but rather the confirmation of cultural evidence] (153). In addition, the idea of a return to the origins takes one to a further consideration of the primal and elementary reasons why people read, in general, and read narrative, in particular.

The simplest response to that question is that people read for the story, and a larger answer is that in stories they seek guidance about fundamental issues of experience: "How do we find significant plots for our lives? How do we make life narratable?" (Brooks, *Reading* 114). Narrative is innate; it is a way of thinking that gives temporal connection and sense to social events:

> In the absence or silence of divine masterplots, the organization and interpretation of human plots remains as necessary as it is problematic. Reading the signs of intention in life's actions is the central act of existence.... If the mastertext is not available, we are condemned to the reading of erroneous plots, granted insight only insofar as we can gain disillusion from them. We are condemned to repetition, rereading, in the knowledge that what we discover will always be that there was nothing to be discovered. (141–42)

If the detective novels of Vázquez Montalbán have become entrenched in the collective Spanish imaginary, this phenomenon is only understood at one level through the analysis of their postmodern textual or ideological complexity. It is necessary, then, to enter into the sphere of ritual relationships between a writer (or a story) and his (its) readers that have taken place from the earliest cultural appearances of narrative.

One of the most beautiful accounts of these relationships is the one provided by Walter Benjamin in the essay entitled "The Storyteller"—one of the several collected in English translation under the apt title of *Illuminations*, a term that suggests the lucidity of a knowledge not attained through analytical reason. Although Benjamin distinguishes the novel from the story because of "its essential dependence on the book" (87), he also highlights what the two have in common among themselves as well as with the larger framework of the epic. In this context, storytelling emerges first and foremost from the impulse toward sense making in the face of death. In a passage also alluded to by Joan Ramon Resina, Benjamin writes that

> not only a man's knowledge or wisdom, but above all his real life . . . first assumes transmissible form at the moment of his death. . . . Suddenly in his expressions and looks the unforgettable emerges and imparts to everything that concerned him that authority which even the poorest wretch in dying possesses for the living around him. . . . Death is the sanction of everything that the storyteller can tell. He has borrowed his authority from death. In other words, it is natural history to which his stories refer back. (94)

Starting from this originary moment, the storyteller weaves a narrative that is opposed to the great form of communication produced by the capitalist world, information. Whereas information seeks to explain and is tied to its specific moment in time, the story limits itself to presenting interpretable events and "does not expend itself. It preserves and concentrates its strength and is capable of releasing it even after a long time" (90).

The story is related to history in a very different way from that of the news fragment; a storyteller does not seek to explain or prove but to represent meaningfully. In this way he comes closest to the historical writing of the chronicle:

> The historian is bound to explain . . . the happenings with which he deals; under no circumstances can he content himself with displaying them as models of the course of the world. But this is precisely what the chronicler does. . . . By basing their historical tales on a divine plan of salvation—an inscrutable one—they [the chroniclers] have from the very start lifted the burden of demonstrable explanation from their own shoulders. Its place is taken by interpretation, which is not concerned with an accurate concatenation of events, but with the way these are embedded in the great inscrutable course of the world. (96)

The storyteller is a "secularized" (96) chronicler who endows life with shape and meaning through the power of memory. Here emerges a distinction between storyteller and novelist: to the "reminiscences" (98) of the former is opposed the totalizing "remembrance" of the latter as a force that searches for the patterns and unity that can hint at a transcendental truth: "the 'meaning of life' is really the center about which the novel moves" (99). And Benjamin joins Georg Lukács in equating this quest for meaning with the force of desire: "'One can almost say that the whole inner action of a novel is nothing else but a struggle against the power of time. . . . And from this . . . arise the genuinely epic experiences of time: hope and memory'" (99).

The story's journey is thus integrally related to the historical course of events, and it is also moral in the widest sense of the word. At its center is the struggle for virtue, not conceived as the self-righteousness of the hero or heroine in melodrama, but as the earnest, and slippery, attempt to play a certain part in the world: "The righteous man has the main role in the *theatrum mundi*. But because no one is actually up to this role, it keeps changing hands. Now it is the tramp, now the haggling Jewish peddler, now the man of limited intelligence who steps in to play this part. In every single case it is a guest performance, a moral improvisation" (106). It is not the quality of virtue that matters, but the knowledge of the forms it takes and the process of its elucidation. Such an emphasis on moral process explains the emphasis on deviance that Peter Brooks notes in the shapes assumed by "traditional storytelling" (*Reading*, 155) as transformed by the nineteenth-century novel:

> Deviance as a question in social pathology offers an opportunity for tracing its arabesque figure as plot. That "arabesque" . . . represents the opposite of the straight line: it is the longest possible line between two points, or rather, the maintenance of the greatest possible deviance and detour between beginning and end, depending on the play of retardation, repetition, and return in the postponement and progressive unveiling of the end. (155–56)

It is not hard to imagine how the novels of the Carvalho cycle might satisfy the axiomatic impulses described by Benjamin. Their serial character serves as insistence on a fundamental, even archetypal, plot: the one generated by the victim who, at the moment of his or her death, steps out of the banality of the anonymous everyday and demands an *account* (both a story and a compensation). As Resina points out, it is this death, and not the fact of crime, that introduces into the narrative a disruption to be rectified: "[it is] the victim [that] introduces heterogeneity in a world reduced to the homogeneity of a dominant point of view. . . . The criminal act is perfectly comprehensible. Codified from the beginnings, it constitutes one of the pillars of social order" (*El cadáver*, 70–71). The fact that the conventions of detective fiction dictate a perennially iterable ending—"what we discover will always be that there was nothing to be discovered"—shifts attention to the process as the most meaningful part of the endeavor. In this process is inscribed the character of the chronicle, and here too the seriality of the Carvalho novels acquires importance, since it functions as the verisimilar representation of Spanish, and, within Spain, of Catalan, society over more than twenty-five years. The passage of time, focused through a single conscience (Carvalho, but even more, his narrator), brings to the fore the fundamental operations of memory and desire in the struggle toward understanding, or at least toward survival.

Again and again, readers will follow the narrative voice as it traces the arabesque patterns of disorder, striving toward a final order that will always be the weakest—and the least important—moment of the story, because they know that in a year or two another novel will appear in which a crime will again take place. Carvalho will once more be summoned to investigate it, but what he will find out throughout the investigation will be more important than its final resolution. One of the things he will discover is the changing face of the righteous man, and the surprising variety of actors who can play that role as well as its opposite. In this way, Vázquez Montalbán's detective novels leave the symbolic world of clear-cut, melodramatic heroes and heroines, in which evil is clearly locatable and localizable, for another world of Gothic descent.

Like melodrama, the Gothic is essentially concerned with good and evil, and sees the world as structured by a bipolar moral conflict. But while "the ritual of melodrama involves the confrontation of clearly identified antagonists and the expulsion of one of them" (Brooks, *Melodramatic*, 17), the Gothic concedes that evil might be anywhere and cannot be subjected to a rule. Rather than attempting to explain all of the natural world according to a rational and moral order, the Gothic recognizes its uncontrollable character. If the Carvalho novels are quite removed from the sphere of castles, dungeons, and sepulchres (although these are implied in the labyrinthine architecture of the city and the ways in which it houses the dead), they remain close to a vision that acknowledges the inevitable presence of evil and the impossibility of decisive moral victories.

The "meaning of life" that the novel strives after is thus that there is no meaning. There is, nevertheless, a certain harmony between story, social history, and natural history that can take the place of primordial truths in the postmodern world. In this search for a totality that is never realized, the reader can nevertheless find something useful—if not necessarily the critique of the alienation of the subject in the capitalist city, at least a reflection on the hate that leads to murder, or a glimpse into the contradictions of a perpetual *charnego*, or the brand of an excellent single-malt scotch. As Benjamin wrote, "each sphere of life has . . . produced its own tribe of storytellers" (*Illuminations*, 85). Each interpreter is the product of his or her tribe, and thus the tribe limits what the interpreter can perceive or transmit. Nevertheless, what counts is the storyteller's ability to provide counsel:

> [Every real story] contains, openly or covertly, something useful. The usefulness may, in one case, consist in a moral; in another, in some practical advice; in a third, in a proverb or maxim. In every case the storyteller is a man who has counsel for his readers. But if today "having counsel" is beginning to have an old-fashioned ring, this is because the communicability of experience is decreasing. . . . After all, counsel is less an answer to a question than a proposal concerning the continuation of a story which is just unfolding. (86)

The story is a unit that the reader can comprehend and repeat, and "the more completely it is integrated into his own experience, the greater will be his inclination to repeat it" (Benjamin, *Illuminations*, 91). The readers of Carvalho novels throughout three decades have integrated them so much into their own experience, that they have made them exceed the status of fiction. The story has jumped out of any specific narrative, and that is why its counsel can be consumed in the form of a film, a TV series, a recipe, a memorized literary passage—"Ya ninguno me llevará al sur" [None can take me South any longer] (Vázquez Montalbán, *Los mares*, 22).

Near the end of the Carvalho cycle (whose specific terminus has been announced repeatedly, but not yet carried out) the series itself, like the victim in each novel, is about to acquire observable and transmissible form. It will be the moment of conclusion and comprehension that Luis Costa hoped for in the passage quoted at the beginning of this chapter, the time when we might understand (create) cohesively the novels' meaning and value. In the critical search for the understanding of the series's place in contemporary Spanish literature—the legitimate search of a legitimate profession—it will be essential to look outside the limits of our repertoire in order to assess, or at least imagine, the ways in which it has provided counsel for that majoritary consumer who is not just the apostate at the other side of culture.

# Afterword: Rummaging Through the Archive

THE PRECEDING CHAPTERS SEEMINGLY ADDRESS DISPARATE AUTHORS, forms, and texts, but these are joined by their character as what I called, in the introduction, borderline or frontier. They are or have been at the borderline or frontier of literature, and they have been so in different ways. The nineteenth-century serial novel appears earlier than the new disciplines of Spanish literary history and philology, which isolate a certain kind of writing as canonical. In its original reception, it remained outside canonical/noncanonical, high/low mappings of Spanish cultural production, allowing for discrete acts of judgment about individual works. Only in time, after the appearance and consolidation of these disciplines (beginning in the 1860s), did its prevalent themes and mode of production equate it with the "negative" term in each of these oppositions, relegating it as a whole to the sphere of the popular (or, more exactly, of nonartistic mass production). The later nineteenth-century work of Benito Pérez Galdós—as a novelist, playwright, journalist, and critic—is borderline in another way: it succeeds in redefining the role of the writer, the responsibilities of the reader, and the definition of the work of art. It is thus symbolic of the advent of the modern, divided literary field (in Bourdieu's terms), and of the pervasive differentiation between "two kinds of works, either great or of no interest at all" that John Guillory still observes in twentieth-century criticism (*Cultural Capital*, 30).

The two chapters that study these nineteenth-century literary events are concerned with the radical break instituted during the period between literature as everything that was written within the cultured spheres (the ones with access to reading and the possibility of acquiring books), and a specialized type of discourse that signaled a specific kind of expression and excluded certain modes of imaginative writing not aligned with this expression. During this time, significantly that of the birth of the bourgeoisie, there appeared a middlebrow space of entertainment, mass-market, production that became the antithesis of everything literature was supposed to embody (much more so than folklore). Thus, part 1 of this study, which traces the transition from the field in which the serial novel appeared to the field that Pérez Galdós helped construct, concentrates on the establishment in Spain of the very line of demarcation between canonical and noncanonical, and its implications for the later production and reception of literary works.

The possibility of exercising taste, discernment, discrimination, applied retroactively to nineteenth-century works that had not yet been the subject of Spanish literary history and criticism (because at their outset these concerned themselves with the medieval and renaissance periods), and lay the ground for the subsequent habits of reading and classification of both the cultured public and, of more concern to this book, the critical institution. The nineteenth century created, in Foucauldian terms (to which I will come back later), a new discursive formation called Spanish literature, different from the referents to which this word applied earlier. In other words, it gave rise to a new repertoire or space of possible statements that could be made about literature, of ways in with literature could itself be uttered, that was culture-specific (although of course Spanish culture intersected others, as well as supranational entities such as "Europe" or "the West"). This new discursive formation would both become entrenched and be constantly modified throughout the twentieth century and into the present. Against this framework, the three chapters of the second part of this book look at points of friction and discontinuity in that discursive formation—again, borderline spaces that tell us something about the way in which it was constituted, enacted, and transmitted.

In modern Spain the literary gradually became a recognizable, if never quite clearly objectifiable, type of discourse, presumably inherently distinguishable *from others*. Chapters 3 and 4 pay attention to examples of this horizontal distinction, by addressing some of the gray areas that emerge in trying to separate literary language from the language of political propaganda and the language of pornography. These chapters address prose works judged in one context or another as either "erotic" (artistic) or "pornographic" (trash), and novels (i.e., writing deployed from a semantically charged genre position suggesting the presence of the literary) attempting to disseminate specific political theses and trigger specific actions, that is, trying to function as propaganda in the political field. From the reading of these works, I attempt to make out some of the connections between this horizontal differentiation among *types* of discourse and a parallel vertical differentiation that categorizes the "truly" literary as canonical (great, privileged, almost sacred, at the very least superior), in opposition to "lower" imaginative discourses that do not quite achieve a presumed minimum level of quality or distinction. In other words, as they have been read, "aesthetic" novels are *better* than propagandistic fiction, and literary erotica is *better* than pornography. The first item in each of these pairs enters the domain of art, whereas the second one does not, so that types of discourse are not only differentiated, but hierarchically ranked—often, in effect, differentiated on the very basis of that ranking. Horizontally or vertically, choices about what fits within the category of literature are based on often unexamined critical presuppositions. The "Literary" is aesthetically stylized, intransitive, thematically or representationally complex, polysemous; it is also associated with certain universalized values: goodness, freedom, national identity and pride, disinterestedness, spirituality, intelligence, critical distance. While the particular indexes deployed at any moment in relation to a given text vary according to the specific context from which the act of judgment is made, there seems to be a limited repertoire from which readers and critics at different points of the political and theoretical spectrum repeatedly draw.

While chapters 3 and 4 perform close readings of specific works, the fifth chapter focuses on the canonical trajectory of a contemporary author. Devoted to Manuel Vázquez Montalbán's position taking in the literary field and its critical treatment, this chapter examines how this writer's detective fiction almost completes a circle in relation to the issues raised by the nineteenth-century serial novel and Galdós's work. The notions of high/low established throughout the 1800s remain operative more than a century later, and the practices of reading and categorization deriving from that period and developed throughout the twentieth century determine a highly problematic instance of reception. Among the cases studied in this book, it is perhaps in this one that the discomfort of the borderline reveals itself most visibly, for here is a living author who is clearly inside the field—inside the highest echelons of the field—and nevertheless embraces everything that is usually excluded from it: the formula story, the bestseller, the sidestepping of critical direction in favor of a "free market" of reading. Critics' abilities to establish knowledge about literature, to order and classify texts, to direct readings according to a binomial structure of thought, are challenged by an author who will neither be on the outside nor play by all the inside rules. Though obviously less successfully than Galdós, Vázquez Montalbán again attempts to redefine the role of the writer, by both returning to the mythical origin of the godlike Egyptian scribe, and to the profane economy of the nineteenth-century scribe. In an intuitive movement of which he himself seems to be differently conscious at different times, Vázquez Montalbán *combines* high and low to recast the writer as a social *mestizo,* thus challenging the critic to also assume a hybrid position and read outside him or herself.

Although I have referred to a circular configuration in the five chapters of this book, and emphasized their continuity as readings from outside the canon, from its frontier with "something else," I do not wish to claim a clean linearity the book does not have, or even seek. Its endeavor is clearly a historical one, as it investigates the constitution, the constantly evolving reiteration of the notion of literature, and the practices related to that knowledge, in the context of Spain (though not necessarily of Spanish academia). But this investigation is limited, and to an extent arbitrary. It could be done in different ways, in different types of articles or books, through different choices of authors and texts, from different theoretical and critical apparatuses, and in different words. While I have referred to readings and criteria utilized by certain theoretical approaches, such as those of feminism and cultural studies, or of essentialist or relativist schools of thought, and occassionally even disagreed with some of their tenets, this book is not intended as a critique of any of those disciplines, all of which have been part of my critical formation. Neither is it intended as an alternative proposal; rather, it is a personal attempt to reflect on how it might be possible to bring the ideas and statements experienced at the level of theory closer to practices undertaken at the level of criticism or even individual reading.

In selecting the primary texts, I have deliberately refrained from ironing out some loose ends. Most of the works alluded to, but not all, are novels, though it would have been quite possible and much neater to perform this same study adhering to this genre throughout. The predominance of novels is due to the fact that this genre is ideal to showcase points of rupture in the fabric of the literary, since from its very appearance—as the first genre addressed at a mass audience, as the first genre that broke with preceptive poetics, as the first genre dependent on commercial distribution—it calls into question the limits of the literary sayable. But rather than focusing primarily on the effects that a genre's emergence and rise to preeminence had on the literary space of possibles, I prefer to concentrate on such a space in itself: how it has been configured in relation to modern Spain and how that macroconfiguration becomes universalized, or is treated as universal, even as it contains within itself multiple, and conflictive, microconfigurations. Rather than conceiving of that configuration as a totality—even to critique it—I prefer to view it, partially, in the metamorphic untidiness that keeps it alive. Thus, I myself shy away from compactness, and turn to very different sources in my explorations. Chapter 4, on eroticism and pornography, includes short stories as well as novels. Chapter 2, on Galdós, addresses his journalism as a cultural text. And, stepping completely outside the bounds of fictional or factual narrative, the same chapter also addresses his theater. Criticism is, of course, also attended to here and at different points in the book, not merely as "secondary" support but as the very object of analysis. Through diverse readings from the archive, I have attempted to outline a description, which can only be fragmentary, of how (through which statements and acts) literature in general, and Spanish literature in particular, has been constructed at certain moments. While the specific criteria through which it is constructed has been different at different points, what is permanent is that it is always configured against an "other": as part of a dual structure of high and low, inside and outside. The five chapters in this book constitute an effort to approach the possibility of other statements and acts that do not ignore literature's history, the history of that dual construction, but reconfigure it in a new way.

Here again is that notion, archive, which I have abstracted into the title of my book. In my desire to transcend canonical thought, I have opposed "archive" to "canon" as a term that describes an alternative conception of literature. The gesture, perhaps rash, was to seize it from John Guillory's *Cultural Capital* (where it had no distinctive status), and to pose it as the guiding formation of my book, a formation that could enclose the canon—not efface it or destroy it or replace it, but encircle it, allowing it to exist as one category of literary text rather than as the sum total of the literary. I will quote Guillory's passage again: "The historical condition of literature is that of a complex continuum of major works, minor works, works read primarily in research contexts, works as yet simply shelved in the archive. Anyone who studies historical literatures knows that the archive contains an indefinite number of works of manifest cultural interest and accomplishment" (30). This author already sees the canon as a selection from the archive—the portion of works brought to the fore and accorded a special status within academic institutions through the instrument of the syllabus. From his formulation one can extrapolate that the archive itself would be the accumulation of things written as literature at one point or another, or which could be considered literature from one position or another. This accumulation is necessarily indefinite and formless, and includes countless objects of "cultural interest and accomplishment" (however these are defined), lying in wait of interested researchers. If we assume that the canon is a particular selection, it becomes less imperative to expose it or transform it; it becomes possible to acknowledge it as a cultural construction without necessarily repeating it; it becomes possible to leave it aside for a moment to attend to a different selection; and it becomes possible to probe its boundaries in order to learn more about both canon and archive. From this point of view, the archive is a material entity, as immense and as indeterminate as it may be: the corpus of writings comprised under the elastic rubric of literature, and constituting the object of my discipline.

While the term "archive" could evoke different visual images, the reference to *shelved works* conjures a very specific one, that of the library, an image that is especially appropriate when the subject is literature, and especially fortunate in the Hispanic context, since it immediately brings to mind the hexagons of Borges's *biblioteca de Babel*. Between Guillory's indefiniteness and Borges's infin003finiteness, the image of the archive-library insinuates the possibility of readdressing the "sacred" texts, and of finding new ones that may tell us something about themselves, as well as hinting at the composition(s) of the archive itself. It is thus that I have imagined myself rummaging through this archive, *checking out* some of its volumes, placing them in relational contexts (in this case in the very frontier between the canon and its outside), learning about them and through them. It is thus that I have imagined myself as one of many researchers, studying and ordering groups of texts that sometimes intersect, and sometimes do not, the groups others have studied, and giving them shapes that are always partial, and yet perhaps always also necessary. From this point of view, the archive is also a *metaphor*—I have put it forward as the symbolic metaphor of this book's endeavor. In this sense it is the imaginary space that exceeds the bounds of the canon, where other systems of thought are possible, and where we are forced to confront the specificity of our universals. It is not a metaphor that works perfectly, and one could easily find its limits, but it is sufficiently adequate to express the pertinent points.

The above are the senses in which I have used the term. Nevertheless, "archive" is not an innocent word, and comes with baggage that surpasses and problematizes the ways in which both Guillory and I have used it. Specifically, it has been theorized by two of the most central thinkers of the twentieth century, Michel Foucault (in *The Archaeology of Knowledge*, 1972) and Jacques Derrida (in *Archive Fever: A Freudian Impression*, first delivered as a lecture in 1994). Both theorists have very different notions of archive and very different uses for the concept, and my application of it conforms to neither (though my general approach evidently leans toward Foucault). To begin with, neither author uses the word literally or metaphorically to refer to literature in particular. Even so, they both present the term in a context of discursive associations that are very relevant to this book. Consequently, it will be useful to review some of those associations to situate further the position I take regarding my subject.

*The Archaeology of Knowledge*, a book many have found "infuriating" (according to its own back cover), is Foucault's attempt to come to terms with what he had been pursuing in previous works; to posit a system, theory, or method to link the types of knowledge he had arrived at about different cultural formations (madness and psychology, illness and medicine, science, language, economics, etc.). To refer to "*medicine, grammar, political economy*" (*Archaeology*, 31)—or literature—to want to write their history, is to confront the elusive nature of their being. Since no one definition can encompass such protean entities, Foucault dwells on the logical impasse their conception presents, wondering on what their unity is based:

> On a full, tightly packed, continuous, geographically well-defined field of objects? What appeared to me were rather series full of gaps, intertwined with one another, interplays of differences, distances, substitutions, transformations. On a definite, normative type of statement? I found formulations of levels that were much too different and functions that were much too heterogeneous to be linked together and arranged in a single figure, and to simulate, from one period to another, beyond individual *oeuvres*, a sort of great uninterrupted text. On a well-defined alphabet of notions? One is confronted with concepts that differ in structure and in the rules governing their use, which ignore or exclude one another, and which cannot enter the unity of a logical architecture. On the permanence of a thematic? What one finds are rather various strategic possibil-

ities that permit the activation of incompatible themes, or, again, the establishment of the same theme in different groups of statement. (37)

Foucault opts for considering these entities as groups of statements constituting *discursive formations* (38), sums of utterances that exhibit a systematicity or regularity defined by their own rules. The very accumulation of statements recognized as "literature" at any specific point depends on a field of possibilities—the "associated field" (98) that can generate or accommodate further literary statements as elements of sameness. It is literature itself that allows any subject to enunciate statements within it, or to recognize statements as belonging to it: the notion's past, its contemporary context, the future responses it can generate. The conditions for the existence of the discursive formation are external (dependent on their time and place), but its rules are internal and particular.

To study a given discursive formation is to describe, from very specific vantage points, how such a group of statements came to be possible, and to constitute a knowledge, discipline, or ideology. It is done by addressing the level of "things said" (what was said as literature or about literature, for example), and only of things actually said, against precise contexts—the subject positions implied by the emission of those statements, the conditions that allowed them to be enunciated, the value they are accorded, their capacity for being repeated and accumulated, the power struggles implied in their appearance and transformations. Those contexts are always relational, never essential, and the ideas of field, network, space of possibilities put forward by Foucault are already very close, though in varying ways, to the relativistic and relational perspectives of the theorists I have presented as guiding my approach in this book—Fish, Smith, and especially Bourdieu and Even-Zohar.

To address all those contexts is "to undertake to uncover what might be called the discursive formation" (Foucault, *Archaeology*, 115–16), but the latter is never the only, or ultimate, object of study. In fact, whatever one might learn about discourse, discursive practices, discursive formations, points in two different directions. This investigation, which Foucault calls "archaeology" (131), aims in an outward direction, toward an overarching cultural domain called the *archive*. The archive is not the collection of a culture's documents, or the institutions that exist to preserve those, but rather an abstract "complex volume, in which heterogeneous regions are differentiated or deployed" (128). The archive is the background of discursive formations:

> [It is] first the law of what can be said, the system that governs the appearance of statements as unique events. But the archive is also that which determines that all these things said do not accumulate endlessly in an amorphous mass, nor are they inscribed in an unbroken linearity, nor do they disappear at the mercy of chance external accidents; but they are grouped together in distinct figures, composed together in accordance with multiple relations, maintained or blurred in accordance with specific regularities. (129)

Neither the discursive formation nor the archive can be expressed as totalities; only their local functioning is available to the researcher. Though the archive is a historical entity proper to a culture, its history defies any generalizations, and the historian can only catch a glimpse of it through its multiple manifestations.

In addition to pointing outward, the archaeology of knowledge points inward, to the very position of the researcher. Foucault is ambiguous about the observation point from which the historian can attempt to "uncover" the discursive formation or the archive. On the one hand, he suggests a necessary distance that can only reveal itself in terms of time: the archive's fragments emerge more clearly "the greater the time that separates us from it" (130). On the other hand, since statements are always part of the discursive formation they address—or at the very least of a *meta-*formation—even if they reorganize and transform it, there is no isolated watchtower from which to enunciate them. Foucault renounces this impossible scientific distance, and, moreover, values just as much the understanding afforded by proximity: "Should [the description of the archive] not approach as close as possible to the positivity that governs it . . . ?" The resulting compromise favors precisely the space of the borderline or the frontier:

> The analysis of the archive, then, involves a privileged region: at once close to us, and different from our present existence, it is the border of time that surrounds our presence. . . . It is that which, outside ourselves, delimits us. . . . [The] threshold of existence [of the description of the archive] is established by the discontinuity that separates us from what we can no longer say, and from that which falls outside our discursive practice; it begins with the outside of our own language *(langage);* its locus is the gap between our own discursive practices. In this sense, it is valid for our diagnosis. . . . It deprives us of our continuities. (130–31)

## AFTERWORD: RUMMAGING THROUGH THE ARCHIVE 225

The attempt to scrutinize a specific instance of discourse becomes an attempt to uncover the discursive formation. The analysis of the discursive formation becomes an attempt to uncover the archive. The description of the archive becomes in turn a way of establishing our own presence within it, of "diagnosing" the insufficiency of our constructions and the presuppositions that govern them.

While it is clear that the concept of archive as I posed it earlier does not coincide with Foucault's, the points of reference his theory provides my approach are surely already apparent. In the very specific studies undertaken in my five chapters, I have been concerned with the statements that have served to construct the literary in the Spanish context, and with the subject positions behind them. I have explored relationally what was, at different points in the nineteenth and twentieth centuries, said as literature or said about literature. The distinction between the discourse of literature and the discourses of literary criticism and theory is implicitly blurred in my study, as I understand it to be in Foucault's scheme and in those of the theorists I have used as direct methodological sources. Not that there is no line between those discourses, since anyone would immediately recognize the concepts to which they refer as distinct, but that both serve to constitute the discursive formation called Spanish literature, to establish its "sayable" in complementary ways. In mapping out the configuration of Spanish literature over the past two centuries, I have paid special attention to the unspoken acts of censorship that allowed it to be established in the ways that it was, and to the sometimes individual, often institutional positions that determined such a space of possibilities. I have addressed these at the level of belief, analyzing some of the assumptions that govern our very perception of and regard for our object of study. And I have looked at them from the point of view of cultural capital, suggesting the difficulties involved in transporting insights easily acceptable at the theoretical level (the canon is a construct; literature is a construct) to the critical stage in which academics have always acted as experts, keepers, and administrators of precisely those objects whose tangible reality theory questions.

To perform this investigation, I have chosen works (or authors) that I saw as borderline between the canon and the archive, whose exclusion from the first of these domains had at some point been made explicit. Thus both the language of the literary texts themselves, and the language in which they had been evaluated, were available for analysis. Perhaps less evidently, I have also situated myself at a frontier. I hope I have made my own partialities explicit—I am a

Puerto Rican woman and an American academic, writing about Spanish literature and culture, and also, sometimes, about a Spanish academia I have experienced tangentially. But I have also attempted to read from just outside or just within the conventions of my field, attempting to become a *mestiza académica*. In striving to denaturalize critical presuppositions and reveal critical discontinuities, I have posited the need to read *otherwise*, sometimes pointing, perhaps nostalgically, to the reading practices of a nonspecialized audience I once belonged to, and sometimes pointing to the hypertheoretical need to constantly read oneself reading—to constantly problematize one's logical and ideological supports.

While Foucault stressed that for him the archive was neither the collection of a culture's documents nor the site of their preservation, it is precisely to such collections and sites that Jacques Derrida turns in his formulation of the term. *Archive Fever* originates as a lecture written precisely for a conference at the Freud House in England, and taking the Freud archive—the archive of psychoanalysis—as its immediate subject. In fact, Derrida's text challenges readers to answer the question he himself poses at a certain point: "In works said to be *theoretical*, what is worthy of this name and what is not?" (5). His speculative notion of the archive must be abstracted from his many critical comments on Freud, psychoanalysis, and their relationship with Judaism, and it is often extremely difficult to extricate the general from the specific. It is nevertheless to the general that Derrida addresses himself, as he employs the languages of deconstruction and of psychoanalysis itself—since he believes the latter already "aspires to be a general science of the archive" (34)—to expound on the transhistorical, universal principles that govern archivization as a human impulse. If Foucault acknowledges only the level of "things said," Derrida on the other hand troubles himself (and "trouble" is a significant idiom in his vocabulary) with the psychic processes that play themselves out in the objectivization of memory.

To ground this exploration, Derrida returns to two originary concepts behind the modern notion of the archive, *arkhe* and *arkheion*. The first of these terms "apparently coordinates two principles in one: the principle according to nature or history, *there* where things *commence*—physical, historical, or ontological principle—but also the principle according to the law, *there* where men and gods *command*, *there* where authority, social order are exercised, *in this place* from which *order* is given—nomological principle" (1). Alongside the inaugural connotations of *arkhe* (which Derrida deems "forgotten"), and as a more continuous matrix, the second term, *arkheion*, introduces and stresses the topological—the site where the archive is kept—and the "archic, in truth, patriarchic, function" (3) of keeping. This conception of the archive emphasizes the accumulation of a body of knowledge, housed at a privileged site, and calling for the social position of the archivist charged with interpreting and administrating:

> As is the case for the Latin *archivum* or *archium* (a word that is used in the singular, as was the French *archive*...), the meaning of "archive," its only meaning, comes to it from the Greek *arkheion:* initially a house, a domicile, an address, the residence of the superior magistrates, the *archons,* those who commanded.... On account of their publicly recognized authority, it is in their home, in that *place* which is their house ... that official documents are filed. The archons are first of all the documents' guardians. They do not only ensure the physical security of what is deposited and of the substrate. They are also accorded the hermeneutic right and competence. They have the power to interpret the archives. Entrusted to such archons, these documents in effect speak the law: they recall the law and call on or impose the law. (2).

Both *arkhe* and *arkheion* bring up the question of power, since the construction of archives seems to be inextricably linked to the privilege of ruling, to the ability to impose the law. Furthermore, as conveyed in these terms the archival impulse tends toward consolidation of that power through the establishment of a whole. The archivist gathers, identifies, and classifies, in fact *consigns,* according to all the possible meanings of that word: "*Consignation* aims to coordinate a single corpus, in a system or a synchrony in which all the elements articulate the unity of an ideal configuration. In an archive, there should not be any absolute dissociation, any heterogeneity or *secret* which could separate ... or partition" (3). In these originary senses, the notion of archive is not too far removed from the notion of canon, both as sacred law or rule, and as the textual body that represents it within the religious sphere or in its transference to secular contexts (juridical, literary, etc.).

As such a unitary structure, the archive is there for its deconstruction, and throughout the rest of *Archive Fever* Derrida will question its stability, searching for the revealing contradictions it, and the law it enacts, harbor, and, perhaps paradoxically, elevating these to the category of science. It is necessary to ponder what makes us build archives, what powers of naming and distinction they deploy, what knowledges they allow us to assemble, and what the *limits* of those knowledges are:

> A science of the archive must include the theory of its institutionalization, that is to say, the theory both of the law which begins by inscribing itself there and of the right which authorizes it. This right imposes or supposes a bundle of limits which have a history, a deconstructable history.... This deconstruction in progress concerns ... the institution of limits *declared* to be insurmountable, whether they involve family or state law, the relations between the secret and the nonsecret, or ... between the private and the public, whether they involve property or access rights, publication or reproduction rights, whether they involve classification and *putting into order:* What comes under theory or under private correspondence, for example? What comes under system? under biography or autobiography? under personal or intellectual anamnesis? In works said to be *theoretical,* what is worthy of this name and what is not? ... In each of these cases the limits, the borders, the distinctions have been shaken by an earthquake from which no classificational concept and no implementation of the archive can be sheltered. Order is no longer assured. (4–5)

The preoccupations detailed above seem to diminish the distance between Derrida and Foucault. Both are concerned with the fragmentary nature of what appears to be cohesive, and both are concerned with the ways in which knowledge and culture can be performances of power.

The first problem with the archive as traditionally conceived has to do with its objects. If archivists gather, appraise, arrange, interpret, preserve, then what is it that all these verbs apply to? Derrida questions the unadulterated existence of "*archivable* content" (17), independent from and not created by the archivist. There is here, as there was in Foucault, no ideal separation between subject and object. This is doubly apparent if one takes into account the specific examples on which Derrida is building his theoretical notion of archive. A good part of the book is a diacritic reading of Yosef Hayim Yerushalmi's *Freud's Moses: Judaism Terminable and Interminable* (1991). Derrida is fascinated with this book's transgression of its genre's conventions: after four scholarly chapters in an academic, historical study, Yerushalmi concludes with a fictive "Monologue" spoken as if before, in fact spoken to, the dead Freud. The author abandons the scientific distance of the observer to invest himself personally in his work, and to inscribe himself in the filial line in which he had situated Freud (whom he had related to his actual father, Jakob Freud, and to his mythical father, Moses). Yerushalmi the archivist cannot sustain his separation from the archive, and the specters of formlessness and incompleteness haunt his writing (as, according to Derrida, they haunted Freud's in *Moses and Monotheism* and "Delusion and Dream in Wilhelm Jensen's *Gradiva*"). Derrida's own distance from Freud and from Yerushalmi is likewise unstable, as the question of Judaism, the question of seeing oneself as the "father" of a discipline, the question of where the academician stands in relation to his object of study, are all relevant to his own experience. Thus historical or scientific knowledges, the modes of knowledge posed by the archive, are shown to rely on fragile boundaries, and the oppositions and hierarchies that ground the archive itself begin to dissolve.

Alongside this blurring of boundaries, and in paradoxical relationship to it, is the archive's absolute need for borders, for the exterior to exist. Against the platonic ideal of pure uncontaminated memory, memory as access and identity *(mneme)*, the archive is "hypomnesic" (11), a prosthetic surrogate for the immediacy of past experience. Nevertheless, here too distinctions disintegrate, and we are left with a larger, overarching paradox. In Derrida's words,

> if there is no archive without consignation in an *external place* which assures the possibility of memorization, of repetition, of reproduction, or of reimpression, then we must also remember that repetition itself, the logic of repetition, indeed the repetition compulsion, remains, according to Freud, indissociable from the death drive. And thus from destruction. Consequence: right on that which permits and conditions archivization, we will never find anything other than that which exposes to destruction, and in truth menaces with destruction, introducing, *a priori*, forgetfulness and the archiviolithic into the heart of the monument. (11–12)

This essential incongruity at the root of the archive is what Derrida calls *mal d'archive*, archive fever. Archives are supposed to bear witness, to be cultural remembrance, but they emerge only as signs of an absence, and the act of archiving is always evidence of a contradictory need to both build and destroy. In this way, a cultural construct intended to objectify the past and make it available becomes the mark of a collective trauma. And the archive itself evades the notion of completeness that it was meant to bear out. Accordingly, as *Archive Fever* advances, Derrida seems consistently to move away from the epistemological grounding of the book's beginning. If, at the outset, it seemed like we would follow him toward a cohesive explanation of the archive, starting from its etymological origins, later on we find that he can no longer refer to the archive as a *concept*, but rather as a *notion* or an *impression* (29). In the end, "one will never be able to objectivize it [the archive] with no remainder" (68).

For Derrida, this is of course a positive value. Rather than seeing the archive as anchored in the past, as the "monument" to something that is dead, Derrida sees it as essentially about the future. The archive is thus an annunciation, rather than an announcement; it implies always the possibility of a birth: "Because the conditions for archivization implicate all the tensions, contradictions, or aporias we are trying to formalize here, notably those which make it into a movement of the promise and of the future no less than a recording of the past, the concept of the archive must inevitably carry in itself, as does every concept, an unknowable weight" (29). This unknowable weight is a figure of desire, and archive fever is no more a metaphor for trauma or illness than a metaphor for fascination and obsession:

> To be *en mal d'archive* can mean something else than to suffer from a sickness, from a trouble or from what the noun *mal* might name. It is to burn with a passion. It is never to rest, interminably, from searching for the archive right where it slips away. It is to run after the archive, even if there's too much of it, right where something in it anarchives itself. It is to have a compulsive, repetitive, and nostalgic desire for the archive, an irrepressible desire to return to the origin, a homesickness, a nostalgia for the return to the most archaic place of absolute commencement. No desire, no passion, no drive, no compulsion, indeed no repetition compulsion, no "*mal-de*" can arise for a person who is not already, in one way or another, *en mal d'archive*. (91)

Rather circularly, Derrida returns from *arkheion* to *arche*. It is as the law of commencement, of an eternally deferred closure or an eternally awaited promise, that the archive impresses itself upon him.

In this book, I have been concerned with the limits of classification as Derrida expounds them. If literature can be construed as a canon or as an archive (that is, as a definite or indefinite corpus), it is precisely the faculties of classification and consignation that are called into critical service. It is we, the literary critics, who have been charged, or have charged ourselves, with the task of selecting, preserving, and institutionalizing the literary archive. The important reminder suggested by *Archive Fever* is that this task is a performance of power, but power can be "performed" in different ways. In acknowledging the always provisional configuration of the archive, and its lack of independence from the archivist, it is possible to open that power to other configurations and other archivists. A deconstructionist perspective on literature is also by necessity compelled to go beyond the dual structure of thought that has been the one constant in the historically changing definitions of the literary. What such a perspective offers is the possibility of ceasing to define literature against what it is not, and to see it in itself and against itself, in the impulses it satisfies as well as in the functions it serves within culture. Against this context, it is not important to arrive at "the" definition of literature, or even to be consistent in how we apprehend it at one time or another. In fact, the *concepts* of coherence, consistency, and closure are directly opposed to the *notions* of remainder, openness, and commencement that are essential to the transcendence of canonical thought.

Foucault was concerned with the epistemology of the archive, with its implications for the construction and organization of knowledge. Derrida, in contrast, attends to its ontological status as a manifestation of being. But though separated by more than twenty years and by two philosophical attitudes, both point in similar directions, toward the limits of "hermeneutic right and competence." As a background for the consideration of the changing nature of Spanish literature, their theories are extremely stimulating. In the first place, they suggest something about the place of theory itself. In the introduction to this book I mentioned Sylvan Barnet and Hugo Bedau's *Critical Thinking, Reading, and Writing: A Brief Guide to Argument,* noting how it divided literary criticism into the functions of interpreting, judging, and theorizing, and how it seemed to isolate the first two, almost as a different endeavor from the third. The fact that this slippage occurs in a rhetorical guide to argument is significant, for arguing implies choosing certain methods to set forth a thesis in order to advance some purpose. It is thus that hermeneutic right and competence are established, and a unity of knowledge is achieved. But to theorize, at least as Foucault and Derrida imply it, is to move away precisely from such unities, and to let go of the need for continuity and consensus. The history of philology and literary criticism is perhaps more revealing when it is turned inside out to disclose the subject positions it embodies, the national and ideological constructions it performs. This does not imply knowing less about literature, or even losing some of the power involved in being its cultural arbiters; it also does not entail the need to abandon literature as an impossible or irrelevant construct. On the contrary, a "philological theory" or "theoretical philology" affords the possibility of understanding literature in its multiple forms and engaging with it from different locations.

In the second place, both Foucault and Derrida suggest a constant displacement from text to archive to researcher (and back again) as objects of study. To inquire into what texts say about cultures and even about human nature is a road to a fundamental self-diagnosis or understanding; and this self-understanding is also crucial to illuminate the objects we construct. But rather than a futile chase after our own tail, such circular inquiry is an exercise in fluidity that enables us to imagine dynamic modes of knowledge. If our disciplines are "phenomena of rupture, of discontinuity" (Foucault, *Archaeology*, 4), it is necessary to embrace local knowledge, unstable categories, mutually reinforcing or mutually exclusive constructions, competences that are momentary. It is necessary to abandon the essential for the relational, and so to be able to account for the existence and import of formations such as literature, or Literature, or the canon, and for our own investment in them, even as we recognize other possible formations. The threshold between the canon and the archive—in the sense in which I initially presented the term as well as in all its theoretical implications—is the point at which we are both willing and driven to set foot in unfamiliar terrains. We can get lost in the Library of Babel, and have a hell of a time while we're at it.

# Notes

## Introduction

1. In the words of James Mandrell, "the impact of theory on the field of Peninsular literary studies has, all told, been negligible" ("Peninsular") 291.

## Chapter 1. Refashioning the Canon

1. Translations of all literary works and primary sources immediately follow the original Spanish quotations. All critical and theoretical sources are quoted either in the original English, or in English tanslation. Unless otherwise noted, all translations are my own.

2. According to Leonardo Romero Tobar, "nineteenth-century novel writers, through the appearance of the great novelists following the Revolution of '68, openly place themselves in the tradition of the publishing market of popular literature" ("Algunas consideraciones," 98), and "the popular novel appears under the three guises of bound volume, fascicle, and *feuilleton* in a newspaper" (103). Jean-François Botrel gives astonishing figures for the production of serial novels (excluding the *folletín*): around 1868 (close to the moment from which the decadence of the genre is usually dated), one-tenth of all new publications (not just novels) is in fascicle; the number of issues per printing ranges from one hundred thousand to 250,000 (Galdós's average audience of some twenty-thousand readers would later be considered exceptional); any one fascicle novel would have been read (in successive printings, I assume) by one-fourth of the literate population, or between eight hundred thousand and one million readers ("La novela por entregas," 131–36). As for newspaper *folletines*, they begin to appear, with mixed contents (not only fiction) after 1834. Soon, "most dailies in Madrid [and in the provinces] begin to adopt this new layout, synonymous with modernity" (Lecuyer and Villapadierna, "Génesis y desarrollo," 16), and by the early 1840s, most *folletín* sections are dedicated to novels. The *folletín* "plays a significant role in the dissemination of novelistic production, at a time when the cost of a book is high" (22; see also Ferreras, *La novela por entregas*). As Montesinos argues, "[books], often voluminous were usually published in serial form" (*Introducción,* 119) and "our specialty was serial literature" (123). He notes the prosperity of publishing houses that reprinted in volume collections the most popular serial novels, such as the *Biblioteca de El Heraldo, El diario de avisos, El Nacional,* and later on the well-known *La Iberia* (126). In summary, from available data one can in-

fer the quantitative importance of the serial production of novels, as well as their influence on those novels that might still be published directly in volume form, and which needed to compete, in terms of cost and contents, with serial fiction.

3. While the information these studies supply is quite extensive, much more can be done. Only a few authors have received extensive consideration—most especially Wenceslao Ayguals de Izco. The scarcity of studies dedicated specifically to Manuel Fernández y González, the second "great" serial novelist both chronologically and in terms of popularity, is conspicuous. Additionally, readers will observe many evident discrepancies between these assessments of the serial novel. Most of those concerned with ideological contents, for example, coincide in their disagreement with Iris Zavala's initial proposition that Ayguals's novels, exemplary within the genre, are at least loosely associated with socialist doctrine, and concerned chiefly with the working class. Another area of discrepancy has to do with readership—whether these novels were addressed chiefly to that working class or to the bourgeoisie, or across class boundaries chiefly to women. These are all areas to which I will return further on in this chapter. In general, however, the coincidences as well as the discrepancies between these texts allow the researcher to reach well-documented conclusions about the phenomenon of the serial novel, and its literary and cultural implications.

4. Catherine Jagoe ("Disinheriting") quotes different figures from Botrel's 1974 "La novela por entregas": in 1860, 37.02 percent of Madrid women could read, as opposed to 9.05 percent in the entire country. Since *Libros prensa y lectura* is published much later than "La novela por entregas," I have chosen the more recent figures. The difference between the two is, however, negligible.

5. My introduction of this vocabulary, which is obviously not the one I handle throughout this book, should serve to refer to Kevin McLaughlin's exceptional work on Balzac and Dickens's participation in the world of commercial, serialized literature. His work, as he explains, is concerned with "how to describe the action by which works of literature seek to define the commerce of which they form a part" (*Writing*, 4). Supporting his thesis on the language of Marx's *Capital*, and on the cultural theory of Adorno and Benjamin, McLaughlin discusses the role of imitation, or citation, and exchange, in the negotiation between the literary and the commercial on the part of the two novelists. His conclusions are very relevant to a consideration of Galdós's parallel negotiation.

6. The scene alluded to from Fernán Caballero's *La gaviota* is that in chapter 19, in which several characters respond to the suggestion made by one of them: "compongamos entre todos una novela" [let's all write a novel together] (264). They criticize the portrayal of women in French *feuilletons*, and review the different possibilities of novel writing available (fantastical, heroic or melancholy, sentimental), concluding that the types of novel best suited to Spanish sensibility are either the historical novel, or the *novela de costumbres* [novel of contemporary customs].

7. Ayguals introduces the *novela por entregas* after a careful process of preparation of the audience's horizon of expectations:

> At the beginning of 1845, Ayguals's enterprise [The Madrid Literary Society] is economically established, with various titles already published, and others in the process of publication. The web of distribution to province capitals is well organized; as are commercial contacts with France and Cuba. The publishing house's publicity seems effective: readers subscribe to the serials and slowly enter a sales machine. . . . The company has acquired, then, the technical traits that . . . make the dissemination of the popular novel easier. Ayguals

has tried novelistic fiction. Everything is ready for our author to begin *constructing,* as rapidly as possible, novels that will fully satisfy the public's expectations. (Benítez, *Idelogía,* 38)

As for the first *folletines,* Lecuyer and Villapadierna recount how "on May 6, 1834, *El Eco del Comercio* is one of the first periodicals to insert into the lower third of its front page, and separated by a double black line, a section that, although it bears no title, is at least formally reminiscent of the famous French *feuilleton*" ("Génesis y desarrollo," 16). At first this section can include varied contents such as articles of customs, home economics, hygiene, urban police matters, court and theater news, bullfighting, literary criticism, economics, legal matters, and scientific matters (17), and only once in a while, "some short story, *novella,* or poem, in one or two parts" (18). Only in the early 1840s does the section begin to be dedicated almost exclusively to novels. According to Romero Tobar, the first Spanish novel to be published as *folletín* is Pablo Piferrer's *El Castillo de Monfeliú* [The Castle of Monfeliu] (*Diario de Avisos,* 1840).

8. I have discussed the use of Cervantes as a model of the historical novel in the articles about Gil y Carrasco and Larra included in this book's bibliography.

9. "One of the arguments that the publishing company deploys most frequently as publicity is that of the relationship between the novel of Ayguals and that of Eugène Sue: the principal purpose is to elicit an immediate reaction from the same public that made *El judío errante* [The Wandering Jew] one of the time's bestsellers. For that reason, the Society establishes direct connections with Sue and his French publishers. Ayguals's dedication to Sue and his translation of *The Wandering Jew* undoubtedly moved the French writer, whose partiality for Ayguals must have opened many Paris doors to the Literary Society" (Benítez, *Ideología,* 41). From the beginning, however, Ayguals will assert his difference from the foreign model, and later on he will distance himself from Sue, claiming Paul de Kock as a new exemplar. This shift, together with his economic interest in the publishing world, is what makes Goldman label Ayguals an "unprincipled opportunist."

10. Even-Zohar develops his ideas on the importance of literature in the constitution of Western nations in the article "The Role of Literature in the Making of the Nations of Europe." He contends that in these societies "it was 'literature' which served as an ever-present factor of socio-cultural cohesion" (22). Socio-cultural cohesion is defined as "a state in which a widely spread sense of solidarity, or togetherness, exists among a group of people, which consequently allows a non-physical means of imparting behavioral norms" (23). In other words, literature functions as the principal, or one of the principal, institutions, that allow the individuals belonging to a collective such as "the Spanish nation" to postpone their personal interests in favor of those of the group, and even to define themselves through their membership in that collective.

11. José Carlos Mainer provides an interesting and thorough account of the "invention" of Spanish literature as an institution and as a canon: as a historical phenomenon originating in the early eighteenth century and influenced by changing conceptions of nationality, by the birth of positivist literary history, etc. Mainer traces the evolution of the notion of literature throughout the nineteenth and early twentieth centuries, paying special attention to the work of philologists Marcelino Menéndez y Pelayo and Ramón Menéndez Pidal in the configuration of the modern Spanish canon.

12. Botrel has shown in *Libros, prensa y lectura en la España del siglo XIX* [Books, Presses, and Reading in Nineteenth-Century Spain] how Spain lagged behind the rest of Europe in nearly all aspects of book production and trade: quality and avail-

ability of paper, economics of the import of material, capital for the modernization of printing presses, etc. (one should note, though, that it is precisely Ayguals de Izco, in his effort to nationalize the novel and improve the conditions of its production, who first brings to Spain a Middleton press, purchased in London after his visit to the 1851 Exhibit of Universal Industry; Benítez, *Ideología,* 57). Elisa Martí López documents the difficulty of matching foreign production. Between 1750 and 1850, she writes, "at least 50% of European novels" come from London or Paris ("Orfandad," 348). The preexistence in France of a novelistic culture and of an extremely organized infrastructure ensures the availability of a multitude of writers (many writers in Spain still do not consider the novel a respectable genre, or are not used to writing novels), and the steady production of installments (many novels in Spain were sporadically produced, or interrupted). Spanish editors of the 1840s procure the simultaneous publication of French novels in Paris and Madrid: "in some cases the Spanish translation is made before the appearance of the novel in the French market" ("Orfandad," 350). This will veritably transfer much of the Spanish publishing business to Paris: "All the editorial activity that precedes and accompanies the publication of a novel happens . . . in Paris; all the commercial energy, responsible for the development of the novel, is transferred to France" (352). According to Victor Ouimette, even the process of book production often takes place outside of Spain: "In France, a whole industry was created for the production and export of Spanish-language books" ("Monstrous fecundity," 384).

13. Regarding Galdós's rejection of the conventions of the serial novel, one of his objections bears special mention at this point, and that is his dislike of the installment form in itself. From early on in his career, it was important to him to publish in volume editions: "En aquel tiempo no había editores de novelas por tomo, y con los editores de novelas por entregas no quería yo, ni podía en modo alguno, entenderme" [At the time, there were no publishers of volume novels, and with the publishers of serial novels I could not, and would not, deal] (qtd. in Ortiz Armengol, "Galdós y Valle-Inclán," 257). In 1870 he wrote "la entrega, que bajo el punto económico es una maravilla, es cosa terrible para el arte" [the installment, a marvel from the economic point of view, is a terrible thing for art] ("Observaciones," 164). As usual, his dismissal does not imply that he does not participate in that economy: already his second novel, *El audaz* (1871) is serialized in the *Revista de España;* Geoffrey Ribbans documents how *La desheredada* (1881) appears in *entregas* by subscription, and many other of his novels will appear serialized in either form. It should, however, be kept in mind, that even as he does, he is actively attempting to establish a distance between serial production and his own. Those of his novels serialized in journals tend to appear "in a *prestigious* publication" (Ribbans, "*La desheredada,*" 69, my emphasis) rather than a newspaper or an overtly commercial publication. Galdós's valorization of the book over the installment also coincides with a moment in which the publication of volumes is becoming materially easier in Spain.

14. The process of institutionalization of the Spanish novel is somewhat, though not exactly, analogous to the process of institutionalization of the German novel, as described by Rakefet Sela-Sheffy in "Strategies of Canonization." Sela-Sheffy describes how the feeling of a need for indigenous production derived from the sense, shared by German intellectuals, of cultural dependence and inferiority with regard to France. Initially, "the predilection for 'Germanness' first originated . . . from *conformity* with the 'cosmopolitan' canon rather than from 'primordial nationalism';

that is, from attempts, already in the previous century [the seventeenth], to cultivate a domestic version of the very same Classicist repertoire, with an aspiration to matching its achievement and finesse" (sec. 3). Nevertheless, "during the second half of the [eighteenth] century, a contradictory tendency gradually prevailed, namely, the search for an alternative source of cultural capital." The appearance of this alternative cultural capital—the newly created German novel—was linked to the emergence of a Romantic aesthetic, in which individual genius replaced the proper adoption of classical (foreign) models as an aesthetic dictum. As in Spain, the espousal of the new genre is hesitant, and its reception distrustful. Thus, "there was a gap, both in time and in content, between the formation of a recognized 'native' literary repertoire, less and less compatible with classicist canonical categories, and the point in which a full recognition of the alternative, indigenously German canon, was possible." The novel, and the new concept of the German canon it helps generate, cannot be fully accepted until traditional ideas about aesthetics and literature can be made to accomodate the new production, and, vice versa, until the new production is successful enough in entering the horizon of expectations to contribute to a change in those aesthetic ideas.

15. Closure in serial novels was a very relative phenomenon, and thus, as I pointed out earlier, second and third parts were frequent. In the continuation to *María, La Marquesa de Bellaflor, o el niño de la inclusa* (1846), although the former protagonist gives the novel its title, the story is no longer mainly about her, and new characters and adventures are introduced. Ayguals also wrote a third part to the saga, *El palacio de los crímenes, o el pueblo y sus opresores* [The Palace of Crimes, or the Poor and Their Oppressors] (1855). The popularity of *María* was immense. It was reprinted innumerable times, and Manuel Fernández y González, probably the second most important serial novelist of the century, claimed it as an intertext in his much celebrated *Luisa, o la mujer del jornalero* [Luisa, or the Laborer's Wife] (1867).

16. True to the serial form, the last page of *Los desheredados* promises that Fernández y González's next novel, *Los hijos perdidos* (1865–66) will follow the story of the little girl, whose name is also Clara. But that is literally *another story*, and within *Los desheredados* she is only briefly described (as a well-dressed baby with something evil in her eyes, following the bourgeois attention to both outside appearance and moral essence).

17. Despite the predilection for the story of the "American dream," I know of no specific connection with Alger, although the two writers were roughly contemporary (with Alger writing until much later in the century). Nevertheless, English was among the several languages Ayguals knew, and he translated Stowe's *Uncle Tom's Cabin* into Spanish very early in his career. He also admired Fenimore Cooper.

18. In *María, o la hija de un jornalero*, Ayguals describes the nature of his social concerns with regard to the working class:

No es nuestro ánimo abogar por esa igualdad absoluta, por esa nivelación de fortunas con que algunos frenéticos han querido halagar á las masas populares. Lo que nosotros deseamos en favor del pueblo es: *igualdad ante la ley; castigo contra el delincuente, no contra el pobre; justicia en pro de la inocencia, y no consideraciones al rico; derechos sociales en todos los españoles; voto en todas las cuestiones para los hombres honrados.* (1:101)

[It is not our intention to advocate that absolute equality, that leveling of fortunes with which some frenetics have wanted to flatter the popular masses. What we want for the people is:

equality before the law; punishment against the delinquent, not against the poor; justice for the innocent, and not considerations for the rich; social rights for all Spaniards; suffrage in all matters for decent men.]

19. I have been describing a social attitude I call *paradigmatic* of the serial novel archetype, but it should also be noted that it generated a reaction, and the consequent production of novels (many serialized) espousing the opposite ideology. An early case in point is Böhl de Faber's *La gaviota*, which severely castigates Marisalada's attempt at social advancement through artistic merit and presents a favorable portrait of the aristocracy and the clergy. Readers should also refer to Hibbs Lissorgues's study of Catholic *folletines*.

20. In this context, it is interesting to note the distaste in serial novels for women who do not fit the type of the beautiful, spiritual, modest, marriageable or married, lady. Most amusing is the ever-present rebuke of *viejas* (hags) (always unmarried), especially those who try unsuccessfully to simulate youth and beauty. An example among several in *María* is the *Marquesa de Turbias-Aguas*, "una vieja coqueta llena de presuncion" [an old coquette full of conceit] (1:183) who tries to stuff herself into the latest fashions:

> Hacíase en consecuencia apretar el corsé en términos, que dividiendo la abultada espalda en dos mitades, formaba dos globos como el pecho; por manera que solo por la cabeza podia conocer el que la miraba si estaba aquella vision de frente ó de espaldas.... Es inútil... decir que sus negros y lustrosos bucles eran postizos, así como su dentadura ... [y en] las abultadas mejillas ... luchaba el mas encendido colorete con los estragos de la vejez. No hemos hablado del cuello de esta joya del bello sexo, porque la marquesa de Turbias-Aguas no tenia cuello. (1:183)

> [She had her corset tightened so that, dividing the bulging back into two halves, it formed two globes just like the breast; such that only by the head could the onlooker know if the spook was facing forwards or backwards.... Needless to say, her shiny black ringlets were false, much like her teeth ... and on the fleshy cheeks, the brightest rouge battled the ravages of age. We have not spoken of the neck of this jewel of the beautiful sex, because the Marquise of Muddy-Waters had no neck.]

The figure reappears in *La bruja de Madrid,* and Fernández y González also revisits it, writing that "no hay pudor más intransigente que el de las viejas, porque, traducido al sentido recto, no es otra cosa que el temor a que se vea el estrago que han causado en ellas los años" [there is no modesty more intransigent than that of hags, because, translated to its right sense, it is nothing less than the fear of showing the ravages of their years] (*Los desheredados,* 1:107). Similarly, although prostitutes are tolerated, spinsters are disapproved of, and particularly those who have not kept themselves sexually pure. Thus, in *María,* the grotesque *Tía Esperanza* protests that "siempre he tenido horror al pecado carnal" [I have always been horrified by carnal sin] (1:181) right before recounting how in her youth a pharmacist "hizo de mí cuanto quiso" [made of me what he wanted]; and a soldier made her commit "cierto desliz ... que me ha costado despues muchos años de cilicios" [a certain indiscretion that has since cost me many years of cilice] (182). Through the tool of humor, serial novelists characterize women outside of marriage as caricature and excedent, thereby strengthening the characterization of domestic space as the only one desirable.

21. Martí López confirms how the serial novel is a side product of the emergence

of the figure of the editor and the modern literary market: "The implementation of capitalist measures in the cultural milieu of the book stimulated the development of the printing press, the emergence of the figure of the editor/publisher, and the unprecedented expansion of the book market. The serial novel is, in this sense, the product most representative of the intervention of new economic and social forces in the traditionally restrictive activity of literature" ("Orfandad," 348).

## Chapter 2. Benito Pérez Galdós and the Canon of Spanish Literature

1. In chapter 4 of my book *Rewriting Melodrama: The Hidden Paradigm in Modern Spanish Theater* I explored Galdós's position with regard to the melodramatic norm prevalent in the Spanish theater of the last third of the nineteenth century. The central thesis of this study is that in referring to melodrama it is necessary to distinguish between the dramatic genre, dominant in Spain from the late eighteenth century through the middle of the nineteenth, and the melodramatic as a moral and aesthetic mode of thought. In this wider sense, the melodramatic pervades the theater of the second half of the century through the hegemonic dramaturgy of José Echegaray (then generically considered *tragedy*), and institutes itself as the central model against which all later playwrights must measure themselves. If, on the one hand, this produces an "Echegarayan" melodramatic school, on the other it generates challenges to the paradigm that achieve different degrees of success. In this context, Galdós's challenge to melodrama—more consistent in his criticism than in the plays themselves—is an attempt at revolutionary rupture that constantly needs to negotiate with the audience's melodramatic expectations. His plays therefore run the gamut from the highly antimelodramatic ethical questions of *Los condenados* to the highly melodramatic polarities of *Electra*, through the complex compromises of plays like *Realidad*.

2. Galdós's account of his revolutionary perspective does not necessarily apply to his own earliest theatrical works, written before the essays in *Nuestro teatro* and never performed. Early plays like *El hombre fuerte* [The Strong Man] (1870), *Un joven de provecho* [A Worthy Young Man] (1864), or *Quien mal hace bien no espere* [Do Wrong, Expect No Good] (1861) were youthful attempts by the writer to break into theater in the period after his first arrival in Madrid. On the other hand, Galdós's critical account of the need for renewal in the theater precedes the premiere of his first staged play, *Realidad* (1892), hailed in advance as a decisive step in the modernization of Spanish drama. In effect, Galdós's recollection of the motives that draw him to theater constrasts starkly with that of Echegaray, who remembers in his *Recuerdos* that he began to write theater "to add a new entry to my budget" (2:22). Rather than trying to find alternatives to existing theatrical modes, Echegaray distills boulevard melodrama to make it suitable for *haute bourgeois* audiences. For a more detailed account, see Ríos-Font, *Rewriting Melodrama*.

3. Although, as writers, Galdós and Echegaray are more or less contemporaries (Echegaray's first play dates from 1874), in the 1880s, as Galdós writes the essays in *Nuestro teatro*, Echegaray is already a consummate and consecrated playwright. His "seniority" in this subfield explains Galdós's appeal to him as a possible reformer, rather than the direct undertaking, at this point, of his own theatrical project.

4. The issue of Galdós's melodramatism has been a subject of a long and interesting debate between Isaac Rubio and Gonzalo Sobejano. Beginning in 1974, the two critics assume opposite positions regarding the playwright's recourse to this "popular" mode of representation. While Rubio charged Galdós with falling prey to the very dramatic structures he was trying to break with, Sobejano emphasized the clear differences between Galdós and Echegaray, the most visible representative of melodrama. Quite recently, in a 1996 article, Sobejano has revised his earlier position, to recognize Galdós's complex incorporation of this "popular" genre especially in those plays with a clear social or political aim.

5. Roberto Sánchez describes Gaspar as "the writer who most conscientiously concerned himself with the reform of Spanish theater during the last decades of the previous century" ("Emilio Mario," 264). He favored the use of prose, the absence of overt moralizing, a greater emphasis on dialogue than on action, and a physical arrangement of the stage that would upset the public's complacency. Gaspar's innovations were nevertheless evaluated by audience and critics according to the criteria applied to melodramatic theater, and his plays were judged deficient rather than revolutionary. Critical rejection and failed performances drove Gaspar to concentrate especially on the *género chico* throughout the last years of his career: "Fed up with trying to direct the audience's taste . . . [I have decided] to devote myself to the *género chico,* from which I expect the regeneration of our drama" (qtd. in Kirschenbaum, *Enrique Gaspar,* 333). For further discussion of Gaspar's project, see Poyán Díaz, Kirschenbaum, and Ríos-Font, *Rewriting Melodrama.*

6. In this context, it is interesting to remember that Echegaray—the most influential nineteenth-century playwright before Galdós—also came to the theater as a previously established public figure (a professor and politician). The procedure followed for the premiere of his first play, *El libro talonario* [The Check Book] (1874) was a sophisticated marketing strategy: the theater announced the play as written by "Jorge Hayaseca," a pseudonym the audience easily deciphered as an acronym of "José Echegaray." On the evening of the performance, Echegaray's identity was revealed, and he was called to the stage for several rounds of applause.

7. According to Bourdieu, modern artists define themselves by opposition to the world of the bourgeoisie: "The literary and artistic field is constituted as such in and by opposition to a 'bourgeois' world which had never before asserted so bluntly its values and its pretension to control the instruments of legitimation, both in the domain of art and in the domain of literature, and which . . . now aims to impose a degraded and degrading definition of cultural production" (*Rules,* 58). Thus, the position Galdós incarnates in the Spanish cultural field (in the novel as well as in the theater) could not have come into being earlier in the century, when the national bourgeoisie was still in the process of establishing itself. It is only against this background that he can begin to stimulate movement toward the invention of position of the modern writer: "Even though it is inscribed in a potential state in the very space of positions already in existence, and even though certain of the romantic poets had already foreshadowed the need for it, those who would take up that position [art for art's sake] cannot make it exist except by making the field in which a place could be found for it, that is, by revolutionizing an art world that excludes it, in fact and in law. They must therefore invent, against established positions and their occupants, everything necessary to define it, starting with that unprecedented social personage who is the modern writer or artist, a full-time professional, dedicated to

one's work in a total and exclusive manner, indifferent to the exigencies of politics and to the injunctions of morality, and not recognizing any jurisdiction other than the norms specific to one's art" (Bourdieu, *Rules*, 77).

8. Insofar as Galdós is concerned with the nature of reality and knowledge, this project also includes exhaustive thought on history and historical discourse. As Geoffrey Ribbans argues in Chapter 1 of *History and Fiction in Galdós's Narratives*, Galdós, without forgoing a nineteenth-century trust in the possibility of historical knowledge, has an acutely modern sense of how language mediates and relativizes it, making any historical narrative "open-ended" (69) and *scriptible* in the sense Barthes gives to the term.

9. In choosing to dedicate this chapter to *El crimen de la calle de Fuencarral* and *La incógnita*, I am cutting the latter text off from the others with which it is usually studied: the 1889 dialogue novel *Realidad* and the 1892 play of the same title. Although the obvious relationship to these other works—versions of the same plot—has provoked excellent critical studies (including those by Sobejano, Tsuchiya, Vernon, and Willem), I hope to demonstrate that taking it out of this context and relating it more directly to *El crimen* than has previously been done can provide useful insights into Galdós's cultural projects. In concentrating on the above-mentioned pair of texts, I am also excluding from my analysis another series of articles written by Galdós on a Madrid crime, the 1886 *El crimen del cura Galeote* (to which I will refer only occasionally throughout this chapter). This decision is partly arbitrary, and partly due to questions of correspondence (in date and topic) between *El crimen de la calle de Fuencarral* and *La incógnita*. Additionally, although *Galeote* concentrates on the subject of crime, it also serves a very different purpose than the *Fuencarral* articles: instead of approaching the events as a mystery (the murderer, Father Galeote, appears from the beginning caught upon the act of shooting the bishop of Madrid), Galdós uses it to expound at length on issues like the deplorable organization and morality of the clergy in Spain, etc. The result is a text that presents many problems outside the scope of this chapter.

10. The crime on Fuencarral Street captured the audience's imagination, and a present-day dramatization of the events (divergent in some ways from Galdós's) can be seen in Televisión Española's 1994 film *El crimen de la calle de Fuencarral*, part of a series on the history of Spanish crime and starring Carmen Maura as Higinia Balaguer. Other nineteenth-century accounts of the crime also exist, either in the form of *causas célebres*, or as anonymous legal accounts.

11. In *Fiction and Diction*, Genette explores "the reasons that might lead factual narrative and fictional narrative to behave differently with respect to the story that they 'report,' simply because that story is in once case (supposed to be) 'true' and in the other fictitious" (56–57). While many (I would say all) of those reasons obviously have to do with reader expectations, he performs a convincing review of narratological techniques that indeed seem to express the difference between both types of discourse.

12. Although Andrade lists the physical categories of criminal, he also makes explicit one reservation about them—that they only apply to the poor, and that the criminal rich rarely fit the same types. Andrade does not problematize the matter further, but it was the subject of much controversy at the time. If money, education, and "breeding" could prevent a person from exhibiting his or her fundamental criminal characteristics, the whole endeavor of categorization (based on traits visible to the scientific eye and impossible to hide) was undermined.

13. Although the way in which Galdós uses description in *El crimen del cura Galeote* is quite different from that in *El crimen de la calle de Fuencarral,* and although it is also evident that his thinking about scientific approaches to crime is different in 1889 from what it was in 1886, the seed of his interest in the subject is already present in *Galeote.* Thus, in this text, Galdós uses the occasion of reporting on doctors' assessment of Father Galeote's mental state to reflect on the role of phrenology and phrenopathy in legal proceedings:

> No queda duda ... [de] que Galeote es un ser degenerado.... ¿Está por eso exento de responsabilidad? ¿Hállase la ciencia frenopática lo bastante adelantada para poder determinar dónde acaba la responsabilidad? ¿Se ha llegado a encontrar el punto exacto en que la justicia debe retirarse, poniendo a los criminales en poder de los médicos? ... Antes que éstos [los expertos legales] lleguen a una inteligencia completa con los alienistas ha de pasar mucho tiempo. (179)

> [There is no doubt ... that Galeote is a degenerate being. ... Is he, for this reason, exempt from responsibility? Is phrenopatic science advanced enough to be able to determine when responsibility ends? Has the exact point at which justice should retreat, leaving criminals in the hands of doctors, been found? ... It will be a long while before they (legal experts) reach complete understanding with alienists.]

As Luis Maristany reminds us, in the early 1880s the *Ateneo* had already been the scene of a debate between doctors and magistrates "on the madness of criminals and, if so, their responsibility. The arguments wielded by the alienists were the usual ones with a phrenological basis, rejuvenated by phrenopaths [frenópatas] like the Belgian J. Guislain" ("Lombroso y España," 369). From this time on, "the name of Lombroso ... [begins to] appear very sporadically" (371), although as mentioned in this chapter, the latter becomes more prominent later on in the decade.

14. On an interesting note, Galdós's quarrel with the sentence seems to follow partly from views on the death penalty implicit in some of his early remarks:

> El error en estas materias no es tan grave cuando se exculpa al criminal como cuando se condena al inocente. Repugnante y horrible sería la figura de José Varela, criminal impune y libre de toda pena; la sociedad que tal consintiera sería una sociedad desquiciada. Pero imagínese a Varela inocente y condenado a muerte.... Esto sería mucho peor que la impunidad. ... Lo que resulta de todo esto es que conviene andar con mucho pulso en materias tan delicadas. (17)

> [Error in these matters is not as serious when the criminal is acquitted as when the innocent are convicted. The figure of José Varela, a criminal unpunished and free from all penalty, would be revolting and horrible; any society tolerating this would be a disturbed society. But imagine Varela innocent and sentenced to death.... That would be much worse than impunity.... What follows from all this is that one better wield a steady hand with regard to such delicate issues.]

15. For a detailed analysis of the metafictional structure of both *La incógnita* and *Realidad,* see Linda Willem, "Turning *La incógnita* into *Realidad:* Galdós's Metafictional Magic Trick."

16. Evidently, Galdós, like Freud himself, is an heir to Schopenhauerean and Nietzchean irrationalism, and within this context, discussions of the unconscious had been taking place for some time. As David S. Luft explains, "philosophical irra-

tionalism established sexuality and whatever mind cannot control as philosophical issues: in this tradition sexuality, women, religion, and the unconscious appeared as threats to reason, usually negatively but sometimes positively" ("Science," 93). The implications of the strength (and gendering) of human urges for traditionally understood notions of morality, religion, and consciousness were a central issue for Galdós, and can be seen in both *La incógnita* and, especially, *Realidad,* through their treatment of the character of Augusta vis-à-vis the relationship between Orozco and Federico Viera. This topic goes beyond my specific thesis in this chapter, and deserves more sustained develoment, but suffice it to point out its relation to the new epistemological and ontological paradigms Galdós is approaching in the 1880s and 90s.

## Chapter 3. Literature and Propaganda: Agustín de Foxá's and Ramón J. Sender's Novels of the Civil War

1. José-Carlos Mainer offers a concise enumeration of these novels in his article "La retórica de la obviedad: ideología e intimidad en algunas novelas de guerra"[The Rhetoric of Obviousness: Ideology and Intimacy in Some War Novels]. An informative source for titles, authors, and contexts is also Trapiello, *Las armas y las letras.*

2. These "others" who might lend consensus are those in a position of relative power from which to determine what will, for a certain group, count as literature, that is, the interpretive community—one of the fundamental concepts in Fish's theory. Because of the constraints of my argument, I am not giving due attention to the many nuances of the concept of interpretive community, which in fact subsumes within itself the notions of "text" and "reader" and is the issuing source of the determination of textual facts (what is a literary text?) as well as of the interpretation of what those facts will be taken to "mean" (and how). These concepts are foundationally developed in the essays of *Is There a Text in this Class?*, to which my readers can turn for clarification.

3. One might surely imagine (in the past, present, or future) societies for which the category, or the institution, of "literature" are not relevant and do not exist, but that is obviously not the case for the Western societies within whose contexts I write.

4. It should be noted that this definition of "novels of the Civil War" is a functional one appropriate for my purposes, and others might obviously be coined in the context of different studies—including, for example, novels by foreigners such as Malraux or Orwell, or not strictly limited to the three years of the war period.

5. The complete Spanish edition was preceded by three 1937 foreign editions: an English one, entitled *The War in Spain,* an American one, entitled *Counter-Attack in Spain,* and a French one entitled *Contre-attaque en Espagne.* One chapter, "Primera de acero" [First Steel Company], was also published in Spain in pamphlet form by the Republican Fifth Regiment.

6. Some essentialist approaches mixed both lines, as did, for example, New Criticism, which focused on literature as both a certain type of imaginative creation and a certain structural way of conveying those contents.

7. It will be obvious to my readers that I disagree with the view expressed by

Suleiman in this book that it is the novel that "signals itself" to us as primarily ideological and didactic rather than our choosing to foreground those features and reading it that way—and this is a point to which I shall return. For now, let me emphasize that, whether inherent or perceived, these are the conventions with which we define (or create) a genre called *roman à thèse*, and according to which we determine its place in literary canons.

8. Antonio Varela inscribes the novel within a different genre or mode, that of romance, defined in this way: "Against the backdrop of a Manichean struggle between forces embodying good and evil, is presented the search for self-identification of a hero who incarnates idealism and good" (*Foxá*, 96). While this is certainly an accurate description of the novel's structure, some of the statements that the choice of Romance leads Varela to make seem puzzling. One example is his minimization of the realist aesthetic of the novel because it would be incompatible with Romance:

> Romance's great achievements in European literature tend to belong to precapitalist times. Since the advent of capitalism and the bourgeoisie, realism and psychology have eroded Romance's hold on serious fiction. *Madrid, de corte a checa* as a political novel of the twentieth century bears some of the trappings of realism and psychology in its presentation, but its basic view of the world is that of Romance. Fascism is essentially incompatible with either the realist or the psychological novel as they are normally understood. (97) Another example: "It is not unusual for traditional Romance to reveal truth through magic, but this is too much to ask of a political novel of the twentieth century" (105). The problems Varela finds in his alignment of *Madrid* with the ancient form of Romance are circumvented by making use of a more proximate genre, the *roman à thèse*, and a more proximate mode, melodrama.

9. The idea of the abuse of modern technology by the masses, which coincides with Ortega's arguments in *La rebelión de las masas*, is suggested especially through the sustained attention in the novel's descriptions to the telephone, "aquel sésamo eléctrico" [that electrical Sesame] (27), "la máquina Yost" [the Yost machine] (30), "el metro" [the meter] (32), the telegraph (77), the train (107), "el lente del objetivo" [the camera lens] (145), the radio (263), and in the hospital the "luz nerviosa, violeta, de los rayos X, sobre los cuerpos desnudos" [nervous, violet light of X-Rays on naked bodies] (277), etc. These are in stark opposition to the objects and the style of the upper classes, as when "bajaba entre los monos azules y máuseres don Carlos, viejecito, con su noble cabello blanco y su traje rozado" [Among the blue overalls and mausers came Don Carlos, old, with his noble gray hair and his worn suit] (297), or in the following scene in which José Félix sees literally a war between two centuries:

> José Félix distinguió al maquinista Pacífico . . . arengando a los obreros. Se lanzaban sobre él los guardias de a caballo, con los sables al aire y se oían los cierres metálicos de las tiendas.
> Contempló José Félix la carroza con los caballos encabritados, rodeada de estudiantes irrespetuosos, silbidos y pedradas. Tocó en el hombro a Pedro Otaño.
> —Mira; dos mundos frente a frente. (70–71)

> [José Felix could make out the Pacific's engine driver . . . haranguing the workers. The mounted guards, with their sables out, launched at him, and one could hear the shops' metal locks,
> José Félix watched the coach's horses rearing up, surrounded by disrespectful students, hissing and throwing stones. He tapped Pedro Otaño's shoulder
> —Look; two worlds facing off.]

10. All of the characters associated with the Nationalist side are equally strongly characterized in positive terms. José Félix, for example, is "alto, romántico y generoso" [tall, romantic, and generous] (*Madrid*, 11), so that his physical nature reflects his moral stature. The most favorable descriptions by far are those of José Antonio Primo de Rivera, presented as the model for all young men to follow. He is "joven, guapo y agradable" [young, handsome, and pleasant], and speaks with "metáforas brillantes" [brilliant metaphors] (170). Or, again, "joven, decidido y poeta" [young, resolute, and a poet] who makes José Félix "deslumbrarse por su gallardía" [dazzled by his grace] (195).

11. He had been imprisoned in Madrid after his return from the 18 July Barcelona premiere of his play *La tonta del rizo* [The Fool of the Curl], where he had expressed onstage his support of the rebel Army, yelling "¡Viva España!" Andrés Trapiello recounts the incident in *Las armas y las letras* [Arms and Letters] (104–6).

12. For a study of the ideological content of *La ciudad alegre y confiada* and the way in which it echoes the reception of Benavente's theater by critics, see González del Valle (both *El canon* and "Ideología política").

13. The son of Colonel Moscardó—defender of Toledo's Alcázar—is executed (*Madrid*, 389) because his father fails to surrender, in a clear intertextual allusion to the legend of *Guzmán el Bueno*, whose son was killed by the Moors for the same reason. The incident is mentioned another time, when José Félix "tours" the site, and an improvised guide remarks that "por este teléfono habló Moscardó con su hijo minutos antes de que lo fusilaran, diciéndole que muriera por Dios y por España" [this is the phone from which Moscardó spoke to his son minutes before he was shot, telling him to die for God and for Spain] (412). On the same page, the narrator relays José Felix's profound impression at seeing among the remains the same people who had fought there: "porque era como visitar las ruinas de Numancia y encontrarse a Escipión en las calles de Soria" [because it was like visiting the ruins of Numancia and running into Escipión in the streets of Soria].

14. Suleiman does not envisage the possibility of a *roman à thèse* being written to persuade readers that there is, say, life on the moon, in which case one might imagine the proposition conceived in terms other than those of an ethical duality. As the subtitle of her book clearly states, she equates *roman à thèse* with "ideological novel." Since this is also the type of novel that concerns me in this chapter, I accept her postulation of the structure of confrontation as the basis of the *roman à thèse*.

15. Mary Vásquez has persuasively argued for *Contraataque*'s identity both as a novel—"a complex, ambiguous, and ambivalent work, . . . built on essential conflict and counterposition, which contains many passages of remarkable beauty and power" ("Narrative Voice," 114)—and as fictive autobiography—"a highly purposive piece of autobiographical fiction designed to offer anticipatory protection to the elusive narrator self portrayed, and veiled, therein" ("Ramón Sender," 225). Although some of her reasons for granting the text novelistic status are more compelling than others—I read differently, for example, the contradictions that she sees as evidence of a multiplicity of narrative voices—she is obviously right in noting how existing conventions allow both generic readings.

16. Sender's characterization of José Millán Astray recalls the general's well-known clash with Miguel de Unamuno, on the occasion of a celebration of the *Día de la Hispanidad* (12 October). Millán Astray interrupted Unamuno's address with the cry of "¡Muera la inteligencia!" [Death to intelligence!] (Trapiello, *Las armas*,

44), and Unamuno criticized him as an invalid whose own deficiencies dictated his influence on the country: "A cripple lacking the spiritual greatness of Cervantes, who was a man (not a superman), virile and complete despite his mutilation; a cripple, as I said, lacking that spiritual superiority, tends to feel relieved as the number of cripples around him increases. . . . General Millán Astray would like to create a new Spain . . . in his own image. And, for that reason, he would like to see Spain mutilated" (qtd. in Trapiello, *Las armas*, 43).

17. Sender's favorable portrayal of communists in *Contraataque* might appear problematic when compared with biographical fact. As Mary S. Vásquez and Andrés Trapiello both document, Sender becomes involved in bitter dispute with the communists soon after the war's outbreak, and remains critical of them throughout his life. This is not, however, the position evident in the novel, which argues for the superior commitment and efficacy of communists over any other Republican group.

18. The chronology of events, especially regarding Sender's cognizance of his wife's death, is one of the more problematic aspects of *Contraataque*, if one attempts to read it for its historical truth. The novel suggests that Sender learned of the assasination in December of 1937, while participating in the defense of Madrid. This timeframe has been disputed by his son, Ramón Sender Barayón, in his book *A Death in Zamora*. Sender Jr. writes that his father knew about his mother's death in early November, and that later the same month he married his second wife, Isabel—a fact not mentioned in *Contraataque* or anywhere else by the writer.

19. Mary Vásquez suggests that self-justification—with regard both to responsibility for his wife's death and to accusations of cowardice and desertion (Trapiello, *Las armas*, 283)—may be the central impulse marking *Contraataque:*

> Ramón Sender Barayón in *A Death in Zamora* quotes Communist General Enrique Lister [*sic*], who in his book *Nuestra guerra* accuses Sender of desertion. The possible veracity of such an accusation has been bruited about in vague terms for years; Francisco Carrasquer offers a heated defense of Sender in his chapter "El raro impacto de Sender en la crítica literaria española." Versions of the accusation place the alleged event in November. An unnamed respondent to Sender Barayón's request in *El País* for pertinent information confirmed the desertion in a letter to Sender Barayón. Might not Sender have sought self-vindication through *Contraataque*, showing himself to be a loyal partisan, part of the Republican unity he so erroneously portrays, and certainly no enemy of the Communists? . . . The text's dual depiction of the Republic's moral right and powerlessness may [also] represent an attempt to assuage what must have been very considerable guilt surrounding the death of Amparo Barayón. Hence the possible textual altering of the date when the extratextual Sender learned of her assassination and the loudness of textual silence with respect to the events described in Sender Barayón's book: the question of Elizabeth and her child. ("Ramón Sender," 225)

20. Although the particular image in the engraving "Yo lo vi" does not represent violent action (as others in the series do), in it Goya resorts most visibly to the convention of the affirmation of personal testimony—the totalizing, privileged vantage point of the artist—to confer a sense of reality and documentary value to his depiction of the war.

21. The two best theoretical accounts of melodrama are, in my opinion, those of Heilman and Brooks, to which the reader can turn for more information on the subject.

22. Political agitation propaganda would generally be pre-revolutionary or revo-

lutionary, preceding post-revolutionary sociological integration propaganda, which would seek to consolidate a value system. In other words, some works of propaganda exist in tension with the majoritary or "official" values of their society, whereas others act to solidify them.

23. The unity and efficacy of Republican forces is affirmed categorically, despite the fact that it is disproven, not only by historical accounts, but by the narrator's own assertions elsewhere. He complains, for example, of the lack of communication between military staff and fighters at the beginning of the war, and shows how two offensives in which he participated were threatened by faulty organization. Additionally, the preferential treatment he gives to communists, in contrast especially with anarchists, undermines his claims to unity and equality of investment.

24. I say that literature "can be" antipodal to propaganda, because Foulkes acknowledges the possibility that literature may itself work as propaganda or "conformist art" (*Literature and Propaganda*, 59). It nevertheless also has the capacity to be "subversive art," setting in motion precisely the distancing resources that can render propaganda useless.

25. Stanley Fish defines the function of criticism and theory as precisely that of persuading, contrasting in this way the New Critical model of demonstration with his proposed model of persuasion:

> In the first model critical activity is controlled by free-standing objects in relation to which its accounts are either adequate or inadequate; in the other model critical activity is constitutive of its object. In one model the self must be purged of its prejudices and presuppositions so as to see clearly a text that is independent of them; in the other, prejudicial or perspectival perception is all there is, and the question is from which of a number of equally interested perspectives the text will be constituted. In one model change is (at least ideally) progressive, a movement toward a more accurate account of a fixed and stable entity; in the other, change occurs when one perspective dislodges another and brings with it entities that had not before been available. (*Text*, 365–66)

26. In referring to the literary field I allude to all the elements included in Pierre Bourdieu's sociological theory about the fields of cultural production, which I detail in chapter 2. Bourdieu seeks to clarify the relationships of interdependence that exist between "high" and "low" production, the structures of interest that support apparently autonomous spheres, and the struggles between the established or consecrated figures and the ones that seek to replace them.

27. The case of futurism is one example, among many possible ones, of how an avant-garde movement can find an ideological affinity with fascism's defense of energy, force, the fascination with the machine. The contradiction between conservative traditionalism and revolutionary impulse reveals itself most evidently in the strange alliance of forces reunited on Franco's side during the Spanish Civil War.

28. For the sake of fairness, I should stress the exception of Mary S. Vásquez's two articles on *Contraataque*. Admittedly, I disagree with her contention that the contradictions in the novel are evidence of a multiplicity of narrative voices—she finds four—and believe rather that they can be productively read without recourse to the artificial division of a single narrative that contains no obvious markers of voice change. Nevertheless, and although her readings of the novel hardly break the large critical silence that has surrounded it, she addresses it as a complex, multiple text worthy of critical attention. Antonio Varela has similarly selected *Madrid de corte a*

*checa* for attention, although he stresses the novel's simplicity and overt dualism, and manifestly considers it para-literary.

## Chapter 4. Eroticism and Canonicity at the Spanish *Fines de Siglo*

1. "'Horrenda Adoración': The 'Feminism' of Felipe Trigo," *Hispania* 76 (1993): 224–34.

2. The issue of Trigo's "canonicity" was, of course, hotly debated. Fernández Cifuentes documents the process by which Trigo, who was coldly received by some intellectuals from the beginning of his career, was increasingly displaced from the canonical, so that in 1917 Alfonso Reyes can declare about his suicidal-writer character (based on Trigo) that he is "at the margins of, or outside, literature" (89). While the eventual relegation of his work had to do mostly with the sexual theme, some writers rejected him for his excessive reliance on an *arte comprometido* concerned more with certain utopias than with the ideal of beauty.

3. In "Horrenda Adoración," I pointed out how Trigo admires an idealized conception of women's bodies, while showing an implicit (and sometimes explicit) disgust for actual female bodily attributes. Trigo dwells amply on the delineation of what James Iffland calls "creaturality": "all that which has to do with the mortal or physical limits of men's [and in this case women's] existence . . . illness, aging and decay, . . . the acts of eating, digesting, defecating, urinating, belching, coughing, breaking wind, copulating, menstruating, sweating, sleeping, snoring, and so forth" (Iffland, *Quevedo*, 61–64). In his utopia of erotic plenitude, men and women would nevertheless be housed separately, and men would witness neither women's normal habits of hygiene nor the childbearing process. Men would be effectively "sealed off" from any physical contact other than sexual intercourse with women at their cleanest, most beautiful selves.

4. In her article on *Las edades de Lulú*, Lou Charnon-Deutsch rejects the text as "extremely disturbing" ("Regarding," 302) in its apparent reversal of the bildungsroman pattern—instead of the character's (and all women's) sexual progression, the critic sees in the novel a "pitiful regression" (307). This opinion is based on the assumption that Lulú's masochism and rejection of her adult self represent "the female subject's submission and fragmentation" (313) and thus have negative "political consequences" and "implications for female subjectivity" (303).

Writing about Mercedes Abad, James Mandrell echoes Charnon-Deutsch's point about women's erotic/pornographic writing in Spain. Mandrell departs from the personal observation that "all [erotica by women] seem—to me—to be *for* men, since all are implicated in the general economy of exchange that is literature" ("Mercedes Abad," 280). He concludes that "if erotica, regardless of who writes it, is written *for* men, then perhaps it is, in the end as in the beginning, pornography, and not a text of love" (281). While both critics write engaging accounts of recent erotic writing by Spanish women, they also base their assertions on a notion of female desire and female interests that subordinates sexual pleasure to politics or "love." As Juan Duchesne would reply, Lulú's adventures could not be more "politically incorrect" (if we were to demand a transparent relationship between traditional political feminism and women's writing) ("Sorprenderla mirando," 66).

5. As mentioned earlier, Andrew Ross studies historical responses to pornography that denounce it on the basis of "singleness of intention" (*No Respect,* 229) or of a necessarily produced effect. Referring specifically to George Steiner's argument, he critiques the type of liberal (as opposed to "liberatory") position that rejects pornography on the aesthetic grounds that it determines certain readings and limits readers' freedom: "The familiar Cold Warrior fear that popular culture already *contains* our response to it, and that it therefore has 'no respect for the reader's' imaginative rights, is presented as a brutish threat wielded by consumer capitalism and monopoly statism alike. Only Literature with its plurality of high intentions allows us to respond with the imaginative freedom that we are accustomed, in the West, to enjoy" (230).

## Chapter 5. Manuel Vázquez Montalbán and the Spanish Literary Institution

1. Although by quoting Fromm I am obviously echoing the cited parts of his criticism, this should not be taken as a blanket agreement with his general theses. In particular, the characterization of critical and cultural theory as a "self-protective . . . monopoly" whose "real agenda" is "power and success in the academy" made by this "independent scholar" (*Academic Capitalism,* Preface, no page numbers) leads him to some conclusions that are, in my view, erroneous. Fromm ultimately does not, as he himself recommends, leave behind the either/or mentality, but rather privileges the authenticity of nonspecialist reading. He only concedes critics a place as intermediaries and helpers (between the work and its truer readers), and resents the use of a specialized professional vocabulary—something for which he probably would not fault a natural or even a social scientist. Additionally, he takes the simple fact of professionalization—that the study and teaching of literature are a professor's job, for which he or she might reasonably expect remuneration and professional advancement—as evidence of truth-obscuring self-interest and "bourgeoisification" (187).

2. In *The Intellectuals and the Masses,* John Carey has traced the development between 1880 and 1939 of the opposition between the intellectuals and the masses created by European thought, and already observable in Alcalá Galiano's statement. In his elaboration of the general thesis that "modernist literature and art can be seen as a hostile reaction to the unprecedentedly large reading public created by nineteenth-century educational reforms" (preface, no page number), Carey makes special reference to the influential philosophy of José Ortega y Gasset as formulated in *La rebelión de las masas.*

3. As McLaughlin reminds us, Balzac was the first French writer to serialize a novel in a journal, and he also considered, in 1833, the possibility of establishing a periodical subscription company. His counterpart in England was Dickens, who inaugurated "the rise of literary mass culture" (*Writing,* 5) with his own *The Pickwick Papers*. Nevertheless, my readers will have noted that I did not establish a parallel in chapter 1 between Ayguals, Fernández y González, and the other Spanish serial nov-

elists mentioned and these two European authors. The reason is the different development of the novel in their different countries. While by the 1830s, as the popularity of serialization began, England and France already had established novelistic traditions, this was not the case in Spain, with the result of the simultaneous institution both of the genre and of the format. This fact—among others, such as the convergence of the author and the publisher in the same individual—prevents the Spanish serial novelists from developing a self-conscious view of their work and of the "paradox" of literary commerce resembling that of Balzac and Dickens. As I argued, such a view will appear in the Spanish literary field with Benito Pérez Galdós.

4. I call *Crónica sentimental de España* "accidental" because of Vázquez Montalbán's anecdote of how, after being discarded, the project was finally (and unexpectedly) written in two weeks at the request of a publisher (*La literatura*, 133–37).

5. *Memoria y deseo* is the title under which Vázquez Montalbán first collected his so-far complete poetry, and it includes the terms he posits as the ultimate keys to his work: "La Memoria como reivindicación frente al demonio del olvido y el Deseo como eufemismo de la esperanza, de la Historia si se quiere: he aquí la tensión dialéctica fundamental de todo cuanto he escrito" [Memory as vindication before the demon of oblivion, and Desire as euphemism for hope, for History if you will: this is the fundamental dialectical tension in everything I've written] (*La literatura*, 137).

6. *El escriba sentado* and *La literatura en la construcción de la ciudad democrática* are themselves conceived of as two parts of one larger plan. Although they differ in format—the first volume collects twenty-six articles, mostly on other authors/texts but revealing of Vázquez Montalbán's philosophy; the second is divided in several chapters loosely connected by the theme of the city as utopia and the role of literature in its construction, with much more direct self-criticism and reflection—the two works together "constituyen la especial biografía de un escritor" as a "serie de reflexiones sobre la operación de escribir en relación con el tiempo histórico" [constitute the special biography of a writer [as a] series of reflections on the operation of writing in relation to historical time] (*El escriba*, 9).

7. According to Bourdieu,

> One cannot give a full account of the relationship obtaining at a given moment between the space of positions [field] and the space of dispositions [habitus], and, therefore, of the set of *social trajectories* (or constructed biographies), unless one establishes the configuration, at the moment, and at the various critical turning-points in each career, of the space of available possibilities (in particular, the economic and symbolic hierarchy of the genres, schools, styles, manners, subjects, etc.), the social value attached to each of them, and also the meaning and value they received for the different agents or classes of agents in terms of the socially constituted categories of perception and appreciation they applied to them. (*Field*, 65)

8. Throughout this chapter I have been advocating attention to the nonspecialist reader, and to the reader or consumer him or herself in literary studies. This approach is clearly related to reader-response theory, and my repeated use of Stanley Fish's arguments throughout the book reveals my debt to certain forms of what has been known by that name. I should point out, however, that many models of reader-response theory have been concerned with the narratee, the implied reader, or a paradigmatic competent or informed reader. Furthermore, in whichever of those guises, the reader has most often been addressed as the actualizer or creator of the meaning or value of a *text*. Consequently, though I would not posit a rupture between

my own line of thinking and the lessons of reader-response, it is important to insist on the centrality of the approach to literature as a system or field within which texts are one of several fundamental components.

9. One such "happening" is the celebration in Madrid of the twenty-fifth anniversary of the Carvalho series, documented by the newspaper *ABC* on 21 February 1997. On this occasion Vázquez Montalbán announced the intended death of the character and the novels by the year 2000. Faced with the threat, his characters "came to life" (played by actors and public figures Pepe Martín, Maruja Torres, and Rosa Regás) to rebel against the author and demand their rights.

10. This characterization of Maugham does not imply that Vázquez Montalbán aligns himself with the position of this writer in the canonical spectrum. Although he does not say so explicitly, the passage might indicate that he would liken himself rather to Graham Greene, or perhaps with either of the two writers, depending on the work in question or the level at which he is read:

> [Virginia Woolf] representa el prestigio de "lo literario," es una autora emblemática de la calidad y, por lo tanto, leerla contagia de esa calidad. Evelyn Waugh es el escritor sutil y atípico, inicialmente sólo valorado por los muy selectos, aún no patrimonial como la Woolf o James Joyce. Graham Greene es el buen escritor de éxito popular, que no incurre en las fórmulas del bestseller, pero que está dotado del don de la *comunicabilidad,* lo que le permite una gran audiencia. Somerset Maugham era . . . el prototipo de autor de bestsellers de una cierta dignidad literaria, conectado con los subgéneros de tradición popular, pero regalando a sus lectores la condición de partícipes de una relación literaria. Por debajo de [estos cuatro autores] . . . podrían contabilizarse centenares de autores de literatura de pasto, cultivadores de fórmulas de segura audiencia y sin ninguna ambición de pasar a la historia de la literatura. (*La literatura,* 175)

> [Virginia Woolf represents the prestige of the "literary," she is an author emblematic of quality and, therefore, reading her transmits that quality. Evelyn Waugh is the subtle and atypical writer, initially valued only by the very select, not yet canonical like Woolf or James Joyce. Graham Greene is the good writer with popular success, who does not fall into the bestseller's formulas, but is endowed with the gift of *communicability,* which affords him a large audience. Somerset Maugham was . . . the prototype of the author of bestsellers of a certain literary dignity, connected with the subgenres of popular lineage, but granting his readers the status of participants in a literary relationship. Below these (four authors) . . . one could count hundreds of writers of ordinary literature, cultivators of surefire formulas, and without any ambition of passing into the history of literature.]

# BIBLIOGRAPHY

Acereda, Alberto. "La actual novela erótica española: el caso de Consuelo García." *Monographic Review/Revista monográfica* 7 (1991): 157–66.

Adams, Hazard. "Canons: Literary Criteria/Power Criteria." *Critical Inquiry* 14, no. 4 (1988): 748–66.

Alborg, Concha. "Ana Rossetti y el relato erótico." *Hispanic Journal* 15 (1994): 369–79.

Alcalá Galiano, José. "El género bufo y laliteratura dramática." *Revista de España* 28 (1871): 188–211.

Aldaraca, Bridget. "'El ángel del hogar': The Cult of Domesticity in Nineteenth-Century Spain." In *Theory and Practice of Feminist Literary* Criticism, ed. Gabriela Mora and Karen S. Van Hooft, 62–87. Ypsilanti, Mich.: Bilingual Press, 1982.

Altick, Richard D. *Deadly Encounters: Two Victorian Sensations*. Philadelphia: University Pennsylvania Press, 1986.

Altieri, Charles. *Canons and Consequences: Reflections on the Ethical Force of Imaginative Ideals*. Evanston: Northwestern University Press, 1990.

Altisent, Marta. "El erotismo en la actual narrativa española." *Cuadernos hispanoamericanos* 468 (1989): 128–44.

Amell, Samuel. "Literatura e ideología: El caso de la novela negra en la España actual." *Monographic Review/Revista monográfica* 3 (1987): 192–201.

Amorós, Andrés. *Subliteraturas*. Barcelona: Ariel, 1974.

Anderson Imbert, Enrique. "Un drama ibseniano de Galdós." *Sur* 16, no. 167 (1948): 26–31.

Andrade, Benito Mariano. *Estudios de antropología criminal espiritualista*. Madrid: Rivadeneyra, 1899.

Andreu, Alicia. *Galdós y la literatura popular*. Madrid: Sociedad General Española de Librería, 1982.

Arenal, Concepción. *La mujer del porvenir*. Ed. Vicente de Santiago Mulas. Madrid: Castalia, 1993.

Armstrong, Nancy. *Desire and Domestic Fiction: A Political History of the Novel*. New York: Oxford University Press, 1987.

Ashley, Barbara Renchkovsky, and David Ashley. "Sex as Violence: The Body against Intimacy." *International Journal of Women's Studies* 7 (1984): 352–71.

Ayguals de Izco, Wenceslao. *La bruja de Madrid*. 1849–50. Barcelona: Taber, 1969. Reprint, with an introduction by Joaquín Marco, Complete original title: *Pobres y ricos, o la bruja de Madrid*.

———. *María, o la hija de un jornalero*. 1845. 2 vols. Reprint, Madrid: Miguel Guijarro, 1868.

———. *La Marquesa de Bellaflor, o el niño de la Inclusa*. 2 vols. Madrid: Ayguals de Izco, 1846–47.

Aymes, Jean-René. "La imagen de Eugène Sue en España (primera mitad del siglo XIX)." In *Del romanticismo al realismo: Actas del I Coloquio de la Sociedad de Literatura Española del Siglo XIX*, ed. Díaz Larios, Luis F., and Enrique Miralles, 391–402. Barcelona: Universitat de Barcelona, 1998.

Baguley, David. "The Nature of Naturalism." In *Naturalism in the European Novel: New Critical Perspectives*, ed. Brian Nelson. New York: Berg, 1992.

Bakhtin, M. M. *The Dialogic Imagination*. Ed. Michael Holquist. Trans. Caryl Emerson and Michael Holquist. Austin: University of Texas Press, 1987.

Barnet, Sylvan, and Hugo Bedau. *Critical Thinking, Reading, and Writing: A Brief Guide to Argument*. 3rd ed. Boston and New York: Bedford/St. Martin's Press, 1999.

Benítez, Rubén. *Ideología del folletín español: Wenceslao Ayguals de Izco (1801–1902)*. Madrid: José Porrúa, 1979.

Benjamin, Walter. *Illuminations: Essays and Reflections*. Ed. Hannah Arendt. Trans. Harry Zohn. New York: Schocken Books, 1985.

Berenguer, Angel, ed. *Los estrenos teatrales de Galdós en la crítica de su tiempo*. Madrid: Consejería de Cultura, 1988.

Berger, Arthur Asa. *Signs in Contemporary Culture: An Introduction to Semiotics*. New York: Longman, 1984.

Berkowitz, H. Chonon. "Galdós' *Electra* in Paris." *Hispania* 22 (1939): 31–40.

Beser, Sergio. "La crítica en la segunda mitad del siglo XIX." In *Leopoldo Alas: crítico literario*. Madrid: Gredos, 1968.

Beverley, John. *Subalternity and Representation: Arguments in Cultural Theory*. Durham: Duke University Press, 1999.

Blanco, Alda. "But Are They Any Good?" *Revista de estudios hispánicos* 23 (1993): 463–70.

———. *Escritoras virtuosas: Narradoras de la domesticidad en la España isabelina*. Granada: Universidad de Granada/Caja General de Ahorros de Granada, 2001.

Blanquat, Josette. "Au temps d'*Electra:* Documents galdosiens." *Bulletin Hispanique* 68 (1966): 253–308.

Blasco Ibáñez, Vicente. *El fantasma de las alas de oro*. Barcelona: Alba, 1997.

Borges, Jorge Luis. *Obras completas*. Buenos Aires: Emecé, 1974.

Botrel, Jean-François. *Libros, prensa y lectura en la España del siglo XIX*. Trans. David Torra Ferrer. Madrid: Fundación Germán Sánchez Ruipérez, 1993.

———. "La novela por entregas: unidad de creación y de consumo." In *Creación y público en la literatura española contemporánea*, ed. Jean-François Botrel and Serge Salaün. Madrid: Castalia, 1974.

Bourdieu, Pierre. *The Field of Cultural Production*. Ed. Randal Johnson. New York: Columbia University Press, 1993.

———. "Fourth Lecture. Universal Corporatism: The Role of Intellectuals in the Modern World." *Poetics Today* 12, no. 4 (1991): 655–69.

---. *In Other Words: Essays Towards a Reflexive Sociology.* Trans. Matthew Adamson. Stanford, Calif.: Stanford University Press, 1990.

---. "Principles of a Sociology of Cultural Works." In *Explanation and Value in the Arts,* ed Laim Kemal and Ivan Gaskell, 173–89. New York: Cambridge University Press, 1993.

---. *The Rules of Art: Genesis and Structure of the Literary Field.* Ed. and Trans. Susan Emanuel. Stanford, Calif.: Stanford University Press, 1996.

Bozal, Valeriano. "Arte de masas y arte popular (1928–1937)." *Cuadernos hispanoamericanos* 435–36 (1986): 745–61.

Brey, Gérard. "Práctica del folletín en la prensa obrera española (1881–1910)." In *Hacia una literatura del pueblo: del follenín a la novela,* ed. Brigitte Magnien, Barcelona: Anthropos, 1995.

Brooks, Peter. *Body Work: Objects of Desire in Modern Narrative.* Cambridge: Harvard University Press, 1993.

---. *The Melodramatic Imagination: Balzac, Henry James, Melodrama, and the Mode of Excess.* New York: Columbia University Press, 1985.

---. *Reading for the Plot: Design and Intention in Narrative.* Cambridge: Harvard University Press, 1996.

Brown, Frieda, et al., eds. *Rewriting the Good Fight: Critical Essays on the Literature of the Spanish Civil War.* East Lansing: Michigan State University Press, 1989.

Brown, Joan, and Crista Johnson. "Required Reading: The Canon in Spanish and Spanish American Literature." *Hispania* 81 (1998): 1–19.

Brown, Reginald. *La novela española, 1700–1850.* Madrid: Dirección General de Archivos y Bibliotecas, 1953.

Brunori, Vittorio. *Sueños y mitos de la literatura de masas.* Trans. Joan Giner. Barcelona: Gustavo Gili, 1980.

Bueno, Manuel. "La Eva futura." *Revista nueva* 2 (August–December 1899): 193–97.

Bürger, Peter. "The Problem of Aesthetic Value." Trans. Shaun Whiteside. In *Literary Theory Today,* ed. Peter Collier and Helga Geyer-Ryan, 23–34. Ithaca: Cornell University Press, 1990.

Butler, Judith. *Gender Trouble: Feminism and the Subversion of Identity.* New York: Routledge, 1990.

Cabañas, Pablo. "Comella visto por Galdós." *Revista de literatura* 26 (1966): 91–99.

Campos, Jorge. "Nota sobre dos capítulos de *La desheredada.*" *Estudios escénicos* 18 (1974): 165–72.

Carey, John. *The Intellectuals and the Masses: Pride and Prejudice among the Literary Intelligentsia, 1880–1939.* London: Faber and Faber, 1992.

---. "Revolted by the Masses." *Times Literary Supplement* 34, 12–18 January 1990, 34.

Carmona González, Ángeles. *La mujer en la novela por entregas del siglo XIX.* Sevilla: Caja San Fernando, 1990.

Carnero, Guillermo. "Sobre el canon literario español dieciochesco." *Insula* 600 (1996): 12–14.

Carney, Hal. "The Two Versions of Galdós' *La loca de la casa.*" *Hispania* 44 (1961): 438–40.

Carrillo, V., et al. *L'Infralittérature en Espagne aux XIXe et XXe siécles*. Grenoble: Presses Universitaires, 1977.

Casalduero, Joaquín. "*Alceste:* Volver a la vida." *Estudios escénicos,* 18 (1974): 113–30.

Cate-Arries, Francie. "Lost in the Language of Culture: Manuel Vázquez Montalbán's Novel Detection." *Revista de estudios hispánicos* 22 (1988): 47–56.

Catena, Elena. "Circunstancias temporales de la *Electra* de Galdós." *Estudios escénicos,* 18 (1974): 79–112.

Cawelti, John. *Adventure, Mystery, and Romance: Formula Stories as Art and Popular Culture.* Chicago: University of Chicago Press, 1976.

———. "The Concept of Formula in the Study of Popular Literature." *Journal of Popular Culture* 3 (1969): 381–90.

———. "Notes toward an Aesthetic of Popular Culture." *Journal of Popular Culture* 5 (1971): 255–68.

Charnon-Deutsch, Lou. "On Desire and Domesticity in Nineteenth-Century Women's Novels." *Revista canadiense de estudios hispánicos* 14 (1990): 395–414.

———. *Narratives of Desire: Nineteenth-Century Spanish Fiction by Women.* University Park: Pennsylvania State University Press, 1994.

———. "Regarding the Pornographic Subject in *Las edades de Lulú.*" *Letras peninsulares* 6, no. 2–3 (1993–94): 301–19.

———. "Voyeurism, Pornography, and *La Regenta.*" *Modern Language Studies* 19, no. 4 (1989): 93–101.

———. "When the Canon Is Not (Good) Enough." *Revista de estudios hispánicos* 23 (1993): 471–79.

Claudín, Víctor. "Vázquez Montalbán y la novela policiaca española." *Cuadernos hispanoamericanos* 416 (1985): 157–66.

Collier, Peter, and Helga Geyer-Ryan, eds. *Literary Theory Today.* Ithaca: Cornell University Press, 1990.

Colmeiro, José F. "La narrativa policiaca postmodernista de Manuel Vázquez Montalbán." *Anales de la literatura española contemporánea* 14 (1989): 11–32.

———. *La novela policiaca española: teoría e historia crítica.* Barcelona: Anthropos, 1994.

Colmeiro, José F., et al., eds. *Spain Today: Essays on Literature, Culture, Society.* Hanover, N.H.: Dartmouth College Dept. of Spanish and Portuguese, 1995.

Compitello, Malcolm Allan. "De la metanovela a la novela: Manuel Vázquez Montalbán y los límites de la vanguardia española contemporánea." In *Prosa hispánica de vanguardia,* ed. Fernando Burgos. Madrid: Orígenes, 1986.

———. "Spain's *Nueva Novela Negra* and the Question of Form." *Monographic Review/Revista monográfica* 3 (1987): 182–91.

Connor, Stephen. "On and Of Literary Value: A Reply to Antony Easthope." *Textual Practice* 5, no. 3 (1991): 326–33.

———. *Theory and Cultural Value.* Oxford: Blackwell, 1992.

Cornea, Paul. "Critique comparée et la question du canon." *Synthesis* 21 (1994): 35–44.

Costa, Luis F. "La nueva novela negra española." *Monographic Review/Revista monográfica* 3 (1987): 298–305.

Craig, David, and Michael Egan. *Extreme Situations: Literature and Crisis from the Great War to the Atom Bomb.* New York: Barnes & Noble, 1979.

Davis, Lennard J. *Factual Fictions: The Origins of the English Novel.* New York: Columbia University Press, 1983.

Dean, Carolyn. "Pornography, Literature, and the Redemption of Virility in France, 1880–1930." *Differences* 5, no. 2 (1993): 62–91.

DeJean, Joan, and Nancy K. Miller, eds. *Displacements: Women, Tradition, Literatures in French.* Baltimore: John Hopkins University Press, 1990.

Dendle, Brian J. "Galdós, Ayguals de Izco, and the Hellenic Inspiration of *Marianela*." In *Papers on Romance Literary Relations,* Marie Wellington, 1–11. Elmhurst: Elmhurst College Press, 1974.

Derrida, Jacques. *Archive Fever: A Freudian Impression.* Trans. Eric Prenowitz. Chicago: University of Chicago Press, 1996.

Díaz Diocaretz, Myriam, and Iris Zavala, eds. *Discurso erótico y discurso transgresor en la cultura peninsular: siglos XI al XX.* Madrid: Ediciones Tuero, 1992.

Díez-Borque, José María. *Literatura y cultura de masas: Estudios de la novela subliteraria.* Madrid: Al Borak, 1972.

Doménech, Ricardo. "En busca del teatro de Galdós." *Estudios escénicos,* 18 (1974): 11–12.

———. "Etica y política en el teatro de Galdós. Aproximación a *Casandra* y *Sor Simona*." *Estudios escénicos,* 18 (1974): 223–49.

———. Introduction to *Quien mal hace, bien no espere,* by Benito Pérez Galdós. *Estudios escénicos* 18 (1974): 253–64.

———, ed. *Estudios escénicos* 18 (1974). Special issue dedicated to the theater of Benito Pérez Galdós.

Dovrin, Karin. *Road of Propaganda: The Semantics of Biased Communication.* New York: Philosophical Library, 1959.

Doyle, Arthur Conan. *A Study in Scarlet.* <http://www.literature.org/authors/doyle-arthur-conan/study-in-scarlet/>.

Duchesne, Juan. "Sorprenderla mirando: Porno-pedagogía en Sade y Almudena Grandes." *Nómada* 1 (1995): 51–66.

During, Lisabeth. "Clues and Intimations: Freud, Holmes, Foucault." *Cultural Critique* 36 (1997): 29–53.

Easthope, Antony. "Literary Value Again: A Reply to Stephen Connor." *Textual Practice* 5, no. 3 (1991): 334–36.

———. "The Question of Literary Value." *Textual Practice* 4, no. 3 (1990): 376–89.

Echegaray, José de. *Recuerdos.* 3 vols. Madrid: Ruiz Hermanos, 1917.

———. *Teatro escogido.* Ed. Armando Lázaro Ros. Madrid: Aguilar, 1957.

——— *El crimen de la calle de Fuencarral: Extracto y juicio del proceso con la carta del exdirector de la cárcel modelo, D. José Millán Astray, en que pide copia de lo publicado en "El país" por el Verdadero Estudiante.* Madrid: Tip. Manuel Ginés Hernández, 1888.

——— *El crimen de la calle de Fuencarral: Juicio oral.* [Madrid], n.d., n.p.

Ellul, Jacques. *Propaganda: The Formation of Men's Attitudes.* Trans. Konrad Kellen and Jean Lerner. New York: Alfred A. Knopf, 1965.

Elton, Willa Sack. "Autocensura del drama galdosiano." *Estudios escénicos*, 18 (1974): 139–54.

Enríquez de Salamanca, Cristina. "Calidad/capacidad: valor estético y teoría política en la España del siglo XIX." *Revista de estudios hispánicos* 23 (1993): 449–61.

———. "The Question of the Political Subject in Nineteenth-Century Spanish Domestic Discourse." *Today: Essays on Literature, Culture, Society*, ed. José F. Colmeiro et al., 103–12. In *Spain* Hanover, N.H.: Dartmouth College Dept. of Spanish and Portuguese, 1995.

Epstein, E. J. *Between Fact and Fiction: The Problem of Journalism*. New York: Vintage Books, 1975.

Even-Zohar, Itamar. "Literature as Goods, Literature as Tools." <http://www.tau.ac.il/~itamarez/papers/lit-g-t.htm>.

———. *Polysystem Studies*. Special issue of *Poetics Today* 11, no. 1 (1990): 27–94. <http://www.tau.ac.il/~itamarez/papers/>.

———. "The Role of Literature in the Making of the Nations of Europe: A Socio-Semiotic Examination." *Applied Semiotics/Sémiotique Appliquée* 1 (1996): 20–30. <http://www.tau.ac.il/~itamarez/papers/>.

Fernández Cifuentes, Luis. *Teoría y mercado de la novela en España: del 98 a la República*. Madrid: Gredos, 1982.

Fernández Gutiérrez, José María. "El lugar de *Jarrapellejos* en el pensamiento de Felipe Trigo." *Revista de estudios extremeños* 44 (1989): 181–205.

Fernández y González, Manuel. *Los desheredados (desventuras de la vida)*. 1857. 2 vols. Reprint, Madrid: Manini Hermanos, 1865.

———. *Los hijos perdidos, segunda parte de Los desheredados*. 2 vols. Madrid: Manini Hermanos, 1865–66.

Ferreras, Juan Ignacio. *La novela por entregas, 1840–1900*. Madrid: Taurus, 1972.

Finkenthal, Stanley. "The Social Dimensions of Galdós' Theater." *Hispania* 59 (1976): 442–49.

Fish, Stanley. *Doing What Comes Naturally: Change, Rhetoric, and the Practice of Theory in Literary and Legal Studies*. Durham: Duke University Press, 1992.

———. *Is there a Text in this Class? The Authority of Interpretive Communities*. Cambridge: Harvard University Press, 1980.

Flores, Antonio. *Fe, esperanza y caridad*. 4th ed. 2 vols. Madrid and Paris: Mellado, 1857.

Foucault, Michel. *The Archaeology of Knowledge and the Discourse on Language*. Trans. A. M. Sheridan Smith. New York: Pantheon Books, 1972.

———. *The History of Sexuality: An Introduction*. Trans. Robert Hurley. Vol. 1 of *The History of Sexuality*. New York: Vintage, 1990.

———. *Power/Knowledge: Selected Interviews and Other Writings, 1972–1977*. Ed. Colin Gordon. Trans. Colin Gordon et al. New York: Pantheon Books, 1980.

———. *The Use of Pleasure*. Trans. Robert Hurley. Vol. 2 of *The History of Sexuality*. New York: Vintage, 1990.

Foulkes, A. Peter. *Literature and Propaganda*. London: Methuen, 1983.

Franc, Isabel. *Entre todas las mujeres*. Barcelona: Tusquets (La sonrisa vertical), 1992.

Fromm, Harold. *Academic Capitalism and Literary Value.* Athens: University of Georgia Press, 1991.

Frow, John. *Cultural Studies and Cultural Value.* Oxford: Clarendon Press, 1995.

Fuentes, Víctor. "More than Three Forms of Distortion in 20th-Century Spanish Literary Historiography: Counterpoint Alternatives." In *Spain Today: Essays on Literature, Culture, Society,* ed. José F. Colmeiro et al. 21–33. Hanover, N.H.: Dartmouth College Dept. of Spanish and Portuguese, 1995.

Ganivet, Angel. *Idearium español.* Madrid: Victoriano Suárez, 1915.

García Gual, Carlos. "Sobre el canon de los clásicos antiguos." *Insula* 600 (1996): 5–7.

García Lara, Fernando. *El lugar de la novela erótica española.* Granada: Excma. Diputación Provincial, 1986.

———. "El sentido de una recuperación: Felipe Trigo." *Cuadernos hispanoamericanos* 332 (1978): 224–39.

García Lorenzo, Luciano. "Bibliografía teatral galdosiana." *Estudios escénicos,* 18 (1974): 215–22.

———. "Galdós desciende a los infiernos." *Estudios escénicos,* 18 (1974): 195–202.

———. *La novela del siglo XIX.* Vols. 23 and 24 of *Literatura española en imágenes.* Madrid: La Muralla, 1973.

Gaspar, Enrique. *Problema.* Madrid: J. Rodríguez, 1881.

Genette, Gérard. *Fiction and Diction.* Trans. Catherine Porter. Ithaca, N.Y.: Cornell University Press, 1993.

Gil, Alfonso. "Notas e impresiones acerca del teatro de Benito Pérez Galdós." *Estudios escénicos,* 18 (1974): 155–64.

Gil, Ildefonso-Manuel. "Dos encuentros con *El abuelo.*" *Estudios escénicos,* 18 (1974): 73–78.

Godzich, Wlad, and Nicholas Spadaccini. "Introduction: The Course of Literature in Nineteenth-Century Spain." *The Crisis of Institutionalized Literature in Spain.* Minneapolis: Prisma Institute, 1988.

Gold, Hazel. "Back to the Future: Criticism, the Canon, and the Nineteenth-Century Spanish Novel." *Hispanic Review* 58 (1990): 179–204.

Goldman, Peter. "Toward a Sociology of the Modern Spanish Novel: The Early Years." *MLN* 89 (1974): 173–90 and *MLN* 90 (1975): 183–211.

Gómez de Baquero, E. *El renacimiento de la novela en el siglo XIX.* Madrid: Editorial Mundo Latino, 1924.

González del Valle, Luis T. *El canon: Reflexiones sobre la recepción literaria-teatral (Pérez de Ayala ante Benavente).* Madrid: Huerga & Fierro Editores, 1993.

———. "Ideología política en varias obras de Jacinto Benavente." In *Boletín de la Fundación Federico García Lorca* 19–20 (1996): 187–212. Special issue entitled *Teatro sociedad y política en la España del Siglo XX.* Ed. Dru Dougherty and María Francisca Vilches de Frutos.

González Frei, Irene. *Tu nombre escrito en el agua.* Barcelona: Tusquets (La sonrisa vertical), 1995.

González López, Emilio. "El drama social contemporáneo: Pérez Galdós y Gómez de la Serna." *Estudios escénicos,* 18 (1974): 131–38.

González Serrano, Urbano. "La crítica en España." *Estudios críticos*. Madrid, 1892.

Grandes, Almudena. *Las edades de Lulú*. Barcelona: Tusquets (Fábula), 1995. Originally published in *La sonrisa vertical*.

Grassi, Angela. *El copo de nieve*. Madrid: Castalia, 1992.

Grau, Jacinto. "El teatro de Galdós." *Cursos y conferencias* 24, no. 139–41 (1943): 39–55.

Greene, Thomas. "On the Category of the Literary." *Canadian Review of Comparative Literature* (1986): 217–24.

Guidieri, Remo. *El museo y sus fetiches: Crónica de lo neutro y de la aureola*. Madrid: Tecnos, 1992.

Guillén, Claudio. *La expresión total: Notas sobre literatura y obscenidad*. Ed. Angel Caffarena. Málaga: Librería Anticuaria El Guadalhorce, 1993.

Guillory, John. *Cultural Capital: The Problem of Literary Canon Formation*. Chicago: University of Chicago Press, 1993.

Gutiérrez, Jesús. "La 'pasión' de Santa Juana de Castilla." *Estudios escénicos*, 18 (1974): 203–14.

Hart, Patricia. "An Introduction to the Spanish Sleuth." *Monographic Review/Revista monográfica* 3 (1987): 163–81.

Hartsock, Nancy. "Postmodernism and Political Change: Issues for Feminist Theory." *Cultural Critique* 14 (1989–90): 15–34.

Hawkins, Harriet. *Classics and Trash: Traditions and Taboos in High Literature and Popular Modern Genres*. Toronto: University of Toronto Press, 1990.

Hebdige, Dick. "From Culture to Hegemony." In *The Cultural Studies Reader*, ed. Simon During, 357–67. London: Routledge, 1993.

Heilman, Robert. *Tragedy and Melodrama: Versions of Experience*. Seattle: University of Washington Press, 1968.

Henshel, Richard L. *Perception in Criminology*. Ithaca, N.Y.: Cornell University Press, 1975.

Heyne, Eric. "Literary Status for Nonfiction Narratives." In *Narrative Poetics: Innovations, Limits, Challenges*, ed. James Phelan, 137–45. Columbus: Center for Comparative Studies in Humanities, Ohio State University, 1987.

Hibbs Lissorgues, Solange. "Práctica del folletín en la prensa católica española." In *Hacia una literatura del Pueblo: del folletín a la novela*, ed. Brigitte Magnien, 46–63. Barcelona: Anthropos, 1995.

Hines, Susan. "What's Academic about Trek." *Extrapolation* 36 (1995): 5–9.

Hinz, Evelyn J. "An Introduction to War and Literature: Ajax Versus Ulysses." In *Troops Versus Tropes: War and Literature*, ed. Evelyn J. Hinz, v–xii. Winnipeg, Canada: University of Manitoba, 1990.

Hjort, Mette, ed. *Rules and Conventions: Literature, Philosophy, Social Theory*. Baltimore: Johns Hopkins University Press, 1992.

Hocquart, Marie-Hélène, and Gérard Brey. "El ejemplo de la prensa obrera francesa. ¿Opio del pueblo o semilla de rebelión?" In *Hacia una literatura del Pueblo: del folletín a la novela*. Ed. Brigitte Magnien, 77–86. Barcelona: Anthropos, 1995.

Hunt, Lynn. "Introduction: Obscenity and the Origins of Modernity, 1500–1800." In *The Invention of Pornography: Obscenity and the Origins of Modernity, 1500–1800*. New York: Zone Books, 1993.

Hutcheon, Linda. *A Theory of Parody: The Teachings of Twentieth-Century Art Forms.* New York: Methuen, 1985.

Huyssen, Andreas. *After the Great Divide: Modernism, Mass Culture, Postmodernism.* Bloomington: Indiana University Press, 1986.

Iffland, James. *Quevedo and the Grotesque.* 2 vols. London: Tamesis, 1978.

Iglesias Feijóo, Luis. "Valle-Inclán y Galdós." *Anales de la literatura española contemporánea* 6 (1981): 79–104.

Iglesias Santos, Montserrat. *La lógica del campo literario y el problema del canon.* Valencia: Ediciones Episteme, 1997.

Insúa, Alberto. *Memorias.* Madrid: Tesoro, 1953.

Jaén, María. *Sauna.* Trans. E. S. Barcelona: Seix Barral, 1988.

Jagoe, Catherine. *Ambiguous Angels: Gender in the Novels of Galdós.* Berkeley and Los Angeles: University of California Press, 1994.

———. "Disinheriting the Feminine: Galdós and the Rise of the Realist Novel in Spain." *Revista de estudios hispánicos* 27, no. 2 (1993): 225–47.

———. "Noncanonical Novels and the Question of Quality." *Revista de estudios hispánicos* 23 (1993): 427–36.

Jann, Rosemary. "Sherlock Holmes and the Social Body." *ELH* 57 (1990): 685–708.

Jauss, Hans Robert. *Toward an Aesthetic of Reception.* Trans. Timothy Bahti. Minneapolis: University of Minnesota Press, 1989.

Johnson, Randal. "Editor's Introduction." In *The Field of Cultural Production,* by Pierre Bordieu, ed. Randal Johnson, 1–25. New York: Columbia University Press, 1993.

Kálmán, G. C. "Signs/Signals of Literariness: Sign Theory vs. Reception Theory." In *Signs of Humanity/ L'homme et ses signes,* ed. Michel Balat and Janice Deledalle-Rhodes. Berlin: Mouton de Gruyter, 1992.

Kaplan, E. Ann. "Is the Gaze Male?" In *Powers of Desire: The Politics of Sexuality,* ed. Ann Snitow, Christine Stansell, and Sharon Thompson, 309–27. New York: Monthly Review Press, 1983.

Kellogg, Richard. "Lombroso and the Born Criminal." *The Baker Street Journal* 35, no. 3 (1985): 143–45.

Kemal, Salim, and Ivan Gaskell. "Interests, Values, and Explanations." In *Explanation and Value in the Arts,* ed. Salim Kemal and Ivan Gaskell. New York: Cambridge University Press, 1993.

———, eds. *Explanation and Value in the Arts.* New York: Cambridge University Press, 1993.

Kermode, Frank. *History and Value: The Clarendon Lectures and the Northcliffe Lectures, 1987.* Oxford: Clarendon Press, 1988.

———. "Institutional Control of Interpretation." In *The Art of Telling: Essays in Fiction,* 168–84. Cambridge: Harvard University Press, 1983.

———. "Literary Value and Transgression." *Raritan* 7, no. 3 (1988): 34–53.

Kirkpatrick, Susan. "Gender and Difference in *Fin de Siglo* Literary Discourse." In *Spain Today: Essays on Literature, Culture, Society,* ed. José F. Colmeiro, 95–101. Hanover, N.H.: Dartmouth College Dept. of Spanish and Portuguese, 1995.

———. *Las Románticas: Women Writers and Subjectivity in Spain, 1835–1850.* Berkeley and Los Angeles: University of California Press, 1989.

Kirschenbaum, Leo. *Enrique Gaspar and the Social Drama in Spain*. University of California Publications in Modern Philology, Vol. 25, no. 4. Berkeley and Los Angeles: University of California Press, 1944.

Kortazar, Jon. "El canon en la literatura vasca." *Insula* 600 (1996): 22–24.

Lecuyer, Marie Claude, and Maryse Villapadierna. "Génesis y desarrollo del folletín en la prensa española." In *Hacia una literatura del Pueblo: del folletín a la novela*. Ed. Brigitte Magniene, 15–45. Barcelona: Anthropos, 1995.

Leps, Marie-Christine. *Apprehending the Criminal: The Production of Deviance in Nineteenth-Century Discourse*. Durham, N.C.: Duke Unviersity Press, 1992.

Levine, Linda Gould. "The Female Body as Palimpsest in the Works of Carmen Gómez-Ojeda, Paloma Díaz-Mas, and Ana Rossetti." *Indiana Journal of Hispanic Literatures* 2 (1993): 181–206.

Lindenberger, Herbert. *The History in Literature: On Value, Genre, Institutions*. New York: Columbia University Press, 1990.

Lissorgues, Solange Hibbs. "Práctica del folletín en la prensa católica española." In *Hacia una literatura del Pueblo: del folletín a la novela*. Ed. Brigitte Magnien. Barcelona: Anthropos, 1995.

*Literatura popular*. Special issue of *Anthropos* 166/167 (1995).

Llanas Aguilaniedo, J. Mª., "Literatura erótica." *Revista nueva* 2 (August–December 1899): 23–24.

Lovell, Terry. *Consuming Fiction*. London: Verso, 1987.

Luft, David S. "Science and Irrationalism in Freud's Vienna." *Modern Austrian Literature* 23, no. 2 (1990): 89–97.

Magnien, Brigitte, ed. *Hacia una literatura del pueblo: del folletín a la novela*. Barcelona: Anthropos, 1995.

———. "Le roman contemporain de l'action: épopée et roman d'aventures." In *Autor de la guerra d'Espagne, 1936–39*, ed. Serge Salaün and Carlos Serrano, 97–105. [Paris]: Presses de la Sorbonne Nouvelle, 1993.

Mainer, José-Carlos. "La invención de la literatura española." In *Literaturas regionales en España*, ed. José Carlos Mainer and José María Enguita, 23–45. Zaragoza: Institución Fernando el Católico, 1994.

———. "La retórica de la obviedad: ideología e intimidad en algunas novelas de guerra." In *Autor de la guerre d'Espagne, 1936–39*, ed. Serge Salaün and Carlos Serrano, 73–95. [Paris]: Presses de la Sorbonne Nouvelle, 1993.

Mandrell, James. "Mercedes Abad and *La sonrisa vertical:* Erotica and Pornography in Post-Franco Spain." *Letras peninsulares* 6, no. 2–3 (1993–94): 277–99.

———. "Peninsular Literary Studies: Business as Usual." *Revista de estudios hispánicos* 27, no. 2 (1993): 291–307.

Marco, Joaquín. *Literatura popular en España en los siglox XVIII y XIX (Una aproximación a los pliegos de cordel)*. 2 vols. Madrid: Taurus, 1977.

———. "Sobre los orígenes de la novela folletinesca en España (W. Ayguals de Izco)." In *Ejercicios literarios*. Barcelona: Taber, 1969.

Maristany, Luis. "Lombroso y España: Nuevas consideraciones." *Anales de literatura española* 2 (1983): 361–81.

Martí López, Elisa. *Borrowed Words: Translation, Imitation, and the Making of the Nineteenth-Century Novel in Spain*. Lewisburg: Bucknell University Press, 2002.

———. "La orfandad de la novela española: política editorial y creación literaria a mediados del siglo XIX." *Bulletin Hispanique* 98 (1996): 347–61.

Martín, Mariano. "Introducción a una lógica de lo absurdo (apuntes sobre el primer Vázquez Montalbán)." *Les langues néo-latines* 80, no. 3–4 (1986): 53–68.

McLaughlin, Kevin. *Writing in Parts: Imitation and Exchange in Nineteenth-Century Literature.* Stanford, Calif.: Stanford University Press, 1995.

[Mesonero Romanos, Ramón de]. "Crónica literaria." *Semanario pintoresco español.* 2d series, no. 24 (16 June 1839): 190–92.

Miralles, Carles. "Sobre canonizar y lo ya canonizado en la literatura catalana." *Insula* 600 (1996): 16–18.

Montesinos, José F. *Introducción a una historia de la novela en España en el siglo XIX, seguida del esbozo de una bibliografía española de traducciones de novelas (1800–1850).* Madrid: Castalia, 1982.

Mora, Gabriela, and Karen S. van Hooft, eds. *Theory and Practice of Feminist Literary Criticism.* Ypsilanti, Mich.: Bilingual Press, 1982.

Moret, Xavier. "Manuel Vázquez Montalbán, escritor: 'Me cuesta más escribir las novelas de Carvalho que las consideradas serias.'" *El País* [Spain] (26 May 1998): 41.

Navajas, Gonzalo. "Género y contragénero policíaco en *La rosa de Alejandría* de Manuel Vázquez Montalbán." *Monographic Review/Revista monográfica* 3 (1987): 247–60.

Navarro, Felipe. "Rencontre avec Manuel Vázquez Montalbán." *Europe: Revue Littéraire Mensuelle* 702 (1987): 163–70.

Ortiz Armengol, Pedro. "Galdós y Valle-Inclán." *Revista de occidente* 10–11 (1976): 22–28.

———. *Vida de Galdós.* Barcelona: Grijalbo Mondadori, 1995.

Ouimette, Victor. "Monstrous Fecundity: The Popular Novel in Nineteenth-Century Spain." *Canadian Review of Comparative Literature* 9 (1982): 383–405.

Pavel, Thomas. "Literary Conventions." In *Rules and Conventions: Literature, Philosophy, Social Therapy.* Ed. Mette Hjort, 45–66. Baltimore: Johns Hopkins University Pres, 1992.

Pereda, Rosa. "Revolución romántica: El poder comercial de la novela rosa multiplica su influencia." *Babelia. El País.* (9 July 1994): 4–5.

Pérez, Janet. "Characteristics of Erotic Brief Fiction by Women in Spain." *Monographic Review/Revista monográfica* 7 (1991): 173–95.

Pérez Galdós, Benito. *El crimen de la calle de Fuencarral.* Madrid: Prensa Moderna, 1928.

———. *El crimen del cura Galeote. Cronicón (1886–1890).* Vol. 7 of *Obras inéditas.* Ed. Alberto Ghiraldo. Madrid: Renacimiento, [1924].

———. "Fernández y González." *Arte y crítica.* Vol. 2 of *Obras inéditas.* Ed. Alberto Ghiraldo. Madrid: Renacimiento, 1923.

———. *Nuestro teatro.* Vol. 5 of *Obras inéditas.* Ed. Alberto Ghiraldo. Madrid: Renacimiento, 1923.

———. *Obras completas.* Ed. Federico Carlos Sainz de Robles. 6 vols. Madrid: Aguilar, 1968.

———. "Observaciones sobre la novela contemporánea en España." *Revista de España* 15 (1870): 162–72.

Pérez Griego, Miguel Ángel. "Formación del canon literario medieval castellano." *Insula* 600 (1996): 7–9.

Pérez Minik, Domingo. "Galdós, ese dramaturgo recobrado." *Estudios escénicos,* 18 (1974): 13–24.

Perkins, David. *Is Literary History Possible?* Baltimore: Johns Hopkins University Press, 1992.

Pesseux-Richard, H. "Un novelista español: Felipe Trigo." In *En mi castillo de luz (Diario de un alma bella),* by Felipe Trigo, 65–127. Madrid: Renacimiento, 1916.

Phillips, Allen W. "Galdós y Valle-Inclán: a propósito de un texto olvidado." *Anales galdosianos* 14 (1979): 105–14.

Pont, Jaume, and Josep M. Sala-Valldaura, eds. *Cànon literari: ordre I subversió.* Lérida, Spain: Fundació Pública de la Diputació de Lleida, 1998.

Poyán Díaz, Daniel. *Enrique Gaspar: Medio siglo de teatro español.* 2 vols. Madrid: Gredos, 1957.

Pozuelo Yvancos, José María. "Canon: ¿estética o pedagogía?" *Insula* 600 (1996): 3–4.

———. *El canon en la teoría literaria contemporánea.* Colección Eutopías, vol. 108. Valencia: Ediciones Episteme, 1995.

Pozuelo Yvancos, José María, and Rosa María Aradra Sánchez. *Teoría del canon y literatura española.* Madrid: Cátedra, 2000.

Pritchett, Kay. "The Function of Irony in Vázquez Montalbán's *Coplas a la muerte de mi tía Daniela.*" *Anales de la literatura española contemporánea* 8 (1983): 47–70.

Pulido, N. "Planeta celebra en Madrid el 25 aniversario de Carvalho." *ABC Digital* [Spain] (21 February 1997): n.p.

Puvogel, Sandra J. "Pepe Carvalho and Spain: A Look at the Detective Fiction of Manuel Vázquez Montalbán." *Monographic Review/Revista monográfica* 3 (1987): 261–67.

Regan, Stephen. *The Politics of Pleasure: Aesthetics and Cultural Theory.* Buckingham: Open University Press, 1992.

Reiss, Timothy. *The Meaning of Literature.* Ithaca, N.Y.: Cornell University Press, 1992.

Resina, Joan Ramon. *El cadáver en la cocina: La novela criminal en la cultura del desencanto.* Barcelona: Anthropos, 1997.

———. "Desencanto y fórmula literaria en las novelas de Manuel Vázquez Montalbán." *MLN* 108 (1993): 254–82.

———. "La figura del criminal en las novelas policiacas de Manuel Vázquez Montalbán." *Indiana Journal of Hispanic Literatures* 2 (1994): 227–39.

Ribbans, Geoffrey. "*La desheredada,* novela por entregas: Apuntes sobre su primera publicación." *Anales galdosianos* 27–28 (1992–93): 69–75.

———. "Los altibajos de la crítica galdosiana." In *La elaboración del canon en la literatura española del siglo XIX,* ed. Luis F. Díaz Larios et al. Proceedings of the second colloquium of the Sociedad de Literatura Española del Siglo XIX. Barcelona: Universitat de Barcelona, 2000.

Ricard, Robert. "El asesinato del Obispo Martínez Izquierdo y el clero madrileño en la época de Galdós." *Anales galdosianos* 1 (1966): 125–29.

Ricoeur, Paul. *Hermeneutics and the Human Sciences: Essays on Language, Action, and Interpretation.* Ed. and trans. John B. Thompson. London: Cambridge University Press, 1981.

———. *History and Fiction in Galdós's Narratives.* Oxford: Clarendon Press, 1993.

Ríos-Font, Wadda C. "'Encontrados afectos': *El Señor de Bembibre* as a Self-Conscious Novel." *Hispanic Review* 61 (1993): 469–82.

———. "Literary History and Canon Formation." In *Cambridge History of Spanish Literature,* ed. David T. Gies. Cambridge: Cambridge University Press. Forthcoming.

———. *Rewriting Melodrama: The Hidden Paradigm in Modern Spanish Theater.* Lewisburg: Bucknell University Press, 1997.

———. "Romantic Irony and Romantic Grotesque: Narrative Self-Consciousness in Mariano José de Larra and Rosalía de Castro." *Hispanic Review* 65 (1997): 39–61.

Romero Tobar, Leonardo. "Algunas consideraciones del canon literario durante el siglo XIX." *Insula* 600 (1996): 14–16.

———. *La novela popular española del siglo XIX.* Madrid: Fundación Juan March/Editorial Ariel, 1976.

Ross, Andrew. *No Respect: Intellectuals and Popular Culture.* New York: Routledge, 1989.

Rossetti, Ana. *Alevosías.* Barcelona: Tusquets (La sonrisa vertical), 1991.

Rubio, Isaac. "*Alma y vida,* obra fundamental del teatro de Galdós." Doménech, *Estudios escénicos,* 18 (1974): 173–94.

———. "Galdós y el melodrama." *Anales galdosianos* 16 (1981): 56–57.

———. "Ibsen y Galdós." *Letras de Deusto* 4, no. 8 (July–December 1974): 207–24.

Rubio Cremades, Enrique. *Costumbrismo y folletín: Vida y obra de Antonio Flores.* Alicante: Diputación Provincial, 1977.

Ruiz Ramón, Francisco. *Historia del teatro español (desde sus orígenes hasta 1900).* Madrid: Cátedra, 1986.

———. *Historia del teatro español (siglo XX).* Madrid: Cátedra, 1975.

Sackett, Theodore Alan. "Galdós dramaturgo, reformador del teatro de su tiempo." *Estreno* 7, no. 1 (1981): 6–10.

———. *Galdós y las máscaras: historia teatral y bibliografía anotada.* Verona: Università degli Studi di Padova, 1982.

Saenz, Hilario. "Visión galdosiana de la religiosidad de los españoles." *Hispania* 20 (1937): 235–42.

Said, Edward. *Representations of the Intellectual: The 1993 Reith Lectures.* New York: Vintage Books, 1996.

Sala, Pedro. "La crítica y los criterios en los tiempos modernos." *Revista de España* 87 (1882): 380–93.

Salaün, Serge. "Apogeo y decadencia de la sicalipsis." In *Discurso erótico y discurso transgresor en la cultura peninsular: siglos XI al XX,* ed. Myriam Díaz Diocaretz and Iris Zavala, 129–54. Madrid: Ediciones Tuero, 1992.

Salaün, Serge, and Carlos Serrano, eds. *Autour de la guerre d'Espagne, 1936–39.* [Paris]: Presses de la Sorbonne Nouvelle, 1993.

Sánchez, Roberto G. "Emilio Mario, Galdós y la reforma escénica del XIX." *Hispanic Review* 52 (1984): 263–79.

Sánchez Beiroa, Ricardo. "La represión en España y en América a través de *Galíndez* de Manuel Vázquez Montalbán." In *Actas del IIIer Congreso Argentino de Hispanistas*, ed. Luis Martínez Cuitino et al, 899–905. Buenos Aires: Universidad de Buenos Aires, 1993.

Sánchez Llama, Íñigo. "Introducción." In *El copo de nieve*, by Angela Grassi, 7–63. Madrid: Castalia, 1992.

Santonja, Gonzalo. "En torno a la novela erótica española de comienzos de siglo." *Cuadernos hispanoamericanos* 427 (1986): 165–75.

Saval, José V. "La lucha de clases se sienta a la mesa en *Los mares del sur* de Manuel Vázquez Montalbán." *Revista hispánica moderna* 48 (1995): 389–400.

Schaefer, Claudia. "Desperately Seeking the Subject: María Jaén and the Promises of Erotic Discourse." *Indiana Journal of Hispanic Literatures* 2 (1993): 207–28.

Schmidt, Ruth. *Cartas entre dos amigos del teatro: Manuel Tolosa Latour y Benito Pérez Galdós*. Las Palmas: Ediciones del Excmo. Cabildo Insular de Gran Canaria, 1969.

Schwartz, Lía. "Siglos de Oro: Cánones, repertorios, catálogos de autores." *Insula* 600 (1996): 9–12.

Sela-Sheffy, Rakefet. "Canon Formation Revisited: Ideology vs. Process Analysis." 1998. Unpublished manuscript.

———. "The Concept of Canonicity in Polysystem Theory." *Poetics Today* 11 (1990): 511–22. <http://www.tau.ac.il/~rakefet/papers/papers.html>.

———. "Strategies of Canonization: Manipulating the Idea of the Novel and the Intellectual Field in Eighteenth-Century German Culture." 1998. <http://www.tau.ac.il/~rakefet/papers/papers.html>.

Sender, Ramón J. *Contraataque*. Madrid: Editorial Nuestro Pueblo, 1938.

Sender Barayón, Ramón. *A Death in Zamora*. Albuquerque: University of New Mexico Press, 1989.

Servodidio, Mirella. "Ana Rossetti's Double-Voiced Discourse of Desire." *Revista hispánica moderna* 45 (1992): 318–27.

Shoemaker, William H. "La acogida pública y crítica de *Realidad* en su estreno." *Estudios escénicos*, 18 (1974): 25–40.

Showalter, Elaine. *Sexual Anarchy: Gender and Culture at the Fin de Siècle*. New York: Penguin, 1990.

Sieburth, Stephanie. *Inventing High and Low: Literature, Mass Culture, and Uneven Modernity in Spain*. Durham: Duke University Press, 1994.

Sims, Robert L. "From Fictional to Factual Narrative: Contemporary Critical Heteroglossia, Gabriel García Márquez's Journalism, and Bigeneric Writing." *Studies in the Literary Imagination* 25 (1992): 21–60.

Sinnigen, John H. "Melodrama y religión: la novelística de Catalina MacPherson." *Revista de estudios hispánicos* 21 (1994): 35–56.

———. "Symbolic Struggles: Literary Study, Social History, Value Judgments." *Revista de estudios hispánicos* 23 (1993): 437–47.

Smith, Barbara Herrnstein. "Contingencies of Value." In *Canons*, ed. Robert von Hallberg, 5–39. Chicago: University of Chicago Press, 1984.

———. *Contingencies of Value: Alternative Perspectives for Literary Theory*. Cambridge: Harvard University Press, 1991.

Sobejano, Gonzalo. "Echegaray, Galdós y el melodrama." *Anales galdosianos* 13 (1978, Anejo): 91–117.

———. "Efectos de *Realidad.*" *Estudios escénicos,* 18 (1974): 41–62.

———. "Forma literaria y sensibilidad social en *La incógnita* y *Realidad* de Galdós." *Revista hispánica moderna* 30 (1964): 89–107.

———. "Política y melodrama en el teatro de Galdós." *Boletín de la Fundación Federico García Lorca* 19–20 (1996): 13–26. Special issue entitled *Teatro, sociedad y política en la España del siglo XX.* Ed. Dru Dougherty and María Francisca Vilches de Frutos.

———. "Razón y suceso de la dramática galdosiana." *Anales galdosianos* 5 (1970): 39–54.

Suleiman, Susan Rubin. *Authoritarian Fictions: The Ideological Novel as a Literary Genre.* New York: Columbia University Press, 1983.

Szondi, Peter. *Theory of the Modern Drama.* Ed. and Trans. Michael Hays. Minneapolis: University of Minnesota Press, 1987.

Tarrío Varela, Anxo. "La formación del canon literario gallego." *Insula* 600 (1996): 18–22.

Thompson, John B. "Editor's Introduction." In *Hermeneutics and the Human Sciences: Essays on Language, Action, and Interpretation,* by Paul Ricoeur. Trans. John B. Thompson, London: Cambridge University Press, 1981.

Torrecilla, Jesús. *La imitación colectiva.* Madrid: Gredos, 1996.

Trapiello, Andrés. *Las armas y las letras: Literatura y guerra civil (1936–1939).* Barcelona: Planeta, 1994.

Trigo, Felipe. *Alma en los labios.* 6th ed. Madrid: Renacimiento, 1919.

———. *La Altísima.* 7th ed. Madrid: Renacimiento, 1920.

———. *El amor en la vida y en los libros: mi ética y mi estética.* 2d ed. Madrid: Renacimiento, 1920.

———. *En mi castillo de luz (Diario de un alma bella).* Madrid: Renacimiento, 1916.

———. *Socialismo individualista: índice para su estudio antropológico.* Madrid: Renacimiento, 1920.

Tsuchiya, Akiko. "*La incógnita* and the Enigma of Writing: Manolo Infante's Interpretive Struggle." *Hispanic Review* 57 (1989): 335–56.

Ugalde, Sharon Keefe. "Erotismo y revisionismo en la poesía de Ana Rossetti." *Siglo XX/20th Century* 7, no. 1–2 (1989–90): 24–29.

Unamuno, Miguel de. *Niebla.* Madrid: Espasa-Calpe, 1991.

———. "Sobre la lujuria." In *Nuevos ensayos.* 316–20. Vol. 3 of *Obras completas.* New York: Las Americas Publishing Co., 1968.

———. "Sobre la pornografía." In *Nuevos ensayos* 321–25. Vol. 3 of *Obras completas.* New York: Las Americas Publishing Co., 1968.

Varela, Antonio. "Foxá's *Madrid de corte a checa:* Fascism and Romance." In *Rewriting the Good Fight: Critical Essays on the Literature of the Spanish Civil War.* Ed. Frieda Brown et al., 95–109. East Lansing: Michigan State University Press, 1989.

———. "Structuring Narcissism: Manuel Vázquez Montalbán's *Los mares del sur.*" *Romance Languages Annual* 6 (1994): 599–603.

Vásquez, Mary. "Narrative Voice and the Toll of War in Ramón Sender's *Contraataque.*" In *Rewriting the Good Fight: Critical Essays on the Literature of the Spanish*

*Civil War.* Ed. Frieda Brown et al., 111–23. East Lansing: Michigan State Univeristy Press, 1989.

———. "Ramón Sender and Wartime Defenses: *Contraataque* as Fictive Autobiography." In *Critical Essays on the Literatures of Spain and Spanish America,* ed. Luis T. González-del-Valle and Julio Baena. Boulder, Colo.: Society of Spanish and Spanish-American Studies, 1991.

Vázquez Montalbán, Manuel. *El escriba sentado.* Barcelona: Grijalbo Mondadori, 1997.

———. *La literatura en la construcción de la ciudad democrática.* Barcelona: Grijalbo Mondadori, 1998.

———. *Los mares del sur.* Barcelona: Planeta, 1997.

———. *O César o nada.* Barcelona: Planeta, 1998.

Vernon, Kathleen. "Chismografía en las novelas de Galdós: *La incógnita* y *Realidad.*" *La Torre* 3, no. 10 (1989): 205–19.

Vilarós, Teresa. "Confesión y parodia en las novelas eróticas de María Jaén." *Nuevo texto crítico* 7 (1991): 147–55.

Villanueva, Darío. "The Evolution of the Spanish Literary System." In *Spain Today: Essays on Literature, Culture, Society.* Ed. José F. Colmeiro, 139–47. Hanover, N.H.: Dartmouth College Dept. of Spanish and Portuguese, 1995.

Von Hallberg, Robert, ed. *Canons.* Chicago: Univeristy of Chicago Press, 1984.

Warshaw, J. "Errors in Biographies of Galdós." *Hispania* 11 (1928): 485–99.

———. "Galdós's Apprenticeship in the Drama." *Modern Language Notes* 44 (1929): 459–63.

Weber, Maryann. "Pragmatic Ploys and Cognitive Processes in *La incógnita.*" *Anales galdosianos* 23 (1988): 57–65.

Weber, Max. *The Protestant Ethic and the Spirit of Capitalism.* Trans. Talcott Parsons. New York: Scribner, 1958.

Wellek, René. "Literature, Fiction, and Literariness." In *Classical Models in Literature,* ed. Warren Anderson et al. Innsbruck: AMOE, 1981.

Willem, Linda. "Turning *La incógnita* into *Realidad:* Galdós's Metafictional Magic Trick." *MLN* 105 (1990): 385–91.

Ynduráin, Francisco. *Galdós entre la novela y el folletín.* Madrid: Taurus, 1970.

Zavala, Iris M. *Ideología y política en la novela española del siglo XIX.* Salamanca: Anaya, 1971.

# Index

Abad, Mercedes 165, 248n
Academia: academics, 12–13, 15, 18, 22, 25, 29, 39, 185–88, 191–92, 194, 196, 201, 219, 225–26, 229, 233n
Acereda, Alberto, 169
Adorno, Theodor, 234n
Aesthetic(s), 13, 17, 26, 31, 36, 38, 40–43, 45–47, 53, 56, 67–68, 72, 75–76, 78, 80–83, 86, 88–90, 115, 121–23, 126–29, 133–35, 156–61, 164, 182–86, 188, 190–91, 195, 210, 218, 237n, 239n, 244n, 249n
Alas, Leopoldo (Clarín), 47
Alberti, Rafael, 78, 133
Alborg, Concha, 170
Alcalá Galiano, Antonio, 49, 192–93, 249n
Alger, Horatio, 59, 237n
Altisent, Marta, 170
Amorós, Andrés, 36
Andrade, Benito Mariano, 101–2, 241n
Andreu, Alicia, 74, 75
Aradra, Rosa María, 31
Archive, 30, 216–18, 220–32
Aristocracy. 40, 51, 57–58, 60–62, 64–65, 67, 69, 72, 86, 116, 129, 158, 191, 238n. *See also* bourgeois(ie); middle class; serial fiction, class in; working class
Armstrong, Nancy, 62
Ayguals de Izco, Wenceslao, 35–37, 39, 50–51, 57, 60–67, 69–71, 234n, 235n, 236n, 237n, 249n; *La justicia divina, o el hijo del deshonor,* 70; *María, o la hija de un jornalero,* 50, 57, 62–67, 69–71, 94, 237n, 238n; *El palacio de los crímenes, o el pueblo y sus opresores,* 237n; *Pobres y ricos, o la bruja de Madrid,* 57, 60, 64–65, 69–71, 238n

Baguley, David, 105
Bakhtin, Mikhail, 68
Balzac, Honoré de, 48–49, 199–201, 234n, 249n, 250n
Barnet, Sylvan, and Hugo Bedau, 14–15, 231
Baroja, Pío, 171
Barthes, Roland, 127, 241n
Baudelaire, Charles, 134
Bedau, Hugo. *See* Barnet, Sylvan
Belda, Joaquín, 165
Benavente, Jacinto, 78, 89, 135, 245n
Benet, Juan, 187
Benítez, Rubén, 36–37, 50, 57, 60–61, 69–70, 235n, 236n,
Benjamin, Walter, 211–15, 234n
Bergamín, José, 133
Bertillon, Alphonse, 100
Bestseller, 189, 191, 203, 207–8, 218, 235n, 251n
Beverley, John, 13, 20
Blanco, Alda, 38, 40, 47
Blasco Ibáñez, Vicente, 45, 74
Böhl de Faber, Cecilia (Fernán Caballero), 35–36, 43, 50, 74, 234n, 238n
Borges, Jorge Luis, 30, 191, 221; "La biblioteca de Babel," 30, 32, 221, 232
Botrel, Jean-François, 36, 41, 45, 54–55, 69, 233n, 234n, 235n
Bourdieu, Pierre, 22– 28, 43, 45–46, 79–82, 84–86, 158, 160, 187, 189, 191, 193–94, 203–5, 216, 223, 240n, 241n, 247n, 250n

269

Bourgeois(ie), 40, 46, 51, 53, 57, 60–65, 67, 69, 74, 80, 85–86, 99, 115–16, 129, 132, 134, 147, 158–59, 166, 185, 197, 202, 217, 234n, 237n, 239n, 240n, 244n, 249n. *See also* aristocracy; middle class; serial fiction, class in; working class
Brooks, Peter, 67, 95, 166, 171, 173, 197, 210, 212–14, 246n
Brown, Joan, and Christa Johnson, 13, 16
Buñuel, Luis, 133
Butler, Judith, 177–79, 182

Caballero, Fernán. *See* Böhl de Faber, Cecilia
Calderón de la Barca, Pedro, 13
Canals, Cuca, 16
Canon: canonicity, literary, 12–13, 15–26, 28–32, 35, 38–40, 42–43, 47, 52, 72–73, 75–77, 88–90, 115–16, 121, 123, 125, 127–29, 152, 156–57, 160–61, 164–65, 172, 183–84, 186–88, 191, 193–95, 201, 216–21, 225, 227, 230–32, 235n, 236n, 237n, 244n, 248n, 251n; Noncanonical literature, 18–19, 29–30, 37–39, 43, 47, 74–75, 77, 193, 216–17
Capitalism, 40, 46, 61, 72–73, 197, 199, 202, 204–5, 211, 214, 239n, 244n, 249n
Carey, John, 249n
Carmona, Angeles, 40
Carrillo, Víctor, 36
Casona, Alejandro, 78
*Causes célèbres*, 99, 241n
Cawelti, John, 56
Céard, Henri, 105
Cela, Camilo José, 13
Cervantes, Miguel de, 13, 16, 20, 35–36, 50–51, 53, 55, 77, 235n, 246n
Charnon-Deutsch, Lou, 12, 38–39, 183–84, 248n
Chateaubriand, François de, 48
Chekhov, Anton, 83
Classic, literary, 12, 20, 51, 206
Close reading, 14, 26, 191, 194
Colmeiro, José F., 190, 196

Commodity, 46, 91, 198–99
Compitello, Malcolm Allan, 190
Complexity: as feature of literature, 14, 30, 42, 115, 160, 162, 183, 189, 191, 194, 211, 218
Conditionalist approaches to literature, 126
Contingency: value of, 12, 17–18, 42
Conventions: conventionality in literature, 15–16, 47, 54–57, 73, 81, 93, 97, 104, 106, 115, 124, 149, 156–57, 162, 188–90, 197, 208–9, 213, 236n, 244n
Costa, Luis, 189, 215
*Costumbrismo*, 35, 54–55, 57. See also *novela de costumbres*
Crime: in literature, 54, 76, 90–91, 99–100, 110–11, 113, 115, 213–14
Criticism: critics, literary, 11–16, 18–19, 22–25, 29, 31–32, 38, 67, 80–81, 87, 122–24, 126–28, 154–56, 158, 161, 183–84, 187, 191–96, 204–5, 207–09, 216–19, 225–26, 230, 247n, 249n. *See also* academia, intellectualism
Cruz, Ramón de la, 82
Cultural capital, 23, 73, 193, 225, 237n
Cultural Studies, 13, 15, 17, 19–20, 127–28, 189, 193, 219
Curriculum, 12–13, 16, 18, 25, 29, 31, 185

Darwin, Charles, 101
Dean, Carolyn, 186
Derrida, Jacques, 222, 226–32; *Archive Fever: A Freudian Impression*, 222, 226–30
Detective fiction, 56, 109, 187–215
Dialogism: in serial novel, 68–72
Dickens, Charles, 249n, 250n
Differentiation: literary, 31, 37, 85, 90, 169, 171, 186, 216, 218
Discursive formations, 217, 223–25
Díez-Borque, José María, 36
Doménech, Ricardo, 76
Douglass, Mary, 177
Doyle, Arthur Conan, 91, 109–10; *The Sign of Four*, 109; *A Study in Scarlet*, 109–10

Duchesne, Juan, 181–82, 248n
Dumas, Alexandre, 48

Easthope, Anthony, 188–89
Echegaray, José, 78–79, 82–84, 87–89, 239n, 240n
Eliot, T. S., 201
Ellul, Jacques, 151
Enríquez de Salamanca, Cristina, 38
Eroticisim: erotica in literature, 11, 31, 164–86, 217–18, 220, 248n
Essentialist approaches to literature, 15–16, 18, 20, 23–24, 126–27, 189, 219, 223, 232, 243n
Espronceda, José de, 35
Ethnic Studies, 17, 127, 161, 193
Etxebarría, Lucía, 208
Even-Zohar, Itamar, 26–28, 52–53, 204, 206, 223, 235n

Feminism 16–17, 37–38, 41, 127, 161, 167, 178, 180, 182–83, 193, 219, 248n, 249n
Fernández Cifuentes, Luis, 171–72, 248n
Fernández y González, Manuel, 39, 44–46, 54, 58–59, 62–66, 69, 94, 104, 234n, 237n, 238n, 249n; *Los desheredados*, 58–59, 62–66, 69, 94, 104, 237n, 238n; *Los hijos perdidos*, 104, 237n; *Luisa, o la mujer del jornalero*, 237n
Ferreras, Juan Ignacio, 36, 41, 45, 54, 55, 233n
Ferri, Enrico, 100, 102
*Feuilleton*, 37, 48, 50, 98, 106, 199, 233n, 234n, 235n. See also *folletín; novela por entregas;* serial fiction
Field: cultural, 27, 84, 89, 115, 163, 194, 240n, 247n; literary, 27, 31, 43, 46, 68, 80, 82, 84–85, 89, 115, 158, 182–83, 186–87, 194, 210, 216, 218, 240n, 247n, 250n
Fielding, Henry, 48
Fish, Stanley, 15–16, 123–24, 155, 223, 243n, 247n, 250n
Flaubert, Henri, 85

Flores, Antonio, 39, 50–51; *Fe, esperanza y caridad*, 50–51
*Folletín*, 35–37, 39, 41, 71, 98, 106, 159, 233n, 235n, 238n. See also *feuilleton; novela por entregas;* serial fiction
Formulas, literary, 50–51, 54–57, 67, 74–75, 189, 204, 218, 251
Foucault, Michel, 21, 170, 217, 222–26, 228, 231–32; *The Archaeology of Knowledge* 222–24
Foulkes, Peter, 152–53, 247n
Foxá, Agustín de, 31, 125, 129–36, 138–39, 141–42, 150, 152, 155, 157–62, 243–48n; *Madrid de corte a checa*, 125, 129–36, 138–39, 141–42, 150, 152, 155, 157–62, 244n
Franc, Isabel, 165, 175–77, 180, 184; *Entre todas las mujeres*, 175–77, 184
Franco, Francisco; Francoism, 129, 137–38, 141, 156, 161, 189, 196, 199, 200, 203, 247n
Freud, Sigmund, 92, 112–15, 226, 228–29, 242n
Fromm, Harold, 191–92, 249n

Gala, Antonio, 187
Ganivet, Ángel, 92, 116; *Idearium español*, 116
García Lorca, Federico, 13, 78, 168, 206
Gaspar, Enrique, 83, 240n; *Las circunstancias*, 83
Gaze, aesthetic, 73, 86, 189, 191
Gaze, sexual, 165–66, 168–69, 171–75, 177–78, 182
*Género chico*, 78, 85, 240n
Genette, Gérard, 93, 126–27, 241n
Gil y Carrasco, Enrique, 35, 50, 235n
Goldman, Peter, 36–37, 43, 55, 235n
Gómez de Avellaneda, Gertrudis, 35
Gómez de la Serna, Ramón, 133–34
González del Valle, Luis, 245n
González Serrano, Urbano, 192
Gothic literature, 97, 188, 214
Goya, Francisco de, 149, 246n
Grandes, Almudena, 165, 172–73, 178–82, 184–86, 248n; *Las edades de Lulú*, 172–73, 175, 178–82, 183–86, 248n

Grassi, Angela, 39, 41, 48, 74; *El copo de nieve,* 74
Greene, Graham, 251n
Greene, Thomas, 188–89
Guerrero Zamora, Juan, 77
Guislain, Joseph, 242n
*Guzmán el Bueno,* 136, 245n
Guillory, John, 12, 17–19, 22, 25, 30, 193–94, 216, 220–22

Hartsock, Nancy, 42
Hauptmann, Gerhart, 83
Hebdige, Dick, 19
Hegemony, 12, 16, 19–21, 24, 43, 52, 113, 177, 179, 185–86
Heilman, Robert, 246n
Hermeneutics, 105, 112, 227, 231
Hernández, Miguel, 127
High culture, 13, 19–20, 37, 136, 165–66, 185, 204, 207–8. *See also* high vs. low; low culture; popular culture
High vs. low, 31, 37, 89, 121, 158, 190, 196, 201, 216, 218–20, 247n. *See also* high culture; low culture; popular culture,
Hinz, Evelyn J., 156–57
History: historiography, literary, 11, 26, 30–31, 40, 42–43, 51, 53, 78, 89, 121, 125, 128, 161, 207, 216–17, 236n
Holmes, Sherlock, 91, 109–11. *See also* Conan Doyle, Arthur
Homosexuality, 18–19, 132, 162, 165, 180–81
Hoyos y Vinent, Antonio de, 165
Hugo, Victor, 48
Hutcheon, Linda, 198
Huyssen, Andreas, 184–85

Ibsen, Henrik, 83
Idealism, 44, 59, 67, 195, 244
Iffland, James, 248n
Identity politics, 18, 20
Intellectualism: intellectuals, 22–25, 28–29, 41, 53, 76, 87, 90, 115, 117, 133, 144, 150, 154, 158, 166, 171–72, 182–83, 236n, 249n
Interpretive community, 17, 19, 39, 205, 243n

Intransitivity: as feature of literature, 122, 127, 129, 150, 152, 162, 188, 218
Irrationalism, 242–43n

Jaén, María, 165, 184; *El escote,* 184
Jagoe, Catherine, 37–38, 40, 42, 44–45, 47, 51, 59, 75, 234n
Johnson, Christa. *See* Brown, Joan
Johnson, Randal, 26

Kaplan, E. Anne, 174–76, 178
Kellogg, Richard, 101
Kermode, Frank, 169–70
Kirschenbaum, Leo, 240n
Kock, Paul de, 235n

Large-scale production: field of, 26, 31, 43–44, 75, 80, 84, 187
Larra, Mariano José de, 35, 50, 235n
Lecuyer, Marie Claude and Maryse Villapadierna, 47–48, 233n, 235n
Leps, Marie-Christine, 91, 99–100
Lesbianism, 175–76, 178, 180, 182
Liberalism: liberals, 18, 23, 147, 183, 185, 193, 205, 249n
Literariness, 26, 72, 124, 126–27, 157, 165, 169, 183–84, 188, 208
Llanos y Torriglia, Félix, 100
Lombroso, Cesare, 91, 100–102, 242n
López Soler, Ramón, 35
Lovell, Terry, 40
Low culture, 37, 196, 201. *See also* high culture; high vs. low; popular culture
Luft, David, 242–43n
Lukacs, Georg, 212

Maeterlinck, Maurice, 83
Magnien, Brigitte, 37, 74, 157–58
Mainer, José-Carlos, 30, 121–22, 126, 159, 235n, 243n
Malraux, André, 243n
Mandrell, James, 183, 186, 233n, 248n
Marañón, Gregorio, 132
Marco, Joaquín, 73
Mario, Emilio, 79, 82, 240n
Maristany, Luis, 100, 242n

# INDEX

Market: literary, 31, 41, 43, 46, 52–53, 73, 81, 87, 187–88, 194–96, 199, 201–7, 217–18, 233n, 236n, 239n
Martí López, Elisa, 51, 53, 236n, 238n
Marx, Karl, 159, 198–99, 234n
Martínez Villergas, Juan, 50
Mass culture, 13, 19, 32, 46, 183–86, 201–2, 207, 249n. *See also* masses; mass literature; production; popular culture; popular literature
Mass literature: production, 44, 84, 185, 216
Masses, 150, 154, 158, 185, 192, 237n, 244n, 249n
Maugham, Somerset, 207, 251n
McLaughlin, Kevin, 198–99, 234n, 249n
Melodrama, 29, 67, 76, 78, 80, 82–83, 85, 87–88, 94–95, 97, 103–4, 109, 115–16, 150–52, 161, 190, 212, 214, 239n, 240n, 244n, 246n
Menéndez y Pelayo, Marcelino, 46, 48, 235n
Menéndez Pidal, Ramón, 235n
Mesonero Romanos, Ramón de, 49, 72
Middle class, 38, 40, 44, 46, 62, 74, 86, 115–16, 196. *See also* aristocracy; bourgeois(ie); serial fiction, class in; working class
Miró, Gabriel, 171
Molina, Tirso de, 13
Monologism: in narrative, 68, 72, 150, 155–56, 160–61
Montesinos, José F., 35, 41, 48, 73, 233n
Moratín, Leandro Fernández de, 82
Moret, Xavier, 201
Morris, Charles, 153
Muñoz Seca, Pedro, 135, 245n

Nabokov, Vladimir, 169
Neruda, Pablo, 133
New Criticism, 13, 127, 243n, 247n
Nietzche, Friedrich, 242n
Nodier, Charles, 48
Nonspecialist reading: readers, 14, 154, 192, 205, 208–10, 226, 249n, 250n
*Novela de costumbres*, 234n

*Novela por entregas*, 50, 71, 234n. *See also folletín; feuilleton;* serial fiction

Orbe, Timoteo, 37, 74
Ordinary language, 72, 123–24, 127–28, 161
Ortega y Gasset, Jose, 134, 244n, 249n
Orwell, George, 243n
Ouimette, Victor, 36, 44, 236n

Pardo Bazán, Emilia, 13
Patrimony: literature as, 12, 21, 24–25, 31, 52, 198, 202, 251n
Pavel, Thomas, 56, 208–9
Pemán, José María, 135
Pérez, Janet, 165
Pérez Escrich, Enrique, 39
Pérez Galdós, Benito, 11, 13, 31, 35–37, 40–41, 43–48, 51, 53–54, 57–58, 73–117, 122, 128, 171, 216–20, 233n, 234n, 236n, 239–43n, 250n; *Alma y vida*, 82, 85–87; *El audaz*, 236n; *Los condenados*, 82, 87–88, 239n; *El crimen de la calle de Fuencarral*, 76, 91, 92–106, 109, 111, 113, 115, 241n, 242n; *El crimen del cura Galeoto*, 241n, 242n; *La desheredada*, 44, 58, 236n; *Electra*, 82, 239n; *La fontana de oro*, 74; *El hombre fuerte*, 239n; *La incógnita*, 76, 91–92, 105–115, 241n, 242n, 243n; *La loca de la casa*, 82; "La novela en el tranvía," 44, 99; *Nuestro teatro*, 81–82, 90, 239n; "Observaciones sobre la novela contemporánea," 35, 44, 47, 53, 115; *Quien mal hace, bien no espere*, 239n; *Realidad* (play), 82–83, 88, 108, 114, 239n, 241n; *Realidad* (novel), 108, 114, 241n, 242n, 243n; "La sociedad presente como materia novelable," 115; *Torquemada en el purgatorio*, 111–12; "Un tribunal literario," 44, 46, 73
Pérez Minik, Domingo, 77
Perkins, David, 53
Polysemy: as feature of literature, 188–89, 191, 194, 218
Popular culture, 16, 37, 191, 205–6, 249n
Popular literature, 11, 50, 185, 189, 233n

Pornography, 31, 165, 168–70, 172, 182–84, 186, 188, 217–18, 220, 248n, 249n
Postmodernism: postmodernity, 16, 42, 122, 162, 186, 190–92, 196–98, 211, 214
Poststructuralism, 122, 127, 190
Poyán Díaz, Daniel, 240n
Propaganda, 11, 121, 135, 137, 151–56, 159, 161–62, 183–84, 217–18, 246–47n
Pozuelo, José María, 31
Pratt, Mary Louise, 193
Psychoanalysis, 112–14, 169, 175, 177, 226

Quality: literary or artistic, 11–12, 14, 16, 20, 39, 42, 45–46, 75, 77–78, 82–83, 90, 122–24, 157, 159, 162–63, 170, 183, 187–89, 193, 203, 218, 251n
Queer Studies, 17, 127, 161, 193

Reader-response approaches to literature, 250–51n
Realism, 35, 40, 42–43, 45, 51, 70, 73–76, 83–84, 88–89, 93–94, 114, 122–23, 129, 135, 160, 166, 210, 244
Relational approaches to literature, 26–27, 29, 221, 223, 225, 232
Relativism: critical, 15–16, 22–24, 92, 108, 112, 125, 156, 219, 223
Resina, Joan Ramon, 190, 196, 211, 213
Restricted production: field of, 26, 43, 47, 80, 84, 89, 187
Reyes, Alfonso, 248n
Ribbans, Geoffrey, 236n, 241n
Ricoeur, Paul, 112–14
Ríos-Font, Wadda, 239n, 240n, 248n
Robbe-Grillet, Alain, 191
Rojas, Fernando de, 13
*Roman à thèse*, 122–23, 129–30, 135–36, 143, 149–52, 155–56, 161–62, 244n, 245n
Romero Larrañaga, Gregorio, 50
Romero Tobar, Leonardo, 31, 36, 49–50, 54, 233n, 235n
Ross, Andrew, 183, 249n
Rossetti, Ana, 165, 174
Rubio, Isaac, 79, 82, 240n
Rubio Cremades, Enrique, 36

Ruiz, Juan, Arcipreste de Hita, 13
Ruiz Ramón, Francisco, 77

Sackett, Theodore, 77–78
Sáez de Melgar, Faustina, 41
Said, Edward, 22–23
Salillas, Rafael, 100
Sánchez, Roberto, 240n
Sánchez Llama, Íñigo, 48
Sand, George, 48–49
Schopenhauer, Arthur, 242n
Schor, Naomi, 44
Scott, Walter, 48
Scribe, Eugène, 81
Sela-Sheffy, Rakefet, 236n
Sellés, Eugenio, 87
Sender, Ramón J., 31, 125, 136–52, 157–61, 243–48n; *Contraataque*, 125, 136–52, 155, 157–61, 243n
Sender Barayón, Ramón, 246n
Serial fiction, 11, 31, 35–75, 90, 94–95, 98, 104, 106–7, 115–16, 138, 191, 208, 210, 213, 216–18, 233–39n, 249n, 250n; Class, 37, 39–40, 44, 46, 57–58, 60–62, 67, 72–74; Heteroglossia, 68–69; Journalism and, 72; Money, 55, 67, 74; Plot, 67. *See also* aristocracy; bourgeois (ie); *follótin; feuilleton;* middle class; *novela por entregas;* working class
Serial novel archetype, 57–61, 67, 75, 90, 116, 238n
Showalter, Elaine, 164
Sieburth, Stephanie, 38, 74–75
Sinnigen, John, 38, 42
Sinués de Marco, María Pilar, 39
Sobejano, Gonzalo, 78, 240n, 241n
Soulié, Frédéric, 48–49
Smith, Barbara Herrnstein, 17, 223
Steiner, George, 249n
Stowe, Harriet Beecher, 237n
Strindberg, August, 83
Sue, Eugène, 48, 51, 159, 235n; *El judío errante*, 51, 235n
Suleiman, Susan, 68, 122–23, 125, 129–31, 135–36, 143, 152, 154–56, 160, 162, 244n, 245n
Szondi, Peter, 83

## INDEX

Tanner, Tony, 169
Taste: literary or artistic, 17, 28, 90, 134, 159, 192, 203, 217, 240n
Thompson, John B., 112
Torrecilla, Jesús, 47, 55
Tradition: literary or cultural, 11, 13, 19, 24, 30, 125, 134, 136, 160, 187, 193, 195–96, 203
Trapiello, Andrés, 243n, 245n, 246n
Trigo, Felipe, 164–72, 177–78, 180, 182, 248n; *Alma en los labios*, 167; *La Altísima*, 167; *El amor en la vida y en los libros*, 166–67; *La sed de amar*, 171; *Socialismo individualista*, 166
Tsuchiya, Akiko, 107–8, 241n

Unamuno, Miguel de, 13, 92, 166, 168, 171, 245–46n

Valle-Inclán, Ramón del, 77–78, 89, 109, 133, 159–60, 171
Value, literary or cultural, 12, 16–17, 20, 26–28, 30, 42, 52, 55, 68, 78, 80, 157–58, 165, 169, 183, 187, 192–93, 205, 215, 223, 250n
Varela, Antonio, 135, 152, 244n, 247n
Vásquez, Mary S., 125, 152, 245n, 246n, 247n
Vázquez Figueroa, Alberto, 187
Vázquez Montalban, Manuel, 11, 31, 159, 187–215, 218–19, 249–51n;

*Autobiografía del General Franco*, 189, 200; Carvalho series, 189–91, 201–2, 206–10, 213–15, 251n; *O César o nada*, 200; *Crónica sentimental de España*, 200, 250n; *El escriba sentado*, 200, 250n; *Galíndez*, 189, 200; *La literatura en la construcción de la ciudad democrática*, 194, 250n; *Memoria y deseo*, 200, 250n
Vega, Lope de, 13, 86
Verlaine, Paul, 134
Vernon, Kathleen, 241n
Vilarós, Teresa, 184
Villapadierna, Maryse. *See* Lecuyer, Marie Claude

Waugh, Evelyn, 251n
Wellek, René, 188–89
Wilde, Oscar, 133
Willem, Linda, 109, 241n
Woolf, Virginia, 208, 251n
Working class, 61, 73–74, 234n, 237n. *See also* aristocracy; bourgeois(ie); serial fiction, class in; middle class

Ynduráin, Francisco, 74–75

Zavala, Iris, 36, 60, 234n
Zamacois, Eduardo, 165, 167, 171
Zola, Emile, 23, 85